PEDAGOGICAL DOCUMENTATION
IN EARLY YEARS PRACTICE

Sara Miller McCune founded SAGE Publishing in 1965 to support the dissemination of usable knowledge and educate a global community. SAGE publishes more than 1000 journals and over 800 new books each year, spanning a wide range of subject areas. Our growing selection of library products includes archives, data, case studies and video. SAGE remains majority owned by our founder and after her lifetime will become owned by a charitable trust that secures the company's continued independence.

Los Angeles | London | New Delhi | Singapore | Washington DC | Melbourne

PEDAGOGICAL DOCUMENTATION

IN EARLY YEARS PRACTICE

SEEING THROUGH MULTIPLE PERSPECTIVES

EDITED BY

ALMA FLEET
CATHERINE PATTERSON
JANET ROBERTSON

Los Angeles | London | New Delhi
Singapore | Washington DC | Melbourne

Los Angeles | London | New Delhi
Singapore | Washington DC | Melbourne

SAGE Publications Ltd
1 Oliver's Yard
55 City Road
London EC1Y 1SP

SAGE Publications Inc.
2455 Teller Road
Thousand Oaks, California 91320

SAGE Publications India Pvt Ltd
B 1/I 1 Mohan Cooperative Industrial Area
Mathura Road
New Delhi 110 044

SAGE Publications Asia-Pacific Pte Ltd
3 Church Street
#10-04 Samsung Hub
Singapore 049483

Editor: Jude Bowen
Associate editor: George Knowles
Production editor: Nicola Carrier
Copyeditor: Gemma Marren
Indexer: Martin Hargreaves
Marketing manager: Dilhara Attygalle
Cover design: Wendy Scott
Typeset by: C&M Digitals (P) Ltd, Chennai, India
Printed by CPI Group (UK) Ltd, Croydon, CR0 4YY

Library of Congress Control Number: 2017939363

British Library Cataloguing in Publication data

A catalogue record for this book is available from
the British Library

ISBN 978-1-47394-460-2
ISBN 978-1-47394-461-9 (pbk)

At SAGE we take sustainability seriously. Most of our products are printed in the UK using FSC papers and boards.
When we print overseas we ensure sustainable papers are used as measured by the PREPS grading system.
We undertake an annual audit to monitor our sustainability.

CONTENTS

List of Figures and Tables   vii
About the Editors   ix
About the Contributors   xi
Acknowledgements   xvii

Introduction   1

PART 1   SETTING THE STAGE   **9**

1 The Landscape of Pedagogical Documentation   11
   Alma Fleet

2 Pedagogical Documentation and Pedagogical Choices   27
   Lise-Lotte Bjervås and Gunilla Rosendahl

3 Developing Pedagogical Documentation within the
   EYFS Curriculum Framework   41
   Nicola Stobbs, Janet Harvell and Michael Reed

   Commentary 1: Living with a Growing Idea   55
   Lasse Lipponen (Finland)

PART 2   LANGUAGES OF REPRESENTATION   **59**

4 The Worlds of the Very Young: Seeing the Everyday in
   Small Pieces   61
   Suallyn Mitchelmore and Alma Fleet

5 Making Learning Visible in Dance and Other Creative Arts   73
   Marc Richard

6 Using Video in Pedagogical Documentation: Interpretive
   and Poetic Possibilities   85
   Sylvia Kind and Adrienne Argent

   Commentary 2: Opening Doors and Windows   98
   Stefania Giamminuti (Italian-Australian)

PART 3   EMBRACING POSSIBILITIES OF CHANGE   **101**

7 Collaborative Decision-Making within Pedagogical
   Documentation   103
   Janet Robertson

8 Pedagogic Documentation and Student Learning   117
   Michael Reed and Nicola Stobbs

9 Making the Outdoors Visible in Pedagogical Documentation   131
   Jane Merewether

10 Diving into the Unknown: The Experience of Pedagogical
   Documentation at Mia Mia   147
   Angela Chng

   Commentary 3: Posing Big(ger) Ideas and Questions   159
   Maria Cooper and Helen Hedges (New Zealand)

PART 4   THE WIDER VIEW   **163**

11 Knowledge and Practice of Pedagogic Documentation:
   Professional Development for Educators   165
   Rosie Walker, Michael Reed and Nicola Stobbs

12 The Potential of Pedagogical Documentation for Leadership
   Enactment   179
   Iris Berger

13 Weavings, Walks and Wonderings: Stories of the Liveliness
   of Pedagogical Narrations   193
   B. Denise Hodgins, Deborah Thompson and
   Kathleen Kummen

   Commentary 4: Situating Pedagogical Documentation
   in a Democratic Context   207
   Andrew Stremmel (United States)

14 Pedagogical Documentation: Where to from Here?   211
   Janet Robertson, Alma Fleet and Catherine Patterson

Index   219

LIST OF FIGURES AND TABLES

Figures

1.1	War	17
1.2	Children's rights	19
1.3	We raised $2000 and donated the money to UNICEF Australia	20
1.4	Links to **LiLi**	22
2.1	Reviewing photographs from last year	30
2.2	Gathering at the gate	31
2.3	Reviewing the visit	34
2.4	Being in the photographs	35
4.1	The identity of hats, lockers and shoes	65
4.2	Emma and Anne playfully explore the humour of hats	66
4.3	Anne and Rebecca re-meet the joy of the bamboo	69
4.4	Sharing the process of pedagogical documentation	70
5.1	Exploring the scarves	77
5.2	Tristan and Isabelle play statues	78
5.3	McKayla's step map	80
9.1	Eloise's photo	139
9.2	My reconstruction of a photograph taken by children in Reggio Emilia	140
10.1	Photographs presented to the child and his attempt to draw himself	152
10.2	The children's puzzle prototypes	154
10.3	Children's drawings of themselves singing	157

Tables

3.1   A comparison of compatibility between underlying
      principles of pedagogical documentation, the statutory
      framework and inspection requirements   47

8.1   A conceptual model: Patterns of teaching and learning   125

11.1 Examples of analytic questioning   173
11.2 Responses from participants   175

ABOUT THE EDITORS

Alma Fleet works with developing early childhood teachers at Macquarie University, Sydney, Australia. Having been a teacher herself (in California and Scotland), and worked for children's services in Australia, she enjoys teaching within the university and with those working with children in both prior to school and school settings. She also enjoys consultancies, presentations and workshops related to educational change across diverse sectors. Recent articles appear in *Reflective Practice: International and Multidisciplinary Perspectives* and the *Australian Journal of Teacher Education*.

Catherine Patterson has taught undergraduate and postgraduate students at the Institute of Early Childhood, Macquarie University, Sydney, Australia, for over two decades. Her teaching responsibilities centre on facilitating the professional growth of student teachers in professional experience courses. Catherine's research explores the realities of teaching and learning for early childhood practitioners. She has supported teachers as researchers at various levels of education, including pre-service student teachers and experienced teachers working with young children.

Janet Robertson works at Mia Mia Child and Family Study Centre at Macquarie University, Sydney, Australia, as the outdoor teacher, a position she has held for 15 years. She is interested in children's thinking, complicating this process with critical pedagogy and at one and the same time, making it visible to the child, co-thinkers and families. Her work is informed by the educational experiences of the schools of Reggio Emilia.

ABOUT THE CONTRIBUTORS

Adrienne Argent is an infant and toddler educator at the Capilano Children's Center in North Vancouver, British Columbia, Canada. She enjoys the process of re-thinking her classroom as an art studio, a space where children can engage in ongoing and collaborative engagements with materials. Many of her pedagogical interests are inspired by contemporary art and the natural beauty of the Pacific Northwest.

Iris Berger has been involved in early childhood education as a classroom teacher, researcher, community organizer, policy consultant and university lecturer since the mid-1990s. Her passion for early childhood education as a distinct and ever-engaging realm of/for research pedagogy began when working with young children in the model classrooms at the Child Study Centre under the auspices of the Faculty of Education, University of British Columbia (UBC), in Vancouver, Canada. She is currently a lecturer and a coordinator with the UBC Institute for Early Childhood Education and Research (IECER).

Lise-Lotte Bjervås works as a senior lecturer at Linnaeus University, Sweden. She conducts research on issues related to documentation, assessment and values education in preschools. Her doctoral thesis is about teachers' views of preschool children in relation to pedagogical documentation. She teaches in the preschool teacher education programme and has previously worked as a preschool teacher. She values her own experiences of working with pedagogical documentation.

Angela Chng has completed both her undergraduate and postgraduate degrees in early childhood. Originally from Singapore, Angela has bicultural perspectives in her everyday work with children and families. She has been working in the sector for the last decade and in that time explored various ways of documenting children's thinking, learning and development. Since 2008, she has been the lead early childhood teacher of the three-to-five-year-olds' classroom in Mia Mia Child and Family Study Centre at Macquarie University, Sydney, Australia.

Maria Cooper has co-authored a number of papers with Helen Hedges, focusing on children's interests, inquiries and working theories to deepen understandings of children's forms of learning and meaning-making.

A senior lecturer in the School of Learning, Development and Professional Practice at the University of Auckland, New Zealand, Maria's research focuses on the phenomenon of 'everyday teacher leadership' in the context of infant-toddler education and care. Her research interests include teacher leadership, partnerships with families and assessment for learning.

Stefania Giamminuti Building on a deep understanding of Australian and Italian perspectives, Dr Giamminuti's doctoral study has informed her thinking, writing and research. In *Dancing with Reggio Emilia: Metaphors for Quality* (2013), she shared her insightful experience with an international community eager to explore potentials of this vibrant thinking community. She continues her work in teacher education at Curtin University, Western Australia.

Janet Harvell became interested in the early years as a parent involved in the local preschool. She then became an associate manager of a 44-place day nursery, before working at a college for eleven years as a quality reviewer, advanced practitioner, programme manager, lecturer and personal tutor. During this time, she supported delivery of the EYPS programme and the emergence of a graduate-led early years workforce, a continuing passion. As a registered nursery inspector, Janet is able to provide another perspective for students enrolled in early years courses.

Helen Hedges is head of the School of Curriculum and Pedagogy at the University of Auckland, New Zealand. Associate Professor Hedges pursues interests in teacher decision-making and co-constructed curriculum. Foregrounding 'the child as thinker' and the framework of 'funds of knowledge', her research explores children's and teachers' interests, knowledge and learning in the contexts of early childhood education. Her research interests extend to teachers-as-researchers and issues of ethical research with teachers and children.

B. Denise Hodgins holds a PhD and an MEd in early childhood education. She has worked in the human services sector since 1989, including in school-age childcare, preschool education, and non-profit programme and service delivery. She is a research associate with the Unit for Early Years Research and Development and a sessional instructor in the School of Child and Youth Care, University of Victoria, Australia. Her work reflects commitment to making visible, and engaging with, issues of equity in, through and for twenty-first-century early childhood pedagogies and research.

Sylvia Kind is an instructor in early childhood education at Capilano University and an *atelierista* at the Capilano University Children's Centre in North Vancouver, British Columbia, Canada. Her work is motivated by an interest in artistic ways of knowing, children's studio practices, experimentations with art as research in early childhood settings, and the intersections of contemporary art and pedagogy.

Laurie Kocher is a lecturer in the early childhood care and education programme at Capilano in British Columbia, Canada. She navigates between the worlds of academia and practice, always with a desire to bring the two together. Her academic background includes doctoral work focused on the pedagogical project of Reggio Emilia, with particular interest in narrative and visual practices of pedagogical documentation.

Kathleen Kummen holds a PhD in early childhood education and is the coordinator of early childhood care and education at Capilano University. Her current work with student early childhood educators is inspired by insights from postfoundational theory, feminist theory and Indigenous studies. Her research interests explore the implications for pedagogy when learning is no longer understood as an event that occurs within the individual through encounters with other humans.

Lasse Lipponen is Professor of Education in the Department of Teacher Education, University of Helsinki, Finland. Published widely, Dr Lipponen's research is directed to children's learning at the intersection of formal and informal learning environments, understanding of children's experiences and perceptions in their life-worlds with digital documentation and participatory research methods.

Jane Merewether teaches in early childhood education at Curtin University, Western Australia. Previously, she was an early years teacher for 18 years. The educational project of the city of Reggio Emilia informs Jane's research, teaching and life. She uses strategies of pedagogical documentation for exploring taken-for-granted ways of thinking about children, teachers, teaching and learning.

Suallyn Mitchelmore is a practicing early childhood teacher and PhD candidate at the Institute of Early Childhood, Macquarie University, Sydney, Australia. Her research focus is on that which is precious and compelling in everyday moments. Suallyn utilizes pedagogical documentation as a methodology that facilitates an inclusive and collaborative platform for the voices of children and adults.

Michael Reed is a senior lecturer at the Centre for Children and Families, Institute of Education, University of Worcester. His teaching involves undergraduate and postgraduate courses focused on the needs of children and families. He also contributes to courses considering effective ways to manage organizations. Mike's research interests focus on enhancing quality provision for young children. He also engages in research with students to consider their professional roles with children. He regularly presents research papers at national and international conferences and writes textbooks about work-based research and early childhood studies.

Marc Richard is an artist and educator, writer, actor, director and choreographer. He has a Masters in dance and a PhD in education, both from York University, UK. He began teaching kindergarten in 1990 and since then has taught at all levels of education, worked as a private arts educational consultant and an artist in education. He is currently a professor in the Faculty of Arts, Animation and Design at Sheridan College in Oakville, Ontario, Canada. Marc's research projects attempt to make the learning visible in creative dance education.

Gunilla Rosendahl is a lecturer in preschool teacher education at Linneus University, Sweden. Her special interests are pedagogical documentation, group learning and an exploratory approach using different modes of expression. Before working at the university, she worked as a preschool teacher for many years and used pedagogical documentation as a tool to reflect and challenge children's learning processes.

Wendy Shepherd is the founding director of the Mia Mia Child and Family Study Centre at Macquarie University, Australia. With her guidance, the centre has developed a widespread reputation for excellence in early childhood education. As the director of Mia Mia, Wendy also makes a valuable contribution to the academic programme at the Institute of Early Childhood, Macquarie University. Prior to her role at Mia Mia, Wendy worked as a teacher in the early years of school and as a preschool director.

Nicola Stobbs completed her teacher education at the University of Worcester, UK. She began her professional life as a primary school teacher with a year six class. After a two-year maternity break, Nicola began working in a preschool, being promoted to manager. As well as running the setting, she became interested in the world beyond preschool and wrote articles for *Practical Pre-School* magazine. The setting was often used as an example of good practice and Nicola was a mentor for many students enrolled in various early childhood tertiary programmes. She is now a senior lecturer at the University of Worcester.

Andrew Stremmel is recognized for his ongoing contributions to teacher education, particularly in the field of teacher inquiry. Professor Stremmel has researched and published widely, including Reggio-inspired pedagogies and academic leadership. With strengths in collaborative dialogue and narrative inquiry, he brings extensive experience to his current position as professor and department head at South Dakota State University, Brookings, SD, USA.

Deborah Thompson is the programme manager at the University of British Columbia Child Care Services. The centre runs an innovative multiage programme combining toddlers and three-to-five-year-olds. Previously, she has worked in the early years field as an early childhood educator and as an early childhood education instructor. She earned a PhD in child and youth care from the University of Victoria, with a thesis entitled 'Caring, Dwelling, Becoming: Stories of Multiage Child Care'.

Rosie Walker's professional heritage is in social welfare where she gained extensive experience in safeguarding and protecting children in both the statutory and voluntary sector. She also managed children's centres for several years before completing her MSc. As a senior lecturer at the University of Worcester, UK, Rosie now coordinates the Foundation Degree in Early Years which includes a number of partner colleges and the university online learning programme.

ACKNOWLEDGEMENTS

As authors and editors it has been a pleasure working with our colleagues. We would like to express our appreciation to the authors, along with the children and families who have contributed to the thoughts evolving here.

In particular, we'd like to thank the international regional coordinators – Laurie Kocher and Michael Reed – as intermediaries between the chapter authors and the editors. Their generous donation of thoughtful energy and infinite patience enabled rich unfolding conversations.

Our thanks also go to Jude Bowen and George Knowles at SAGE for their interest and perseverance in facilitating this exciting publication.

Finally, we'd like to acknowledge the ongoing enthusiasm and support from our families, colleagues and friends.

Alma, Catherine, Janet

INTRODUCTION

Pedagogical documentation is becoming recognized internationally as a metaphor for a way of working that encapsulates teachers and children as co-researchers; being present in the moment while deeply investigating matters of interest over time. It is a process that enables educators, families and children to learn alongside each other, while supporting planning and recording processes. Known variously as pedagogical documentation, pedagogic documentation, educational documentation and pedagogical narration (among other descriptors), this way of working is inspired by the educators of Reggio Emilia, Italy, and interpreted in locally relevant ways in many countries. As international interest in the power of pedagogical documentation has grown, educators have become keen to learn about experiences of their colleagues in other places. This book draws together examples from a number of countries to share the delights and concerns of those working with pedagogical documentation. At the same time, we hope it may overcome feelings of isolation experienced by those working on these ideas in less-than-supportive environments. The chapters highlight multiple approaches from diverse countries and readers will need to think critically about the most appropriate approaches for their own contexts.

Throughout the book, chapters are grouped together to illustrate possible linkages of issues and ideas. Each group of chapters is followed by an invited commentary from a professional in the early childhood community. These responses between chapter writers and respondents hint at conversations that create a dialogic frame for ideas and possibilities. Participants in these conversations – either as authors or respondents – include early childhood practitioners, researchers, centre directors, programme managers, university academics and others. This conversational tone is designed to prompt readers to consider multiple possibilities of pedagogical documentation and to engage with the unfolding conversations. While each section has its own integrity, it is not necessary to engage with the contents of the book in a linear fashion. Chapters are designed to enable readers to connect with personally relevant examples to deepen their appreciation of the potentials of pedagogical documentation.

To highlight contextual similarities and differences, we will now turn to country-positioning contributions from Australia, Britain and Canada. The contributing authors were invited to consider regulatory contexts, issues and current challenges in their region. No generalizations are intended, either for countries offering opinions and examples, or for those whose work is not included here.

Australian context

Janet Robertson and Wendy Shepherd

In her poem 'My Country', Dorothea Mackellar (1911), wrote about the wild landscape of Australia. Her use of metaphors described vast bush-land, mountains, deserts and coastal rainforests, anthropomorphizing 'A wilful, lavish land'. In this poem, there is also a hint of the history of colonization of Australia by the British government in the 1770s as Mackellar, situated in the colonialist mindset, makes no mention of the first people of this land, whose rich culture and communities were nearly wiped out by white convicts and settlers. Just over a century later, *The Early Years Learning Framework* (DEEWR, 2009: 13) redresses this silence: 'Educators recognize that diversity contributes to the richness of our society and provides a valid evidence base about ways of knowing. For Australia, it also includes promoting greater understanding of Aboriginal and Torres Strait Islander ways of knowing and being.'

Historically, education and care of children under five years was not considered the responsibility of governments; parents who worked had no choice of children's services. Philanthropists began the first crèches and kindergartens, as children and their health became a cause for concern within the increasingly gentrified community. Out-of-home education and care began, but without governmental guidelines. Eventually, as programmes flourished, and the rights of children gained political interest, regulations were developed in the early 1970s in line with legislation for protection of children. In 2011, the process began to unify and standardize regulations for the education and care of Australia's youngest citizens. Until then, there had been a mélange of different regulations and delivery modes, across three levels of government. The current National Quality Framework and Standards has at its core the protection and wellbeing of children (ACECQA, 2012); these documents refer to child-centred learning and play and include responsibility for documenting children's learning.

The issues that Australian educators tussle with around the role of pedagogical documentation seem to be perennial. The reason to document is clear: it is a legislated requirement. It is the 'how much, when and who is it for', that confronts educators. Firstly, there is often confusion about the difference between reporting (for example, for an audit) and recording (documenting events) and pedagogical documentation, which is a principle driving curriculum and pedagogy in concert with colleagues and children. Worse still, some educators see documenting as making a Christmas present of happy snaps for families contained in a scrapbook called a portfolio. For others, however, documenting learning is about teachers and children thinking aloud, driving the progress of their pedagogy and curriculum, in dynamic and reflective processes.

The second issue is another roadblock: how much documenting are teachers 'required' to do. No regulation specifies the amount! We would, nevertheless, always advocate for meaningful documentation rather than recording trite information. If pedagogical documentation is a *habit of mind and practice*, then processes of planning, forecasting and reflecting are rolled into one. If it is made visible with children as co-constructors, then it is the teachers' 'everyday' responsibility, and part of the daily routine.

Tied into this issue is the perceived problem of time: time to write, think, reflect, collaborate and still participate in the daily teaching life of busy early childhood sites. When teachers believe that pedagogical documentation is something *in addition* to what they do each day, rather than an opportunity to reframe their pedagogy and *instead* embed it, then documentation loses a certain dimension. It becomes a quality versus quantity dilemma; a 'must do' instead of a professional strategy for thinking about pedagogy.

Who leads, writes and explores the pedagogy in documentation is another issue in a country bedevilled by an industrial legacy of a divide between 'child-care' and 'preschool'. Australian early education started from two institutions, established in New South Wales (NSW) in the late 1800s and early 1900s – one preparing teachers for nursery (long day care) and the other for preschool. Although the central belief was that teachers were required in both forms of early education, this got lost over the years as the conception of offering early education *or* care spread across the nation, eventuating in a divide, with long day care very much the poor cousin. Consequently, there has been a tendency for university-qualified early childhood teachers to teach in preschool/kindergarten settings, and those with diploma qualifications to work in long day care programmes. Other supporting educators may be working towards minimal qualifications and have little understanding of the documentation landscapes. This is changing, but salary scales and conditions mitigate against the government intention that there be teachers in long day care programmes. Nationally, each four-year-old child is entitled to 15 hours of preschool education per week. In some states and territories, long day care programmes outsource this responsibility; children are taken to a preschool programme (which may only operate during school terms), rather than having a degreed teacher work within the long day care programme.

These issues are not insurmountable; neither is the perceived problem of what exactly is pedagogical documentation.

British context

Michael Reed and Rosie Walker

The United Kingdom: Northern Ireland, Wales, Scotland and England each have parliaments and assemblies which recognize the way early childhood education provides social and economic benefits and enhances children's wellbeing in each nation. Policy frameworks translate into a range of early education provision on the ground, for example, community-based provision which offers full day or sessional (morning or afternoon) education and care; community-based inter-professional children's centres as well as before-school, after-school, holiday care and childminders who offer home-based education. Some of this provision is private, some developed by voluntary organizations, and some by schools that have developed nursery and early education classes. To use England as an example: in 2013, there were about 17,900 full day care settings, about 13,400 after-school settings, 12,800 before-school settings, 7,200 holiday settings, and 46,100 childminders. In terms of support for working families, there are currently free childcare sessional places for children equating to 15 hours per week; there are plans to introduce in some areas 30 hours' worth of free childcare places. There is special provision to support access to childcare for disadvantaged two-year-olds.

Each nation sets out specific early education curriculum requirements and all early education settings are regulated and inspected. Practitioners who lead and work within these settings are known as leaders, managers or supervisors and are qualified at graduate level, or will have undergone further education vocational training to a level where they can lead a setting. Childminders must complete an approved training course appropriate to infants and children.

Each of the nations has established quality goals and minimum standards for early years practice; having in place clear curriculum and learning standards for children which includes their social and educational wellbeing and ensuring that those who work with children and families promote family and community engagement in early childhood education and care (ECEC) by knowing what goes on and 'what works' through research and documenting children's learning. Differences appear in the ways each nation develops and enacts policies about how children should be cared for and educated, and how policies are formed and subjected to review. This inevitably means that regulatory expectations and change are often driven by social and political trends.

In terms of regulation and inspection, each nation has in place a curriculum framework, childcare standards and regulatory bodies which monitor those standards. This influences what is recognized as quality practice; there is a genuine desire to extend such quality provision to all groups in society. It means settings adopting a process of self-evaluation involving all those closely involved and asking key questions about their provision and the distinctiveness of that provision – in effect, advocating the importance of a cycle of child-focused observation, documentation and reflection to consider how best to support children's learning.

It is within this context that the values and principles of pedagogical documentation are becoming increasingly visible within the UK in Scotland and England. This is evidenced in a recent report on pedagogical practice in England (Wall et al., 2015). The report asserts that there is now a concerted effort to value the interpretation educators place on how children learn, which would appear to recognize how pedagogic documentation may influence thinking and practice. It is an approach which sits well within an early education setting where the leader focuses on and develops educational practices and which is often referred to as pedagogic leadership. Hujala and Eskelinen (2013) suggest that pedagogic leadership involves making connections between practices in an early education setting, so that everything leads towards meeting the educational and welfare needs of the children. In this way, the teaching and learning is the driving force. It is an approach which requires practitioners to work together and learn from each other to consider what children know, understand and can do. It underpins the way educators attempt to understand what characterizes effective learning and use this information to help children learn, to consider what learning opportunities need to be refined and how best to monitor progress. This approach can sit within a regulatory framework as it is flexible – and adults, formally, informally, consciously or otherwise, help children to learn (Ofsted, 2015).

Canadian context

Laurie Kocher

Canada is the second largest country on the globe, boasting an endless variety of landscapes spread across six time zones. It is a bi-lingual country, with both French and English as national languages. At the same time, it is an ethnically diverse country, with a multitude of additional languages, histories and cultures. Thirty-five million people call Canada home.

The history of Canada, in large part, is the history of the colonization of Aboriginal peoples. Collectively, First Nations, Inuit and Métis peoples are the various Aboriginal peoples in Canada. After a tragic history of the placement of over 150,000 children in residential schools (1860s to 1990s) as an effort to remove and isolate children from the influence of their families, traditions and cultures, and to assimilate them into the dominant European culture (or, as has infamously been said, 'to kill the Indian in the child'), efforts are now underway to address these grievous wrongs. With the publication of the Truth and Reconciliation Commission's report (December, 2015), there will be increasing emphasis on holistic education that embraces Aboriginal values and acknowledges and redresses past wrongs.

Altogether, Canada's childcare landscape is complex and difficult to navigate. Universal, government-funded early learning programmes for children do not begin in the majority of Canada's provinces/territories until children are five years old. Canada's childcare system – or rather, non-system – has been described as a 'patchwork of care' service. At present, Canada's scant public support for childcare is largely limited to subsidies for mothers in low-income families to enable them to enter and remain in the workforce. The province of Quebec is a notable exception, where universal childcare, introduced in 1997, provides subsidies for families using childcare services. In many parts of the country, licensed childcare spaces that employ qualified early childhood educators are available for about 20 per cent of children requiring care. Waiting lists are long and fees are high, often amounting to more than mortgage/housing costs. Families somehow make do with a patchwork of arrangements, including parents working opposite shifts; making informal arrangements with neighbours, families and friends; utilizing licensed or unlicensed family home childcares or licensed centres (not-for-profit and profit options); hiring in-home nannies; working from home where possible and so forth.

Polling shows considerable interest in increased public investment in childcare. In fact, in the 2015 federal election, three of the four major political parties included discussion of a pan-Canadian, national childcare programme as a major platform issue. The ideology of the previous Conservative government was predicated upon a belief that childcare is an individual responsibility and not a social issue. Policy-makers have fostered conflicted public opinion about the role of women and the care of young children as an excuse for inaction.

The recently elected Liberal government has pledged to develop a new National Early Learning and Care Framework with the mandate to deliver affordable, high-quality, flexible and fully inclusive childcare for all Canadians. There is an opportunity for federal government leadership to spearhead the development of a national framework. Childcare advocates are cautiously hopeful.

Across the country, individual provincial early learning frameworks have been developed. These include statements of common principles, approaches and tools to guide practice in early childhood settings. Each document was locally constructed using a variety of approaches. Despite their different paths to development, the frameworks host many similarities. Families and communities are viewed as partners who strengthen each programme's ability to meet the needs of children. Respect for diversity, equity and inclusion are embraced as essential for optimal development. A planned curriculum, anchored by play, is recognized as best able to capitalize on children's natural curiosity and exuberance to learn. Most jurisdictions continue to add to their sources to enrich programming. The documents are largely written for those who work directly with young children and their families. They inform staff expectations of the children and help to document their own and the children's progress. Many, although not all, have been heavily influenced by the pedagogical documentation practices of the educational project of Reggio Emilia in Northern Italy.

Like childcare, provision of preschool education (for three-to-five-year-olds) is a private service offered either by not-for-profit or for-profit agencies. Typically, preschool is a part-time programme offered half days, two to five days per week. It does not meet the needs of working families for childcare. Families may scramble to cobble together preschool and childcare services, although some programmes offer both within the same location. Children's advocates argue that childcare and preschool should come under the jurisdiction of the education sector in order to provide a more seamless, publicly funded system. Currently, programmes for young children fall under a different umbrella of social services.

Teacher training, whether for childcare or preschool, is the same. Most early childhood educators will complete, at a minimum, a two-year post-secondary credential, although four-year degree credentials are becoming more common. Teacher education programmes, located in colleges or universities, have become revolutionized by the inclusion of postfoundation theories (for example, postmodern, poststructural, feminist, postcolonial). These postfoundational theories have the potential to disrupt normalizing early childhood education discourses that create and maintain social inequities, and to respect differences and diversities. Given the importance of diversity in Canada, these are relevant shifts.

In conclusion

These country-positioning papers have explained some of the complex socio-political contexts that are reflected in many of the chapters of this book. In acknowledgment of these complexities, chapter authors were invited to use their own voices to explore concepts related to pedagogical documentation. As a result, styles, genres and perceptions vary across chapters, illustrating how the inspiration from the educators of Reggio Emilia has been taken up in diverse ways in a number of countries. We hope these multiple interpretations provoke your thinking and cause you to question your assumptions about this way of working with children, families and colleagues.

References

ACECQA (Australian Children's Education and Care Quality Authority) (2012) National Quality Framework. www.acecqa.gov.au/national-quality-framework (accessed 18.03.16).

DEEWR (Australian Government Department of Education, Employment and Workplace Relations) (2009) *Belonging, Being & Becoming: The Early Years Learning Framework for Australia*. Canberra: Australian Government.

Hujala, E. and Eskelinen, M. (2013) 'Leadership tasks in early childhood education', in E. Hujala, M. Waniganayake and J. Rodd (eds), *Researching Leadership in Early Childhood Education*. Tampere: Tampere University Press, pp. 213–234.

Mackellar, D. (1911) 'My country'. www.dorotheamackellar.com.au/archive/mycountry.htm (accessed 30.05.16).

Ofsted (Office for Standards in Education, Children's Services and Skills) (2015) *Teaching and Play in the Early Years: A Balancing Act?*. Reference: 150085. www.gov.uk/government/publications/teaching-and-play-in-the-early-years-a-balancing-act (accessed 25.01.17).

Truth and Reconciliation Commission of Canada (2015) *Final Report*. www.trc.ca/websites/trcinstitution/index.php (accessed 01.06.16).

Wall, S., Litjens, I. and Taguma, M. (2015) *Early Childhood and Care Literature Review: England*. Paris: Organization for Economic Co-operation and Development (OECD). www.oecd.org/unitedkingdom/early-childhood-educa tion-and-care-pedagogy-review-england.pdf (accessed 01.06.16).

PART 1
SETTING THE STAGE

1

THE LANDSCAPE OF PEDAGOGICAL DOCUMENTATION

ALMA FLEET

Having previously set the scene, this chapter now proposes a schema to conceptualize pedagogical documentation in terms of the Local Interpretation of Larger Ideas (**LiLi**). Challenging formulas, this approach to a 'wicked problem' invites creativity and inspiration alongside accountability. A narrative of 'war and peace' situates the reader in this landscape.

Introduction

This chapter offers glimpses of the diverse landscapes of pedagogical documentation, a sense of the richness offered by this way of working. It highlights the importance of philosophy and processes as well as multiple possible products, illustrating complexity as a strength that can meet systemic accountability and employer requirements, as well as generating professional pride and unexpected insights as part of being with young children and their families. Acknowledging differing geographical and socio-political contexts, it is inevitable that each school, children's service or educational system attempting to understand pedagogical documentation will evolve 'particular' located understandings and practices.

Embracing a 'wicked problem'

We propose approaching the challenge of defining pedagogical documentation as a 'wicked problem', in the sense evolved by Bellamy (2007). Speaking from the perspective of environmental resource management, she referred to 'wicked problems' as those that 'defy efforts to delineate their boundaries and to identify their causes, and thus expose their problematic nature' (Rittel and Webber, 1973: 167). Bellamy addressed Adaptive Capacity in relation to these problems through seven component attributes: Participatory, Deliberative, Multi-layered, Nested, Accountable and Responsive, Just, and Well-informed (2007: 108) – a list which resonates with intellectually engaged educators.

Although seen through a lens of governance in Northern Australia (Patterson et al., 2014) rather than education, at the common sense level, these essential attributes sit comfortably with a **LiLi** schema for relating to pedagogical documentation, as explained below. To look at the 'wicked problem' of the nature, roles and 'doing' of pedagogical documentation, the categories of Adaptive Capacity can be interpreted as follows (definitions from Bellamy, 2007: 108):

Participatory defined as: 'engagement with stakeholders being inclusive of the range of values of people involved or affected by [the] decision-making. Critical for building trust and legitimacy'; therefore building on socio-cultural frames and enabling inclusion of multiple voices through participation of varied adults and children.

Deliberative defined as: 'accommodating debate, dissent, mediation and negotiation. Critical for developing shared understanding and trust and enhancing adaptive capacity'; therefore supportive environments need to be fostered for respectful, reciprocal exchange.

Multi-layered defined as: 'not neatly hierarchical … Critical to adaptive responses at appropriate levels'; therefore implications for individual or groups of children will be considered alongside implications for adults, employers and systems.

Nested defined as: 'multiple centres or authorities for creating opportunities for understanding and for servicing needs in spatially heterogeneous contexts. Critical for providing flexibility for adapting to local contexts … and creating appropriate learning and decision-making opportunities'; therefore pedagogical documentation sits within everyday practice as an ongoing generative vehicle for authentic living research.

Accountable and Responsive defined as: 'relating to both local communities and higher authorities in terms of decisions and actions … responsive to changing circumstances, performance, knowledge and societal objectives and preferences. Critical to efficiency and adaptive capacity … to respond to and shape change in the long term'; therefore flexibility and clarity of purpose and presentation progress the goals of pedagogical documentation – including consideration of participants and relevance to readers.

Just defined as: 'social justice in relation to the distribution of benefits and involuntary risks. Critical to enhancing the adaptive capacity of vulnerable groups and society as a whole'; therefore issues of power imbalance or bias need to be considered in deciding on children or content to be included/excluded from experiences and their representations.

Well-informed defined as: 'embracing new forms of knowledge to deal with complexity and uncertainty associated with change in interconnected social and natural systems. Critical to social acceptability and adaptive governance capacity'; therefore opportunities offered by pedagogical documentation can be explored through multi-media, professional learning and with open-minded intellectual curiosity and creativity. Advocacy becomes enhanced.

While reflecting on these characteristics and making the amorphous process of pedagogical documentation manageable, we suggest consideration of the **LiLi** schema (pronounced LyeLye – not Lily!) proposed by Fleet (2015a, 2015b). The schema is a way to consider *Local Interpretation of Larger Ideas*: embracing intuitive processes that can galvanize this way of working, it proposes a set of core components, examining these from the perspectives of professional decision-making inherent in documenting pedagogically.

To illustrate this multi-faceted definition in the context of **LiLi** and the characterization of pedagogical documentation as a 'wicked problem', a narrative will be shared. This story is partial, as layered thoughts and experiences in the lives of four-year-old children, their families and educators, will not slide into this space. It will, however, give readers an opportunity to visualize what might be meant in response to the question: What exactly are we talking about when we refer to pedagogical documentation?

Seeing pedagogical thinking in action

Before moving into an example, let's position the following narrative in a larger landscape. Generally, when educators refer to 'pedagogical documentation', they refer to inspirational professional practices in the community-based centres (and one primary school) in Reggio Emilia, a Northern Italian town that has been interpreting these ideas since the end of World War II. Their thoughts are encapsulated in numerous publications, including editions of the *Hundred Languages of Children* (Edwards et al., [1993] 2012) and catalogues associated with travelling exhibitions of the same name.

Representations emerging from the thoughtfulness of adults and children working together also appear in other guises, including Learning Stories in New Zealand (Carr and Lee, 2012) and Pedagogical Narrations in Canada (Pacini-Ketchabaw et al., 2015). Overviews of pedagogical documentation are available elsewhere, such as in the freely available *What's Pedagogy Anyway?* (Fleet et al., 2011). It would seem, however, that misunderstandings surround this construct (as is often the case with 'wicked problems'), resulting in potentially superficial forms of recording (e.g. reporting in various 'day book' formats), or illustrated reports (e.g. to support accountability requirements). Without capturing reciprocal, responsive, relational encounters with analysis of possible interpretations of unfolding investigations or events, however, the work cannot fairly be labelled as 'pedagogical documentation'. The term is not a 'catch-all' for all forms of visual recording; it implies philosophical positioning related to the image of the child (particularly as proposed by the educators in Reggio Emilia), roles of educators, usage of time and space, the facilitative role of physical and affective environments, and positioning of thinking within the local and larger community. Pieces of representation may be quite brief, involving one or two children, or extended and revisited over longer periods of time.

There are several ways in which the following example is shared. Each is an excerpt of a larger piece as the work evolved over three months; through conversations, chats with children and families, and various forms of pedagogical documentation. Firstly, the teacher introduces her thinking. Then, an overview provides context for this investigation of a topic not often explored with young children, but which was filling the news and concerning hearts and minds at the time. While many materials were presented in panels and/or posters for families entering and leaving the centre, the entire process is considered part of pedagogical documentation.

Suet Mei Lee writes as the lead educator with this group of (mostly) four-year-olds. She works with Viviana Botero Lopez, director and educational leader in a community-based centre. After sharing some of their thinking, the work will be considered in the context of the **LiLi** schema.

Children's exploration of war, peace and social justice

In an early reflection, Suet wrote:

> I had an idea of having this conversation with my children for weeks. I had done my research trying to understand what is happening in Syria so that I could prepare for any questions that children might have … There were many things that held me back from starting this discussion. How do I start this? The discussion might go 'wrong' (unpredictable questions). The other teachers in the room might not agree with this. What about the parents? They might not like it!
>
> But I decided to do it.
>
> During the discussion, I wrote down everything that the children said. I wasn't sure what to expect … I re-thought and re-read repeatedly what the children said. All I could think is how lucky I am to be able to see the world through their lens. As adults, we often complicate things around us. For children, it is simple yet wise and straight to the point … I am keen to learn and know more about children's interpretation of the concept of war and maybe peace …

Project overview

This summary identifies highlights of the project for Suet and Viviana.

> As adults, we are exposed to different information around the world thanks to media, and the current situation in Syria is no exception. We can decide how to react to this information, whether to take part or not. Nonetheless, young children are also being exposed to this information, but their reactions and perceptions can be challenging to deal with in a childcare setting. As early childhood educators, Viviana and I decided to follow this project with children knowing that the outcome was unpredictable.
>
> With Viviana's support I embraced this potentially risky issue and captured children's voices and thoughts concerning this war. Children explored the concepts of war, peace and social justice through many group discussions. The discussions emphasized children's theory
>
> *(Continued)*

(Continued)

building, their construction of knowledge as a group as well as their making-sense of an issue not present in their everyday lives.

We explored the role of humanitarian organizations with the children and they discussed ways to raise funds to support refugees. The children decided to make jewellery and Christmas cards to sell to the local community to support children affected by the war in Syria. This re-emphasized the role of children and educators as active agents who can address 'big issues', recognizing that we are all part of a global community who have the right to live in peace and experience 'belonging'.

The following snippets include excerpts from a PowerPoint presentation and from large panels that were constructed as part of the pedagogical documentation process, to include children's thoughts and educator reflections:

Aidan: [*Comparing the size of Syria and Australia on the map*] It is too small for them to build schools and hospitals!

Benjamin: So the buildings were destroyed? Do they have cars on the street? Maybe the cars explode and burn down the buildings.

Emily: Yes! You know there is a pipe at the back of the car and sometimes the gas comes out and cause explosion!

Suet and Viviana reflect:

As we can see, the children seemed to find it challenging to link their current life experiences to what they thought might be happening in Syria. So, we decided to introduce the concept of 'war' and we asked the children: What does war mean?

Charlotte: That means peoples are fighting.

Rafael: And they use weapons to fight.

Emily: Like guns.

Benjamin: And cannonballs.

Charlotte: And swords.

Rafael: When you use weapons, you hurt peoples. And the cannonballs will cause explosion that destroyed the buildings.

Emily: That is why we don't use gun and weapons in Banksia. Because we are all good people here and no one should get hurt.

Benjamin: This war will never end. Because is a fight! Someone needs to stop immediately. If not, this will never end.

Figure 1.1   War

Suet and Vivian reflect:

> Through discussion, children are making sense of abstract issues ... They are using trial and error with different concepts that they are familiar with, but their interpretations are very wise and meaningful.

In one of the group conversations, Yolandy reported:

I watched the news about Syria with my daddy and mummy ... In the news they show some people who are carrying weapons like guns. All the buildings are destroyed and there are big pieces of rocks on the floor ... there are peoples sitting on the street because they are hurt. I saw this man and his face was red. I thought it was face painting and maybe because he was angry. Actually it was his blood all over his face ... it was very sad to see. They all look very sad and worried ...

This conversation moved on quickly to the consideration of *How can we help?*

Emily:	We can go over there and help them to run away.
Rafael:	We can't because it is not safe in Syria!
Charlotte:	But someone needs to bring the food and water to them.
Emily:	I know! We can pack some of the food at home and Suet can fly over there and give it to them!
Benjamin:	I know! We can give them money! Suet, you can give them money!
Aidan:	I will bring a gold coin and a silver coin in tomorrow from home.
Emily:	We can go to the bank and ask for some money too!
Charlotte:	We can ask our daddy and mummy to give us some money, too!
Benjamin:	Suet, I have a question. How money is useful, if there isn't any food in Syria? They won't be able to use money to buy those foods!

As these concerns were discussed, time passed and life in the centre continued to unfold, but with media attention still directed towards the war in Syria, the children continued to explore possibilities to raise funds to help refugees. Ideas began to emerge:

Liv:	We can paint some rocks and sell them!
Emily:	We can also sell some stuff made out of papers. We have a lot of papers here!
Benjamin:	We can sell used books. Or we can make books that help people to know more about Syria.
Charlotte:	We can make some bracelets and sell them.
Aidan:	We can write something on the paper so people will know we need to the money to help the Syrians.
Chloe:	We could also make some cards Suet!

Suet analysed this evolving investigation in terms of the national *Early Years Learning Framework* (DEEWR, 2009). In that accountability context, she reflected that:

> It was clear to me that children demonstrated increasing awareness of the needs and rights of others. They broadened their understanding of the world that they live in and were keen to take actions in assisting the others who are in need of help. The children showed a

strong sense of empathy and care towards the others (DEEWR, 2009). More than that, they showed a strong sense of belonging, being and exploring their becoming (as they participated fully and actively in their community) (ibid.).

She continued to work with the children to tease out their understanding of concepts of war, peace and human rights, including drawing as another 'language' of investigation. Conversation returned to practical ways to help – a key component supporting the development of agency and social responsibility rather than generating fear or helplessness. The children and educators then worked to make their plans a reality – making jewellery, cards and paperweights to sell at a fundraising event for families and nearby university community.

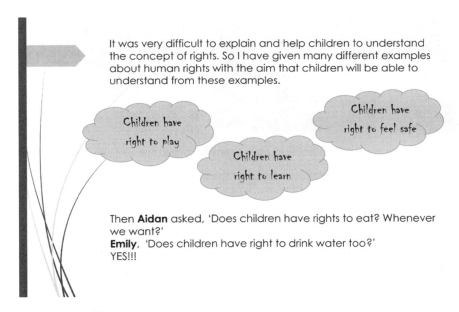

Figure 1.2 Children's rights

We searched for 'Volunteers that help Syrian refugees' on Google. After careful consideration, the children decided to choose UNICEF Australia.

> **Emily:**   I choose UNICEF because they used money to buy medicine for the Syrian people. This is important. So they won't get sick.
> **Chloe:**   UNICEF also provide winter clothes for them. This will help to keep them warm.
> **Rafael:**   And UNICEF provide education so children will be able to learn.

The day before the fundraising event, Aidan and Isabel helped organize the labels that showed the others the cost of items that we would be selling.

On the day of the event, Aidan introduced our handmade cards to one of our previous parents.

Figure 1.3   We raised $2000 and donated the money to UNICEF Australia

So, how does this approach sit with LiLi?

The aim of this schema is to: 'investigate decision-making frames inherent (and often invisible) when an educator pursues pedagogical documentation as a way of being with children. It aims to identify decision points that enhance or constrain the efficacy of this professional practice' (Fleet, 2015b). By making these *implicit* components *explicit*, there is both some reduction in complexity and awakening of the breadth of areas for consideration. The apparently contradictory nature of these two goals reflects the realities of working in a sector torn between requirements for linear accountability and desire for humanistic educational environments nurtured in relationships.

LiLi originated to highlight conversations in Australia, but may be relevant elsewhere. Theoretical frames associated with **LiLi** can be summarized in terms of seeing:

- pedagogical documentation as non-linear, interdisciplinary sites of possibility rather than product-oriented record-keeping (Rinaldi, 2006)
- professional decision-making positioned within a socio-constructivist frame (Berger and Luckmann, 1966)
- foregrounding of relationships in pedagogical processes (Hill et al., 2005)
- participatory rather than transmissive pedagogies (Formosinho and Pascal, 2015), therefore, from a transformational perspective
- pedagogical documentation as a component of socially just practice (Fleet et al., 2006, 2012).

It highlights five areas where there seems to be a shift from past orientations to more current frames of reference, as follows:

The Space: From a conception of the importance of 'the environment' referring to physical layout and specific resources towards a focus on CONTEXT as a sociocultural frame

The Individual: From a planning focus on each child's 'interests' or developmental stage towards consideration of the child's perceptions and PERSPECTIVES

The Group: From a focus on cooperating to 'work together' towards a focus on CONNECTEDNESS through collaboration

The Site: From a focus on trying to 'involve' families towards a focus on partnerships with COMMUNITIES, with

The Goal, therefore, of moving from focusing on 'responsible autonomy' towards focusing on SOCIALLY JUST PRACTICES through embedded equity agendas. (Fleet, 2015a)

While each starting point continues to be important for consideration, each may be potentially limiting. Expanding possibilities provide broader scope for growth and also reflect an interest in ideas offered by thinkers in Reggio Emilia.

'But isn't documentation supposed to be about recording?' some might ask. Well, partially. While artefacts for record-keeping are part of the processes of pedagogical documentation, a product is not the purpose. Working in relationship with adults and children enables consideration of curriculum, of children's learning and development, of the affective culture of the centre, of goals of families and each larger community. Along the way, photos are taken, conversations transcribed, investigations planned, observations recorded, outcomes considered. Multiple possibilities exist for consolidating these elements. Energy put into these efforts and insights required to move in fruitful directions must be accompanied by thinking professionals working in collaboration with others, by ongoing analysis of what is being revealed about pedagogy, about children's unexpected ideas, concerns, theories, priorities, discoveries. Pedagogical documentation is more than reporting; it is a multi-faceted way of growing alongside children which includes recording, using documentation as a stepping stone, as a vehicle for sharing with children, families and other professionals as well as guiding future planning. At its best, this work can be living, inspirational and revelatory. It can also be perceived as a time-consuming chore. In that case, the potentials of pedagogical documentation have probably not been understood.

LiLi can assist educators' decision-making about recording and professional practices. Core elements can be seen with reference to the examples of shared engagement in provocations from the war in Syria:

- a relevant project *context* that is socially culturally situated
- individual children's perceptions and *perspectives* being sought respectfully and enabled to evolve over time, particularly through explorative investigation
- multiple opportunities fostered for collaboration encouraging the development of authentic *connectedness* within and across groups
- sharing with families and encouraging engagement with and contributions from *communities*
- enabling progress towards the goal of *socially just practices* through embedded equity agendas.

These conceptualizations can be represented as shown in Figure 1.4.

THE SPACE

Seeing a context in which indoor and outdoor spaces are living systems of people, ideas and cultures

THE INDIVIDUAL

Standing in someone else's shoes to consider and build on varying perspectives

THE GROUP

Pursuing connectedness through meaningful relationships across ages, places and groups

THE SITE

Being positioned within a community context including socially just practices and equity agendas

---

Figure 1.4 Links to LiLi

While always expecting professional decision-making and intellectual curiosity, this interpretation of an investigation enables *Local interpretation of Larger ideas*. It builds on links to literature and children's theory-making, embraces families, valuing reciprocity and being interactive, while often including cyclical investigations. While it does not predetermine formats or generalize expectations, it does require written analysis for the way of working and evolving representations to be considered pedagogical documentation. Subsequent distribution may include blogs or newsletters, posters, portfolios or workshops. Purpose will determine the size and efficacy of the evolving experiences, relevant aggregation and presentations.

Relating children's explorations to the 'wicked problem' of pedagogical documentation

Returning to components of 'Adaptive Capacity' to tackle the 'wicked problem' of pedagogical documentation, one might ask whether this problem is shaped by record-keeping as required by legislation? Partially. Regional requirements vary widely across instrumentalities but no one (as far as we are aware) explicitly requires the doing or keeping of something named 'pedagogical documentation'. In itself, therefore, expectation does not make documentation a 'problem'. Everyone needs to devise effective ways of working with children in safe, sound, facilitative, enjoyable and perhaps inspirational educational environments and to record something about these actions. Whatever happens in those environments needs to be planned, implemented, evaluated and reported. There are infinite numbers of ways of tackling any part of this equation. For the moment, we are focusing on the elements of Adaptive Capacity as related to productive, effective and worthwhile engagement with pedagogical documentation.

Does this extended explanation mean that pedagogical documentation is only relevant for major issues or events, to be attempted by people with generous time allocations, who are Reggio-informed, with all elements essential throughout? No. Insightful pieces can be presented (particularly as work in progress) on a page reflecting encounters unfolding one afternoon. The experiences are more likely to generate pedagogical potential, however, if the initial idea is considered, shared with families, explored, followed up, perhaps when a key child next attends the site. If the data and/or information offers possibilities for further thought, highlights unexpected theory-making or discovery by a child or small group of children, then taking a few minutes to download a photo, describe a snippet of context and the unfolding interaction (non-verbal for the youngest ones) becomes energizing. That leads to analysing elements making the situation or event noteworthy, while looking for patterns or threads of engagement or dispositions over time to add additional richness to the seeing, hearing, thinking and interpreting. Such worthwhile work is more likely to unfold if there is supportive infrastructure, including interested colleagues, a thoughtful professional environment, and an informed educational leader (see, for example, Shepherd and Robertson, 2012). That was the context for work reported in this chapter: the lead educator has never been to Reggio Emilia, has been teaching for less than five years and speaks English as an additional language. She works in a context, although with professional, well-informed leaders who promote professional learning opportunities, provide time for collegial reflection, and a culture of collaboration and intellectual curiosity. When asked about whether the recording while doing this investigation assisted in the thinking of educators and/or the planning with or understanding by children of the purpose of the project, she wrote:

> I think recording the events gave me the opportunity to go back and read repeatedly about what the children had said. The revisiting process helped me to understand as well as learning how to be responsive to children's desire and determination of helping the Syrian refugees ... Recording events also reshaped my thinking and understanding of children's learning. Children being persistent, showing their sense of belonging as part of the global community and showing empathy and care towards the peoples who are in need. Throughout this project, I felt like a student, who put on a different lens, and relearned the world that I have lived in for 25 years from the children. I want to say that I learned to look at the world with simplicity but really, the children's interpretation of the world is very wise. For children, revisiting the discussions we had before seemed to enable them to think deeper about the concept of war and peace and their rights as children and humans.

Conclusion

Pedagogy is shaped by interpretations of philosophy and perceptions of accountability: it is more than curriculum or programme implementation. If concerned about whether or not pedagogical documentation can make a worthwhile contribution in contexts of stringent accountability, it is worth considering perspectives offered elsewhere (Fleet et al., 2014). Further, as we are reminded by Giudici et al. (2001), it is a case of seeing assessment (and community expectations) as 'making learning visible'.

Journeying with pedagogical documentation includes thinking around and then discussing with colleagues several foundational points including:

Who is the documentation for?
Who contributes to the processes involved?
When are decisions made that affect the shape and content of the documentation?
What is the pedagogy of the documentation? (Fleet, 2015a)

The answers to these questions help shape what happens next. Thinking in terms of **LiLi** demonstrates that:

- locally contextualized knowledge shapes pedagogical decision-making
- respectful time and space are necessary for co-researching with children
- intellectually complex decision-making by educators benefits from supportive infrastructure and collegial facilitation. (Fleet, 2015b)

Engaging with this 'wicked problem' includes an invitation to position yourself in this intriguing landscape: the goal must be to engage with children in ways that value their humanity. This work matters; today only comes once. The provocations of pedagogical documentation can thread through multiple layers of living and learning together; relish the invitations inherent in the process!

References

Bellamy, J. (2007) 'Adaptive governance: The challenge for natural resource management', in A.J. Brown and J.A. Bellamy (eds), *Federalism and Regionalism in Australia: New Approaches, New Institutions?* Canberra: ANU E Press, pp. 95–118.

Berger, P. and Luckmann, T. (1966) *The Social Construction of Knowledge: A Treatise in the Sociology of Knowledge*. Soho, New York: Open Road Media.

Carr, M. and Lee, W. (2012) *Learning Stories: Constructing Learner Identities in Early Education*. London: Sage.

DEEWR (Australian Government Department of Education, Employment and Workplace Relations) (2009) *Belonging, Being & Becoming: The Early Years Learning Framework for Australia*. Canberra: Australian Government.

Edwards, C., Gandini, L. and Forman, G. (eds) ([1993] 2012) *The Hundred Languages of Children: The Reggio Emilia Experience in Transformation* (3rd edn). Santa Barbara, CA: Praeger.

Fleet, A. (2015a) 'Where perceptions, interests and professionalism intersect: Journeying with pedagogical documentation', presented at the National Quality Standard Conference: Reshaping Documentation (various Australian cities).

Fleet, A. (2015b) 'Making professional decision-making visible through pedagogical documentation', presented at European Early Childhood Education Research Association (EECERA) Conference, Barcelona.

Fleet, A., Patterson, C. and Robertson, J. (2006) *Insights: Behind Early Childhood Pedagogical Documentation.* Sydney: Pademelon Press.

Fleet, A., Patterson, C. and Robertson, J. (2012) *Conversations: Behind Early Childhood Pedagogical Documentation.* Sydney: Pademelon Press.

Fleet, A., Patterson, C. and Robertson, J. (2014) 'Assessment: A critical companion to early childhood pedagogy', in M. Reed and R. Walker (eds), *A Critical Companion to Early Childhood.* London: Sage, pp. 296–306.

Fleet, A., Honig, T., Robertson, J., Semann, A. and Shepherd, W. (2011) *What's Pedagogy Anyway? Using Pedagogical Documentation to Engage with the Early Years Learning Framework.* Sydney: Children's Services Central. www.cscentral.org.au/Resources/what-is-pedagogy-anyway-.pdf (accessed 30.06.16).

Formosinho, J. and Pascal, C. (eds) (2015) *Assessment and Evaluation for Transformation in Early Childhood.* London: Routledge in association with the European Early Childhood Education Research Association (EECERA).

Giudici, C., Rinaldi, C. and Krechevsky, M. (eds) (2001) *Making Learning Visible: Children as Individual and Group Learners.* Reggio Emilia, Italy: Reggio Children.

Hill, L., Stremmel, A. and Fu, V. (2005) *Teaching as Inquiry: Rethinking Curriculum in Early Childhood Education.* Boston, MA: Pearson Education.

Pacini-Ketchabaw, V., Nxumalo, F., Kocher, L., Elliot, E. and Sanchez, A. (2015) *Journeys: Reconceptualizing Early Childhood Practices through Pedagogical Narration.* Toronto: University of Toronto Press.

Patterson, J., Smith, C. and Bellamy, J. (2014) 'Enabling and enacting practical action in catchments: Responding to the wicked problems of nonpoint source pollution in coastal subtropical Australia', *Environmental Management*, 55 (2): 479–495. Doi: 10.1007/s00267-014-0409-5.

Rinaldi, C. (2006) *In Dialogue with Reggio Emilia: Listening, Researching and Learning.* London: Routledge.

Rittel, H.W.J. and Webber, M.M. (1973), 'Dilemmas in a general theory of planning', *Policy Sciences*, 4 (2): 155–169.

Shepherd, W. and Robertson, J. (2012) 'Making a space for pedagogy: The story about Mia Mia – a work in progress', in A. Fleet, C. Patterson and J. Robertson (eds), *Conversations: Behind Early Childhood Pedagogical Documentation.* Sydney: Pademelon Press, pp. 217–233.

2

PEDAGOGICAL DOCUMENTATION AND PEDAGOGICAL CHOICES

LISE-LOTTE BJERVÅS AND GUNILLA ROSENDAHL

This chapter offers exploration and reflection through voices from a Swedish preschool. With a focus on pedagogical choices, the authors share experiences of toddlers and teachers offering insights to conversations and organization. Links with families are highlighted through the evolving processes of documentation.

Introduction

This chapter builds on a case study conducted in a Swedish preschool where the teachers have long experience of using pedagogical documentation. The term 'preschool' is used in Sweden for the first step in the educational system. Although preschool is not mandatory, almost every child aged between one and five years attends.

The teachers at this preschool have organized for an exploratory approach and developed a common reflection culture. Each year, the whole preschool chooses a common theme with the focus on exploring some aspect of the city. This year they have chosen to investigate transformations in the city by letting the children follow both longer-lasting changes, for example, construction of a new house, and more temporary changes in the city depending on weather and seasons. The children are also given opportunities to create changes in order to contribute to transformation in the city.

In this case study, we have followed the group with the eight youngest children, aged one to two years, and their two teachers. We have participated in the teachers' planning meetings four times during one semester and made audio recordings. On these occasions, we also posed questions about pedagogical choices in their work with pedagogical documentation. The parents, teachers and the head of the preschool have approved the publication of photographs used here. The chapter focuses on the teachers' choices in their work with pedagogical documentation before the project starts, during the project work and in their encounters with parents.

Preparation for documentation

When the teachers talk about pedagogical choices connected to the project work and documentation, they emphasize the importance of being well prepared. Before a new project, they must feel curiosity and inspiration and may need to acquire new knowledge. They stress that they must formulate overall issues in a careful way, issues which become guidelines and help them to sharpen their gaze and discover the children's strategies. Ahead of the new project, the teachers discuss what they should choose to focus on while they are documenting; this must be something connected to the selected issues.

When thinking about projects for toddlers, teachers may plan to take the children out of the preschool to extend their learning. There are a number of decisions to be made regarding the choice of an appropriate place. The teachers identify many aspects that they take into account. It should be a place that invites transformation and is close to the preschool so the toddlers can walk and don't need strollers. The place also needs to be free from cars so toddlers can move around and explore without being limited by teachers who must say 'No.' The previous year the youngest children investigated a nearby bird statue. The statue with its associated bird bath was an interesting place for these children; three of them, Emma, Johan and Viktor, are still part of the toddler group. According to the teachers, the existing relationship these three children have with the bird statue is a valuable starting point and therefore one reason for the choice of place for this year's project. Another reason is that cooperative learning is also enhanced when starting with a place that some children already have experienced.

Pedagogical choices in the process with the children

When the teachers introduce the project, they use selected pictures from the documentation of the previous year, since in their experience this helps children to remember and retell for their friends. This time, the pictures show the bird statue that Emma, Johan and Viktor already know. The teachers' intention is to begin in old experiences with the help of documentation, but then open up for new possibilities and for the unexpected. Their idea is that the children who already have experience of the bird and the place can act as a driving force in beginning the project.

The teachers show the chosen pictures, printed in a large format, so the toddlers are able to see simultaneously without crowding, in order to enable communication among them.

According to the teachers' experiences, it depends on the activity when deciding how many children should be invited to participate. The teachers want to be able to see and listen to each child. Hence, when it is time for the first walk to the place where the bird statue is, they chose to take four children. In this case, two of the toddlers who already have investigated the place have the task of showing it to two of their new peers. The teachers explain that it is manageable for them with four children who are walking and holding hands; one of the teachers has time to take pictures and the other has time to write down the children's communication. There is also time for the teachers to see and pay attention to what the toddlers discover during their joint exploration. The teachers argue that pedagogical documentation is a tool that can be used to create opportunities for cooperative learning since it shows what is going on for everybody. One child's discovery becomes everyone's discoveries. What the individual child does becomes visible and a concern for the whole group. At the same time the teachers claim that work with pedagogical documentation helps them perceive individual children's interests and strategies.

It requires careful organization at the preschool to enable two adults to walk out with only four children. At this preschool, the whole teaching team supports a joint pedagogical ideal including how to work with pedagogical documentation. When the two teachers are working with the four toddlers, their colleagues take care of other children. A shared reflective culture, where all teachers are involved in reflections about on-going project works for different groups of children, supports the teachers' willingness to cooperate in such a way.

When teachers gather the children in the morning, they start a discussion together with the children. Perhaps it ends in the decision that today there will be a walk to the bird statue. This discussion is documented in the folder containing the teachers' planning. The teachers might take a photograph of the children preparing for the walk. As they have created a culture of

Emma: That!
Johan: Water!
Lisa: Look!
Johan: Clap, clap!
Lisa: Look there!
Johan: Ah, look bird, water!
Viktor: There! [*Points to the sculpture and the water*]
Lisa: Look mouth [*points to the beak*]
Johan: Water and bird!
Emma: Water, bird!

Figure 2.1   Reviewing photographs from last year

documentation, they only need to look at each other and they have an agreement about taking a picture and thereby give a situation a value.

While the children are gathering at the gate, the teachers begin to document, to show that they are connected to the project again. They explain that they need bodily awareness when they are documenting and supporting the children's cooperative learning. As a result, the children hold hands on the walk, while the teachers go next to support their communication, but also to have their hands free to be able to document. One of them emphasizes: 'We are busy in the hands, but not in thought.

Figure 2.2   Gathering at the gate

Because we are busy, the children can keep the focus and they have a bigger responsibility to keep together.'

Afterwards, during a circle time when the children retell the walk with the help of the documentation, the teachers sit next to them or a little behind, preferably not with a child in their lap. They try to make it possible for the children to move around and communicate about the pictures. One of the teachers underlines:

> When there are two children who are communicating, we sit back a little so we don't come between the two who are trying to communicate. It's about that cooperation, it has to sit in our bodies too. This is bodily knowledge. It's about small things, how we are positioning ourselves and how we are placing pictures on the table. You can destroy it with your body and become a brake pad, or you can babble on too much so the children's words can't be heard.

The teachers also highlight the value of coming prepared to the circle so attention then may be on the shared processes. They consider it as significant to decide in advance who should write and who should take photos so that an unclear division of roles does not lead to lack of concentration among the children.

Focus of documentation

When the teachers document the children's exploration of the place, they focus on what the place invites, and the repertoire of physical movements and verbal expressions that develop between the toddlers. For example, Emma tells her friends how to stand on the ramp and say 'ready, ready, go' and run, and then the children do and say the same.

When teachers document the children's exploration, they try to be attentive to what it is that sets the group in connection with the place, things and with each other. They try to capture both verbal and non-verbal expression. One teacher points out: 'We capture the children's interest through documentation. We see what they do with the body. When they don't have the verbal language, we capture gazes, a hand pointing out, and we have to catch stuff like that instead.'

They ask themselves what these children are interested in and how they may support this and challenge the children further. This makes it possible for the toddlers to continue their investigation and deepen their understanding. Sometimes, the toddlers come up with new ideas and sometimes it is the teachers who do. When the teachers are planning the next walk they find the starting point in a previous documentation, but sometimes a child brings forward new proposals. They give one example:

> Johan said 'Paint' directly when we asked: 'Tell me what you want to paint!' And he answered, 'Paint out there,' and then Emma said, 'Paint brush.' We said that we could bring the paintbrushes out and paint on the bird. We made a choice to embrace Johan's idea. We could have done it another day but he has this idea now. It works like that with toddlers. Perhaps it is more about acting immediately. With the older children, we can say, 'We have written it, but we will do it on Tuesday.' But to say that to a toddler, what does it mean for a child, one year old?

The pictures taken on this occasion will later be used in conversation with Johan's parents. Then the purpose is to show the parents through the documentation how the preschool invites Johan to come up with ideas, which he can realize in the group.

Selection of documentations

The teachers begin by introducing one place for the toddlers: the place with the bird statue. After all the children have visited the place and started to explore it, the teachers look through all documentation and chose pictures they want to share. They present the documentation as a big mind map on a low table where the toddlers gather. The teachers have chosen pictures to illustrate items that captured the toddlers' attention on their visit: the bird statue itself, the water in the bird bath, the rocks, the sloping ramp, line of stones and a bench, as well as what the children were doing at these places. Children's comments about the place ('Where!' 'Stones!') will be documented and added to the mind map.

When it comes to choosing pictures, the teachers say that they take into account different aspects in different contexts and for different purposes. They often choose only to take photos of the children's hands when they are acting. This can be an advantage for the children looking at the photographs, because if the focus is on the object, then there will not be so much pointing out each other. When the teachers focus on the movements, however, the whole child needs to be in the picture, otherwise movements will not be visible for the children. The teachers have selected some pictures to be shown in black and white, since the contents become clearer when the children's colourful clothes are not dominating. Other pictures that they choose to show in colour, and in this documentation the colour photographs make the light shimmering in the water recognizable.

The educational environment in relation to pedagogical documentation

At circle time, the children and teachers gather at a round table that is a suitable height for toddlers to sit or stand and study the documentation. The children use their whole body when they point and communicate about the pictures and one teacher says: 'We have noticed that it can be a very advanced language even with the little ones. They are coming together through the language and the words get a value. There is a strong drive to conquer the words for the sake of the fellowship, in order to participate.'

The teachers have also made a reflection wall with large format, plastic-wrapped photos; one of them explains:

> We are building up a reflection wall. The children will be involved in putting up the pictures. We think that we can take pictures of the walks. The reflection wall should be living, not finished; we can take down the photo and take it with us, even when we go outside, and then we put it back again.

Figure 2.3   Reviewing the visit

The teachers also tell about benefits they have discovered with the pictures on the table and the wall. The toddlers meet and communicate with the help of the documentation, although the teachers are not present. When parents come and pick up their child and ask what has been done today, sometimes the child goes to the documentation, points, and then the parent understands and can join in dialogue.

Sometimes, the teachers choose to project pictures from the documentation onto the wall. Then, the toddlers can play in the picture and according to the teachers, this supports them to deepen their relationship with the place.

Figure 2.4 Being in the photographs

Pedagogical choices in collaboration with parents

In their work with pedagogical documentation, the teachers would like to direct the parents' attention towards what the children have done and experienced in preschool together with their peers. The teachers would like parents to understand that while questions like what and how the children have eaten and if they have slept well are important, they are not the most significant questions when parents come to pick up their children. To encourage parents to become more interested in what has happened in pedagogical practices, teachers talk with them about pedagogical documentation as an important tool to involve them into the children's learning processes.

When documenting, teachers also have the parents in mind. They ask themselves: 'What needs to be documented in order to give parents insight into and understanding of what their children experience and learn in preschool?' With the help of documentation, they want to expand the parents' image of what a preschool can be. One pedagogical choice they made in relation to parents was to document the children at the gate before the walk. According to the teachers, such pictures can demonstrate to parents how they trust children. It shows that they have chosen not to use strollers and they want children to hold each other's hands when they are walking. It can show parents that the children communicate more with each other without an adult walking between them.

The teachers explain that, during parent meetings, they choose to show documentation as a slideshow. They also point out, however, that they could further develop these opportunities by stopping the slide show a few times and discussing processes with the parents. One of the teachers says: 'The slideshow is a sort of recap of what we've done. We want to show the parents all the processes. We want the parents to participate and contribute. What do they think about the places we have chosen?'

One teacher also said that parents tell them what children do when they are at the place together with their children. The teachers are curious to hear this because it may contain ideas for further investigation. Another choice that they mention is that they could engage the parents more at the beginning of the semester by inviting them to be involved in the choice of issues for the project. According to the teachers, this would create expanded opportunities for parents to be involved and influence what the children would experience at preschool right from the beginning.

Building relationships with pedagogical documentation

In a review of our increasingly individualized society, Bauman (2001) points out that what makes a society is what holds us together. At this preschool, the teachers have the hope that through project work the children will create a better relationship with their city and become active participants in society. This effort is visible in all the choices the teachers make in the pedagogical process with the toddlers. The aim is to create a group where each individual is made visible, but also connected to each other and the surroundings. Teachers direct their attention towards both individuals and the whole group of children, and their pedagogical documentation shows how they value differences and use them to expand children's learning. This is in line with what Dahlberg and Moss (2005: 2) underscore, namely that preschools don't need to be institutions where 'the Other' is made into 'the Same'. Instead, they can be places open 'for diversity, differences, and otherness, for new possibilities and potentialities' (ibid.: 2). The teachers show in practice Dewey's ([1916] 2007) thoughts about the necessity to learn, as a part of an education, how to use other peoples' experiences as a complement to one's own limited experiences.

The teachers' work with pedagogical documentation has supplied them with valuable tools to create relations between the child, the group and the city, and to support children's cooperative learning processes. One tool is to formulate questions as guidelines in the work. This is assessed by teachers as useful for finding focus for the documentation. Preparation is important since it evokes curiosity to know more, and wonderment when the unexpected arises (Dahlberg, 2015). Wonderment is considered to be the foremost prerequisite for experiences and learning by Dahlberg et al. (2013) and it is something that the teachers emphasize, too.

Another useful tool for cooperative learning is previous documentation. These teachers have consciously chosen to build on some children's previous experiences, and with the support of this documentation ask the children to recall their memories. In this way, children can share what they have learned with new peers. This can be interpreted as illustrating what Dewey ([1916] 2007) defines as education. He emphasizes that education means to reconstruct and reorganize experience and thus provide meaningful experience and increase the sense of connection and continuity of the activities one is involved in. When children share their memories, documentation becomes an active agent contributing to learning, which is a role that Lenz Taguchi (2010) stresses when she describes pedagogical documentation as a tool for creating knowledge, learning and change. In order to support cooperative learning, these teachers consider it significant that the children have access to and can meet and communicate about documentation all the time. This can be compared with the discussion from Dahlberg et al. (2013) describing the creation of meaning. They point out that interaction with others makes the world meaningful; they underline that pedagogical documentation makes it possible for children to retell and revisit what has happened.

The teachers' work with pedagogical documentation highlights the value of a supporting organization and supportive forms of work, including a culture of reflection. Teachers at this preschool have chosen to organize time and space in a way that creates possibilities to work with children in small groups. This case study also reveals that the teachers' work with pedagogical documentation makes it possible for toddlers to be involved in the planning of the day. The teachers welcome the children's ideas and strive to include their perspectives in learning opportunities. In a practice which values negotiation, children's participation may be seen as an ethical and a democratic approach (Åberg and Lenz Taguchi, 2005) and this permeates the teachers' talk about their work with the children and with pedagogical documentation.

Finally, the teachers see that with the help of pedagogical documentation, parents are not only able to be involved in their children's experiences, but they also gain understanding of the pedagogical practices. In line with this, Åberg and Lenz Taguchi (ibid.) ask how parents can be expected to influence professional practice if teachers cannot describe the child's everyday life at preschool and explain the children's learning. In this case study, it is evident that teachers see pedagogical documentation as having a valuable role in representing what happens at the preschool for parents.

Conclusion

In summary, pedagogical documentation appears to help individuals to be connected to others and to the world. It takes advantage of ordinary moments in children's lives at the preschool and turns them into special moments of learning or discovery. It helps deepen adults' understanding of children's learning and creates opportunities to strengthen relationships between children, teachers and families. The teachers in this chapter have shown courage in sharing insights into their experiences; their thoughts illustrate the rich possibilities of pedagogical documentation, while acknowledging the complexities of decision-making within their preschool community. It is through the sharing of such experiences that teachers learn from one another and the profession continues to grow and develop.

References

Åberg, A. and Lenz Taguchi, H. (2005) *Lyssnandets Pedagogik: Etik och Demokrati i Pedagogiskt Arbete*. Stockholm: Liber.

Bauman, Z. (2001) *The Individualized Society*. Cambridge: Polity Press.

Dahlberg, G. (2015) 'Mötet med Reggio Emilia', in A. Barsotti, G. Dahlberg, H. Gothson and T. Jonstoij (eds), *Hundra Sätt att Förundras: Pedagogik i en Föränderlig Omvärld*. Stockholm: Liber, pp. 42–74.

Dahlberg, G. and Moss, P. (2005) *Ethics and Politics in Early Childhood Education*. London: RoutledgeFalmer.

Dahlberg, G., Moss, P. and Pence, A. (2013) *Beyond Quality in Early Childhood Education and Care: Languages of Evaluation* (3rd edn). Abingdon: Routledge.

Dewey, J. ([1916] 2007) *Democracy and Education*. Sioux Falls, SD: NuVision Publications.

Lenz Taguchi, H. (2010) *Going Beyond the Theory/Practice Divide in Early Childhood Education: Introducing an Intra-Active Pedagogy*. London and New York: Routledge.

3

DEVELOPING PEDAGOGICAL DOCUMENTATION WITHIN THE EYFS CURRICULUM FRAMEWORK

NICOLA STOBBS, JANET HARVELL AND MICHAEL REED

This chapter considers policy contexts and the roles of educational leaders as those concerned with early childhood education grapple with the complexities of accountability and recording requirements. It enables the consideration of policy and practice across four differing national contexts in the UK.

Perspectives from the UK

The UK is made up of four nations: England, Northern Ireland, Wales and Scotland. Each accepts that early childhood education and care (ECEC) should be an integral part of education and social policy; and, moreover, that promoting early childhood education brings a wide range of social and economic benefits (Litjens and Taguma, 2010; Wall et al., 2015). Each nation enacts policies developed by their elected parliaments and assemblies, inevitably influenced by each nations' distinctiveness and the availability of finance. Differences appear in practice in the way each nation develops and enacts policies. These are shaped over time and subjected to review to ensure contemporary issues are being addressed.

Documenting children's learning in the UK is an accepted part of early education practice, forming part of every nation's curriculum requirements. There are, however, many approaches used to record what children do within a diverse range of early educational settings. These approaches are underpinned by discourse which includes the influence of Rinaldi (2006) in asserting the rights of the child, integrating Loris Malaguzzi's reflective interpretations of learning, and theoretically framed by the work of Vygotsky (1978) regarding the interactions between educator and child. To this is added the value of constructing narratives that represent the child and the child's interests (Bruner, 1986). Whether the enlightened views of these commentators have been translated into a curriculum framework that sees value in documenting children's learning is open to debate. Documenting learning in the UK is often seen as providing an opportunity to reflect on what a child can do, but tends to have less impact on analysing learning in order to refine the learning environment, being sometimes too closely associated with assessment rather than considering characteristics of children's learning.

Pedagogical documentation, however, is a different matter; it means documenting learning with the child at the centre and is purposeful with regard to the characteristics of children's learning. Recordings form the basis for collective professional analysis and refinement to the learning environment. Unfortunately, that form of documentation is less visible in the UK. Its implementation relies on the education and experience of the leader within the early education setting; their influence cannot be underestimated. An effective leader employs documentation to make visible both the actions and the underpinning motivations in children's play, ensuring that recording learning acts as a bridge between child, educator and parent. They will also ensure that it provides a basis for dialogue, analysis and questioning as well as refining the learning environment and learning opportunities. The key question is whether leaders can use the approach as part of meeting the regulatory requirements which underpin early education policy and the day-to-day actions of educators.

When considering the complexities of early education, one may lose sight of what systems and policies look like to those most closely involved.

We, therefore, introduce vignettes to illustrate some of the possibilities and barriers associated with implementing pedagogical documentation currently facing educators in the UK.

Four vignettes

Jane, Fiona, Caitlin and Ellie became friends when they met on a study visit to the infant-toddler centres of Reggio Emilia, Italy, where they were inspired by the use of pedagogical documentation and its potential for observing and analysing children's learning.

Jane works in a busy childcare centre in England. She was aware of regulatory requirements imposed by the government but was confident that she could combine pedagogical documentation with assessment requirements. When she introduced this at a staff meeting, the team seemed initially enthusiastic but now she finds that she has to reiterate how it is a way of examining learning as well as monitoring children's progress towards the early learning goals of the statutory curriculum.

Fiona works in a university nursery in Scotland and is part of a small, well-qualified and motivated staff team. They already knew about pedagogical documentation and embrace both the process and the concept. Staff share observations of the children every week to plan for the children's interests. As time goes by, people have noted that maintaining the effort involved is difficult and so Fiona has decided to bring together other practitioners using the approach to reflect on the purpose of documenting children's learning. However, she struggles to find sufficient numbers of those using the approach in her locality to share perspectives.

Caitlin works in a school nursery in Wales and is also committed to the principles of pedagogical documentation. However, her head teacher is not an early years specialist and hopes to raise standards by ensuring that children are set targets to progress towards agreed national outcomes. She is not supportive of introducing another method of what she sees as assessment when a national strategy for coding children's understanding of key concepts is not yet secure among school staff. Caitlin's colleagues seem glad to have detailed guidelines of what children should know and how to grade them. Caitlin sees learning as more than a transmission of knowledge, but struggles to find allies among her peers.

(Continued)

(Continued)

Ellie works in a rural setting in Northern Ireland. Although she, too, saw the potential of pedagogical documentation while in Reggio Emilia, she finds that she has to spend much time discussing with staff the 'right balance' of adult- and child-led activities. They struggle to know when to intervene and when to enable free-flow play. She realizes that she has a long way to go until the team sees potential value in pedagogical documentation.

These vignettes illustrate how the four nations within the UK struggle with employing pedagogical documentation within their own systems and curriculum frameworks. It suggests that, to be successful, the approach requires those in leadership positions to balance not only the opportunities afforded by the approach against its constraints, but also identify how it sits within the demands of regulatory curriculum frameworks. This chapter explores these issues and concludes with a discussion that suggests pedagogical documentation is a tool enabling practitioners to reflect deeply on *how* children learn as well as *what* they learn. It is an effective part of an integrated approach to support the development of learning opportunities and assist educational planning. It also has potential to elevate the early years workforce from being 'good enough' (Georgeson and Campbell-Barr, 2015: 323) to one that is able to speak out about the strengths of young children.

Pedagogical documentation in England

The English curriculum framework for early education, the Early Years Foundation Stage (EYFS) (DfE, 2014), was recently reviewed and refined. Its construction purports to underpin features associated with effective early learning, as identified by Sylva et al. (2009). In practice, it could be argued that the curriculum holds contradictory views of the child and its family, as well as what is valued in processes of learning and teaching. For example, the curriculum is supported by a statutory framework, divided into three sections outlining requirements for: (i) learning and development, (ii) assessment and (iii) safeguarding and welfare. Documentation of children's learning sits within the areas of both learning and assessment, but how this occurs and the depth of analysis given to how children learn is a matter for individual settings, consequently relying on the qualities and experience of leaders. In a review of qualifications in England (Nutbrown, 2012), leadership quality was identified as important to ensure the educational and welfare needs of children by promoting good practice in collaboration with others. The review emphasized the role of an early years educator and resulted in a progressive series of qualifications leading to the status of Early Years Teacher (DfE, 2013). These qualifications focus on a graduate leader who is aware of effective learning characteristics and can use this knowledge to help children learn by refining learning opportunities. This process includes the ability to effectively monitor and document progress. Such leaders are expected to be facilitators in practice and mentors to trainee practitioners, paving the way for a culture of pedagogic leadership to become established (Papatheodorou and Moyles, 2009).

However, this structural approach by the government to formulating and regulating national policy has its critics. It is suggested that practitioners in England are 'at the bottom of the epistemological hierarchy' (Moss, 2013: 141), a view drawn from the way practitioners may be seen as educators, but in reality have little autonomy to consider the pedagogical base they might employ. Some argue that the political system has used the professionalization of the workforce, seen initially as a way of raising the status of early years education, as a vehicle for control, effected through the use of regulatory standards that 'represents adherence to a mechanistic reductionist project, wherein those who represent the power elite (government departments and agencies) act as regulators of the behaviour of the subordinate (practitioners)' (Osgood, 2006: 6). Indeed, Plum (2012: 491) suggests this has resulted in a focus on 'technical rationality' at the expense of 'teacher autonomy'.

It can be argued that a tension has emerged between the structural patterns of learning and development set out in the statutory requirements of the EYFS and the process features exemplified in advice given to practitioners regarding their day-to-day interactions with children. For example, a developmental 'ages and stages' view of documenting and assessing learning is at odds with the socio-cultural approach to learning in the non-statutory guidance of the EYFS known as *Development Matters* (Early Education, 2012). This document suggests a *positivist* stance as educators evidence children's learning against predetermined early learning goals, while simultaneously taking an *interpretivist* stance in recording children's learning dispositions against the 'Characteristics of Effective Learning' (DfE, 2014: 9; see also Moyles and Worthington, 2011; Rix and Parry, 2014). This means that early educators need the wherewithal, experience and education to equip them to understand and blend approaches (Grieshaber, 2008). They also need the confidence and support to work with others to devise locally meaningful documentation, rather than relying on representing children's interests by drawing together a chronology of progress, commonly referred to as 'learning journeys'. This is a narrative document compiled for each child by an early educator, comprising notes, photographs, drawings and observations which are mapped against developmentally arranged early learning goals (DfE, 2014). These 'journeys' may provide useful information about children's learning and are often cited as being aligned to the learning stories found in New Zealand's Te Whāriki curriculum. However, the original learning stories were intended to re-create selfhood via the creation of 'alternative narratives', co-authored by children, teachers and families to enable an understanding of shared culture (Carr and Lee, 2012). In contrast, the learning *journeys* used in England suggest a linear route. Most are stored in the setting and shared occasionally with families. Some parents are unsure how to interpret the codification of the early learning goals, while practitioners may be disillusioned with the time learning journeys take when they can see little value in them. This suggests an underlying unease that what is being documented is 'superficial' and 'misunderstood' (Basford and Bath, 2014: 127). Instead of making *learning* visible, it would appear they are being used as a tool for accountability in order to make '*practice* visible' to administrators and inspectors (Plum, 2012: 496).

Although many educators in England align their practice to the perceived demands of Ofsted, it is clear that regulatory systems allow for a variety of rigorous approaches to documenting learning. For example, Ofsted (2015a) stress the need for a setting to have a clear pedagogic value base and to carefully consider the effectiveness of teaching in meeting the needs of all children, with impact demonstrated by the progress children make from recorded baselines. This approach easily resonates with the use of pedagogical documentation and demonstrates a more productive process than emphasizing the recording of children's progress, as opposed to supporting understanding of children's learning. This latter approach can result in discussions based on educators' understanding of children's learning and how this can be used to provide an enabling environment to support children's progress.

Table 3.1 illustrates potential overlap between the requirements of the inspection process, the statutory framework and pedagogical documentation. The statements do not align, but are general points for illustration.

The table shows that regulators do not perceive the introduction of pedagogical documentation negatively. Instead, it offers encouragement to practitioners to engage in pedagogic leadership and to find meaningful

Table 3.1 A comparison of compatibility between underlying principles of pedagogical documentation, the statutory framework and inspection requirements

Statements taken from Fleet et al. (2012: 6)	Statements taken from the Statutory Framework for the EYFS (DfE, 2014)	Statements taken from the Early Years Inspection Handbook (Ofsted, 2015b)
Pedagogical documentation means: • Following children's and educators thinking and finding ways to make that thinking visible … • Asking questions about the learning that occurs … • More than just gathering evidence, it is about making learning visible … • Reflection on learning that has taken place	• Every child is a unique child, who is constantly learning and can be resilient, capable and self-assured (p. 6) • Children learn and develop well in enabling environments, in which their experiences respond to their individual needs and there is a strong partnership between the practitioners and parents and/or carers (p. 6) • Early years providers *must* guide the development of children's capabilities (p. 7) • Practitioners *must* consider the individual needs, interests and stage of development of each child in their care, and must use this information to plan a challenging and enjoyable experience for each child in all areas of learning and development (p. 8) • Practitioners *must* respond to each child's emerging needs and interests, guiding their development through warm, positive interactions (p. 9) • Ongoing assessment … is an integral part of the learning and development process. It involves practitioners observing children to understand their level of achievement, interests and learning styles, and to then shape their experiences … (p. 13) • Assessment *should not* entail prolonged breaks from interaction with children, nor require excessive paperwork. Paperwork *should be* limited to that which is absolutely necessary … (p. 13) • At the end of the EYFS (the final term of the year in which a child reaches age five) … each child's level of development *must* be assessed against the early learning goals (p. 14)	• Inspectors must spend most of the inspection time gathering first-hand evidence by observing the quality of the *daily routines* and activities of children and staff (p. 17) • Inspectors should consider the impact of staff knowledge, qualifications, training and expertise (p. 37) • Inspectors should observe the quality and timeliness of adults' interventions and how well any learning that children demonstrate is built on by the adults working with them (p. 37) • Direct observation should be supplemented by a range of other evidence including assessment on entry, progress checks of two-year-olds, formative assessment, the EYFS profile … evidence of planning for next stages (p. 37) • The inspector should examine the information that the provision gathers about what children know, can do and enjoy when they start to attend. Evidence of starting points can also be gained by talking to staff and parents (p. 43) • The inspector must use the evidence to evaluate how well the provider and practitioners know about, and understand, the progress children are making towards the early learning goals (p. 44)

ways of documenting children's learning. It suggests that there are ways to demonstrate how children can progress towards the early learning goals of the statutory framework, but is not prescriptive regarding what form this progress monitoring should take. What is important is that confident pedagogic leaders who 'can create a space for a vivid and critical discussion about pedagogical practice' (Dahlberg et al., 2007: 145) are developed. However, some caution is needed. The aim of most settings in England is to be rated 'Outstanding' by Ofsted (2015b). This is awarded to settings that can show the developmental progress of children towards measurable outcomes. The leader of a setting must be confident they can both document learning and record outcomes that meet 'regulatory expectations'. A lack of such evidence will inevitably be perceived as contributing to a low grade following inspection, with consequences for morale, financing and potential withdrawal of parental patronage. This again underlines the importance of carefully leading, managing and implementing pedagogical documentation into a learning community.

Pedagogical documentation in Scotland

There is no specific mention of pedagogical documentation in the Scottish Curriculum for Excellence (3–18 years); however, its potential may sit within the requirement to recognize achievement through profiling and reporting (Scottish Government, 2010), whereby learners reflect on the process of their learning.

There is some evidence of engagement with pedagogical documentation in Scotland: practitioners record children's theories and make their learning visible (for example, Wharton and Kinney, 2015; Warden and McNair, 2015). Notwithstanding these examples, an independent review of the early years workforce concluded that 'the workforce needs to be developed substantially in size and quality' (Siraj and Kingston, 2015: 12) with an emphasis on both undergraduate and postgraduate course design and leadership skills, suggesting that there is a way to go before pedagogical documentation is common practice.

Pedagogical documentation in Wales

While pedagogical documentation was not a term used in the Welsh Early Years Foundation Phase (EYFP) (Welsh Assembly Government, 2008), educators were encouraged to learn alongside the children and use evidence-based approaches to reflect on their professional practice.

This evidence could be published research; alternatively, it could be research based on the practitioner's own theories of how children learn. However, a review of the Foundation Phase by Siraj in 2014 (cited in Prowle et al., 2015) found significant room for improvement regarding the delivery of the EYFP. It was suggested that without appropriate support and resources for educators, implementation had been ad hoc (Prowle et al., 2015). In proposing a way forward, Prowle et al. recommended that staff training be underpinned with theoretical knowledge of how children learn and develop and that head teachers provide strong leadership, fostering a 'culture of commitment' (ibid.: 201) to the Foundation Phase. A further recommendation suggested the implementation of a systematic approach to tracking and planning based on observations and responsive to the learning needs of the child. This has resulted in a prescriptive document, whereby practitioners make judgements of children's progress, categorized as either bronze, silver or gold, against developmental outcomes (Welsh Government, 2015).

Pedagogical documentation in Northern Ireland

Northern Ireland's Foundation Stage (FS) (CCEA, 2007) was underpinned by a child-led, play-based pedagogy; however, despite some ascribed advantages (Doherty and Walsh, 2015), there were difficulties associated with insufficient training regarding theoretical perspectives on play. In 2012, the 'Curricular guidance for pre-school education' (CCEA, 2012) was produced, suggesting activities to promote development and learning. Pedagogical documentation does not feature in the guidance and it is stipulated that, although 'children's efforts and achievements should be recognized, shared with them and recorded' (ibid.: 9) in profiles, 'observations take time', so only 'useful information' should be recorded. The *Learning to Learn* document (DENI, 2012) accepted that progress was still needed in terms of up-skilling the workforce and improving leadership, suggesting that there is a desire to develop pedagogical practice, but a realization that this will occur over time.

Moving towards a model for introducing pedagogical documentation

All nations of the UK share a desire for evidencing children's learning. However, it seems that each nation is at a different stage of knowledge and understanding about how this can be translated into practice. There is evidence from England and Scotland that educators are 'trying to see and understand what is going on in the pedagogical work and what the child is capable of without any predetermined framework or expectations of norms' (Dahlberg et al., 2007: 146). They are starting to ask how learning occurs, rather than assuming – as in transmission models of learning — that learning occurred because teaching occurred (Wien et al., 2011).

Importantly, pedagogical documentation can also reveal the educator's thinking and their views about learning (Lancaster, 2006; Dahlberg et al., 2007; Wien et al., 2011). It enables the focus to return to children's learning rather than meeting curriculum requirements. It is 'their images and their words to gather, their insights, their confirmation, or their disagreement, in a shared dialogue, so that in the long run the children's interests and learning can be supported' (Dahlberg et al., 2007: 147). The key word here is 'interests', and it is worth noting that the EYFS (DfE, 2014: 5) clearly recommends that educators should plan 'around the needs and interests of each individual child'. It can be argued that pedagogical documentation provides a way of gaining insights about those interests and avoids objectifying children in terms of their development, elevating them to actors in society and co-constructors of culture (Turner and Gray Wilson, 2010: 7).

As Kalliala and Samuelsson (2014: 116) state: 'there are few phenomena that generate only benefits … we have to ask: what is being neglected while we are busy documenting?' Is it enough to demonstrate 'technical rationality' at the expense of 'teacher autonomy' (Plum, 2012: 491) as long as children make progress towards goals? When ascribing to an ideological stance that challenges the instrumental view of the child as an economic investment (Soler and Miller, 2003), the early years practitioner will need to navigate the tensions of conforming to 'regulatory expectations whilst attempting an approach that sits more closely with a democratic pedagogy' (Basford and Bath, 2014: 127).

Conclusion

There are leaders (Bennett, 2001; Wien et al., 2011) of early educational practice who appreciate that an observer of children can never know with surety what children are feeling and who look beyond what a child can do – who see assessment as more than recording deficit developmental levels, and instead listen with emotional and intellectual empathy to the voice of the child. It is these educators who may find that pedagogical documentation provides an ethically safe learning environment for both practitioners and children (ibid.). However, this involves having a sound knowledge of the characteristics of children's learning and the ability to adapt and challenge established systems. As Wood notes, practitioners who choose to take a locally derived, relativist, responsive approach to quality while working within the constraints of the EYFS (DfE, 2014) 'need to be prepared for the fact that understanding children's perspectives can challenge dominant policy discourses and practices in pedagogy, curriculum planning and assessment' (Wood, 2010, cited in Wood, 2013: 156). Whether there are sufficient pedagogical leaders willing to ascribe to this agenda in the UK is currently far from certain. The inevitable conclusion is that those in a position of influence must learn, develop and articulate the value of pedagogical documentation and introduce it within courses of professional development, particularly within university programmes preparing the pedagogic leaders of tomorrow. Until those in positions of influence are willing to do this, it could be argued that practitioners will continue to have little autonomy regarding practice and will remain at the bottom of the 'epistemological hierarchy' (Moss, 2013: 141), acquiescent to remaining 'good enough' (Georgeson and Campbell-Barr, 2015).

This chapter has revealed why the earlier practitioner vignettes are realistic, although there are still grounds for optimism about ways forward for pedagogical documentation in the UK. Regulation has a place, but if a professional workforce is desired, then educators have to be empowered to make decisions and influence educational decision-making. In this case, it means considering how children learn as well as what they learn.

References

Basford, J. and Bath, C. (2014) 'Playing the assessment game: An English early childhood education perspective', *Early Years*, 34 (2): 119–132.

Bennett, T. (2001) 'Reactions to visiting the infant-toddler and preschool centers in Reggio Emilia, Italy', *Early Childhood Research and Practice*, 3 (1). http://ecrp.uiuc.edu/v3n1/bennett.html (accessed 20.01.17).

Bruner, J. (1986) *Actual Minds, Possible Worlds*. Cambridge, MA: Harvard University Press.

Carr, M. and Lee, W. (2012) *Learning Stories: Constructing Learner Identities in Early Education*. London: Sage.

CCEA (Council for the Curriculum, Examinations and Assessment) (2007) 'The Northern Ireland Curriculum Primary'. http://ccea.org.uk/sites/default/files/docs/curriculum/area_of_learning/fs_northern_ireland_curriculum_primary.pdf (accessed 23.01.17).

CCEA (2012) 'Curriculum guidance for pre-school education'. http://ccea.org.uk/sites/default/files/docs/curriculum/pre_school/preschool_guidance.pdf (accessed 23.01.17).

Dahlberg, G., Moss, P. and Pence, A. (2007) *Beyond Quality in Early Childhood Education and Care: Languages of Evaluation* (2nd edn). Abingdon: Routledge.

DENI (Department of Education, Northern Ireland) (2012) *Learning to Learn: A Framework for Early Years Education and Learning*. www.deni.gov.uk/sites/default/files/publications/de/learning-to-learn-framework-document-2012.pdf (accessed 20.01.17).

DfE (Department for Education) (2013) *More Great Childcare: Raising Quality and Giving Parents More Choice*. www.gov.uk/government/publications/more-great-childcare-raising-quality-and-giving-parents-more-choice (accessed 20.01.17).

DfE (2014) *Statutory Framework for the Early Years Foundation Stage: Setting the Standards for Learning, Development and Care for Children from Birth to Five*. www.foundationyears.org.uk/files/2014/07/EYFS_framework_from_1_September_2014__with_clarification_note.pdf (accessed 20.01.17).

Doherty, A. and Walsh, G. (2015) 'The Foundation Stage Curriculum in Northern Ireland', in D. Boyd and N. Hirst (eds), *Understanding Early Years Education across the UK: Comparing Practice in England, Northern Ireland, Scotland and Wales*. London: Routledge, pp. 60–99.

Early Education (2012) *Development Matters in the Early Years Foundation Stage*. London: Early Education.

Fleet, A., Patterson, C. and Robertson, J. (2012) *Conversations: Behind Early Childhood Pedagogical Documentation*. Sydney: Pademelon Press.

Georgeson, J. and Campell-Barr, V. (2015) 'Editorial: Attitudes and the early years workforce', *Early Years*, 35 (4): 321–332.

Grieshaber, S. (2008) 'Interrupting stereotypes: Teaching and the education of young children', *Early Education and Development*, 19 (3): 505–518.

Kalliala, M. and Samuelsson, I.P. (2014) 'Introduction: Pedagogical documentation', *Early Years*, 34 (2): 116–118.

Lancaster, P.Y. (2006) 'Listening to young children: Respecting the voice of the child', in G. Pugh and B. Duffy (eds), *Contemporary Issues in the Early Years*. London: Sage, pp. 63–75.

Litjens, I. and Taguma, M. (2010) *Revised Literature Overview for the 7th Meeting of the OECD Network on Early Childhood Education and Care*. Paris: OECD.

Moss, P. (2013) *Early Childhood and Compulsory Education: Reconceptualising the Relationship*. London: Routledge.

Moyles, J. and Worthington, M. (2011) 'The early years foundation stage through the daily experience of children', Occasional Paper, No. 1 TACTYC. http://tactyc.org.uk/occasional-paper/occasional-paper1.pdf (accessed 20.01.17).

Nutbrown, C. (2012) *Foundations for Quality: The Independent Review of Early Education and Childcare Qualifications: Final Report*. www.gov.uk/government/uploads/system/uploads/attachment_data/file/175463/Nutbrown-Review.pdf (accessed 20.01.17).

Ofsted (Office for Standards in Education, Children's Services and Skills) (2015a) *Teaching and Play in the Early Years: A Balancing Act?* Reference: 150085. www.gov.uk/government/publications/teaching-and-play-in-the-early-years-a-balancing-act (accessed 25.01.17).

Ofsted (2015b) *Early Years Inspection Handbook: Handbook for Inspecting Early Years in England under Sections 49 and 50 of the Childcare Act 2006.* www.gov.uk/government/uploads/system/uploads/attachment_data/file/458588/Early_years_inspection_handbook.pdf (accessed 23.01.17).

Osgood, J. (2006) 'Deconstructing professionalism in early childhood education: Resisting the regulatory gaze', *Contemporary Issues in Early Childhood*, 7 (3): 5–14.

Papatheodorou, T. and Moyles, J. (eds) (2009) *Learning Together in the Early Years: Exploring Relational Pedagogy.* London: Routledge.

Plum, M. (2012) 'Humanism, administration and education: The demand of documentation and the production of a new pedagogical desire', *Journal of Education Policy*, 27 (4): 491–507.

Prowle, A., Davidge-Smith, L. and Boyd, D. (2015) 'The Welsh Foundation Phase', in D. Boyd and N. Hirst (eds), *Understanding Early Years Education across the UK: Comparing Practice in England, Northern Ireland, Scotland and Wales.* London: Routledge, pp. 159–204.

Rinaldi, C. (2006) *In Dialogue with Reggio Emilia: Listening, Researching and Learning.* London: Routledge.

Rix, J. and Parry, J. (2014) 'Without foundation: The EYFS framework and its creation of needs', in J. Moyles, J. Payler and J. Georgeson (eds), *Early Years Foundations: Critical Issues.* Maidenhead: Open University Press, pp. 203–214.

Scottish Government (2010) *Curriculum for Excellence Building the Curriculum 5: A Framework for Assessment: Recognising Achievement, Profiling and Reporting.* www.gov.scot/resource/doc/335943/0109859.pdf (accessed 23.01.17).

Siraj, I. and Kingston, D. (2015) *An Independent Review of the Scottish Early Learning and Childcare (ELC) Workforce and Out of School Care (OSC) Workforce.* www.gov.scot/Resource/0047/00477419.pdf (accessed 23.01.17).

Soler, J. and Miller, L. (2003) 'The struggle for early childhood curricula: A comparison of the English Foundation Stage Curricula, Te Whāriki and Reggio Emilia', *International Journal of Early Years Education*, 11 (1): 57–68.

Sylva, K., Melhuish, E. and Sammons, P., Siraj-Blatchford, I. and Taggart, B. (2009) *Early Childhood Matters: Evidence from the Effective Preschool and Primary Education Project.* Abingdon: Routledge.

Turner, T. and Gray Wilson, D. (2010) 'Reflections on documentation: A discussion with thought leaders from Reggio Emilia', *Theory into Practice*, 49: 5–13.

Vygotsky, L. (1978) *Mind and Society: The Development of Higher Mental Processes.* Cambridge, MA: Harvard University Press.

Wall, S., Litjens, I. and Taguma, M. (2015) *Early Childhood Education and Care Pedagogy Review: England.* Paris: OECD. www.oecd.org/unitedkingdom/

early-childhood-education-and-care-pedagogy-review-england.pdf (accessed 01.12.15).

Warden, C. and McNair, L. (2015) 'A Scottish perspective: Development of a value based curriculum', in D. Boyd and N. Hirst (eds), *Understanding Early Years Education across the UK: Comparing Practice in England, Northern Ireland, Scotland and Wales*. London: Routledge, pp. 100–158.

Welsh Assembly Government (2008) *The Foundation Phase: Framework for Children's Learning for 3-to-7-Year-Olds in Wales*. www.ibe.unesco.org/curricula/unitedkingdom/wlk_pp_lpr_fw_2008_eng.pdf (accessed 23.01.17).

Welsh Government (2015) 'Foundation Stage profile'. http://gov.wales/topics/educationandskills/earlyyearshome/foundation-phase/foundation-phase-profile/?lang=en (accessed 23.01.17).

Wharton, P. and Kinney, L. (eds) (2015) *Reggio Emilia Encounters: Children and Adults in Collaboration*. London: Routledge.

Wien, C.A., Guyevskey, V. and Berdoussis, N. (2011) 'Learning to document in Reggio-inspired education', *Early Childhood Research and Practice*, 13 (2). http://ecrp.uiuc.edu/v13n2/wien.html (accessed 10.11.15).

Wood, E. (2013) *Play, Learning and the Early Childhood Curriculum* (3rd edn). London: Sage.

Commentary 1: Living with a Growing Idea

Lasse Lipponen

Department of Teacher Education, University of Helsinki

Interest in pedagogical documentation continues to grow. We are, however, at the very beginning of understanding all of the educational and research uses and consequences of documenting and using documents in early childhood settings. The contributions by Fleet (Chapter 1), Bjervås and Rosendahl (Chapter 2), and Stobbs, Harvell and Reed (Chapter 3), advance our scientific understanding of pedagogical documentation. More especially, they expose the complex issues of pedagogical documentation and professional decision-making. Describing and analysing a decision-making process, the authors cross the boundary of the classical divide between content and process, and demonstrate the meaning and consequences of the multi-voiced nature and multiple functions of pedagogical documentation. These chapters stress the importance of pedagogical documentation as a way of being and living with children.

The chapters, however, are not only about pedagogical documentation and decision-making, but they all ask, either implicitly or explicitly, more profound questions: what exactly are we talking about, when referring to pedagogical documentation, and how should we understand it both theoretically and as social practice? Despite giving slightly differing answers, these three chapters share at least one common idea, namely, that moving around terrains of early childhood settings, people always produce and leave traces, either material (like notes) or symbolic and immaterial manifestations (like memories) (Cussins, 1992; Ferraris, 2013). In the process of pedagogical documentation, we are giving form to experiences by producing objects that congeal them into 'thingness' (Wenger, 1998); traces are turned into inscriptions, and finally, perhaps inscriptions into documents.

Documents, such as photographs, notes, pictures and curriculum, play crucial roles in pedagogical documentation and, in studies introduced in these three chapters, in decision-making. Despite the central role of documents in pedagogical documentation, I think that in most of the studies, documents are mainly taken as neutral tools. There exist a few theories that take the role of documents (or artefacts in general) seriously. From a Vygotskian (1978) point of view, documents carry deep cultural meanings. As the chapters demonstrate, documents are always complex, fluid and transitional, have a multi-voiced nature (Engeström, 1990), and they always imply more possible uses, and consequences, than their intended one. In decision-making, documents mediate communication between different parties by offering a point of shared reference. In the case of children, documents such as photos help to mediate children's memories and experiences and, in doing so, provide support in transforming life as lived to life as told, and vice versa (Lipponen et al., in press).

The multi-faceted and very special nature of documents is nicely conceptualized and argued by Ferraris (2011, 2013). Not just any trace or inscription can be considered as a document. According to Ferraris (2011, 2013), documents are special kinds of things in a social sphere. They are constructed through traces (for example, photos, notes), and inscriptions. A trace that is registered and used for a particular purpose – and is shared by more than two people – can be understood as an inscription. Only an inscription with institutional value can be regarded as a document. Thus, the minimum requirement to consider something as a document is that it has social significance. Because of their nature, having institutional value, documents are powerful tools: they can have control and influence over people and events and, as the three chapters show, serious consequences for the construction of social reality in early childhood settings (Ferraris, 2013).

Thus, if we want to develop and transform pedagogical practices or decision-making in early childhood settings with pedagogical documentation, there are at least three things we should seriously consider. Firstly, we need to enhance the formation of inscriptions, and keep them alive, especially through pedagogical documentation. This includes specific inscriptions for further actions instead of mere traces (descriptions): easily pedagogical documentation turns into a pure registration of facts, without any intention of using the traces later. Secondly, we need to recognize inscriptions with institutional value: these are tools with transformative nature. Recognizing inscriptions with institutional value means following the chain of consequences they produce in space and time for everyday decision-making. These two concerns open up possibilities for shared decision-making, and building up, for example, more participatory early childhood education. Thirdly, we need to understand more deeply the life cycle of documents. As stated by Thompson (1979), things (objects) are in many cases transient – lasting only for a short time – they very easily lose their value and turn into rubbish. This can, of course, happen with documents as well. Or, on some occasions documents can become durables. From this point of view, the interesting question is, what happens to documents after they have been used to reflect and mediate decision-making? Do they somehow remain durable in people's daily lives in early childhood settings, or is their destiny to become rubbish? And if they are refound, and rubbish is put into practice, how does this happen, and do they become documents once again? These three chapters open up possible directions for answering these three demands.

References

Cussins, A. (1992) 'Content, embodiment and objectivity: The theory of cognitive trails', *Mind*, 101: 651–688.

Engeström, Y. (1990) 'When is a tool? Multiple meanings of artifacts in human activity', in Y. Engeström (ed.), *Learning, Working and Imagining: Twelve Studies in Activity Theory*. Helsinki: Orienta-Konsultit Oy, pp. 171–195.

Ferraris, M. (2011) 'Social ontology and documentality', in G. Sartor, P. Casanovas, M. Biasiotti and M. Fernández-Barrera (eds), *Approaches to Legal Ontologies, Social Ontology and Documentality*. London: Springer Science Business Media, pp. 83–97.

Ferraris, M. (2013) *Documentality: Why it is Necessary to Leave Traces?* (tr. R. Davies). Bronx, New York: Fordham University Press.

Lipponen, L., Rajala, A., Hilppö, J. and Paananen, M. (in press) 'Exploring foundations for visual methods used in research with children', *European Early Childhood Education Research Journal*. DOI:10.1080/1350293X.2015.1062663.

Thompson, M. (1979) *Rubbish Theory: The Creation and Destruction of Value*. Oxford: Oxford University Press.

Vygotsky, L.S. (1978) *Mind in Society: The Development of Higher Mental Processes*. Cambridge, MA: Harvard University Press.

Wenger, E. (1998) *Communities of Practice: Learning, Meaning, and Identity*. Cambridge: Cambridge University Press.

PART 2

LANGUAGES OF REPRESENTATION

4

THE WORLDS OF THE VERY YOUNG: SEEING THE EVERYDAY IN SMALL PIECES

SUALLYN MITCHELMORE AND ALMA FLEET

Underneath the large noisy events lie the small events of silence. (Deleuze, 1994: 163)

Through narratives of little everyday moments, this chapter opens possibilities for documentation as experiences lived by very young children and the educators sharing their lives. Highlighting pedagogical meaning within the delights of playing with hats or reaching for bamboo, these moments unlock previously overlooked ways of being in children's environments.

Introduction

Every day, in group settings for young children, we re-meet familiar practices and routines. Often, it is because of their persistence and familiarity that we give little consideration to the richness of what is actually happening within these interactions that shape our behaviours. This chapter seeks to open up and challenge the notion of the ordinariness or inevitability of daily practices and actions, and to bring value to the everyday as a space of transformation, invention, possibility and optimism (Schilling, 2003; Moran, 2005; Sheringham, 2006). Following the postwar liberation of France, cultural theorists such as Lefebvre, de Certeau and Barthes turned their attention to examining the intersubjective nature and critical potential of 'everydayness' or the daily quotidian (Sheringham, 2000; Highmore, 2002). Derived from theories of the everyday, 'quotidian inquiry' is a way of bringing visibility and voice to the unseen qualities that underpin, shape and reshape everyday practices. Two pieces of pedagogical documentation will be shared here to illustrate the richness embedded within the 'everydayness' of the daily quotidian. By documenting everyday interactions, we not only reveal the endless variations of practices from one day to the next, but more so the persistence of values that are embedded within the lived experience of the daily quotidian. Simultaneously, we see the potentials of pedagogical documentation for illuminating these practices.

The quotidian: The concept of 'everydayness' and its value within early childhood education

When we think of 'the everyday', our mind takes us to the benign, to the routine happenings that we re-meet from one day to the next, more often than not with little consideration of their place in our life. Quotidian inquiry asks us to not just stop and look at these routine happenings, but more so, to value the critical potential of the everyday. By tuning into what is initially hidden by habit or, indeed, by a sense of ordinariness, and focusing on the minute variations that manifest within quotidian practices, we reveal the everyday as a space of invention 'that is endlessly forming and reforming' (Sheringham, 2006: 398). The nature of quotidian practices is that they generate beginnings through the touchstone of past experiences and the re-meeting of a new day. This gives quotidian practices the quality of invention: 'It is not just repetition that makes daily activities part of the everydayness, but the endless variation and sedimentation which, according to Réda or Certeau, turn the quotidian into a sphere of invention' (Sheringham, 2006: 361). Quotidian inquiry belongs to the French tradition of theorizing the everyday, the cultural theory of everyday life. Sheringham describes the quotidian as the performative nature of the everyday: 'Everydayness lies in the practices that weave contexts together; only practices make it visible' (2006: 360). It is the unseen nature of the quotidian, with its capacity to hold practices and actions together, that has made it the focus of investigations which aim to reveal the social and political contexts that are hidden within everyday life (Lefebvre, 1987; Schilling, 2003; Moran, 2005).

Lefebvre states: 'Why wouldn't the concept of the everydayness reveal the extraordinary in the ordinary?' (1987: 9). To critique the everyday is to challenge the notion of the ordinariness or inevitability of daily practices and actions, and to bring value to the quotidian as a space of transformation, invention, possibility and optimism by giving visibility to the unseen qualities that underpin our lived experiences (Moran, 2005; Sheringham, 2006). While the quotidian is constituted through the persistence of everyday experiences, it is in a constant process of being intersubjectively reshaped, as individual subjectivities engage with and re-meet their everyday quotidian practices that something new is born.

Quotidian inquiry undoubtedly has value within early childhood education, particularly within pedagogical spaces of children under the age of three. Through its underpinning of valuing 'everydayness', appreciating quotidian practices means that, as educators, we do not privilege one part of the curriculum over another. Mealtimes hold the same value as sharing a favourite story or exploring the garden, thus opening up multiple viewpoints and resisting the normalization of practice (Rinaldi, 2006). When we value the everyday, we never overlook what might seem mundane or par for the course; rather, we bring to our routine practices a lens that acknowledges the capacity of the quotidian to construct shared values and reveal development happening within everyday interactions.

The daily happenings of children under the age of three are often punctuated by familiar patterns, necessitated through meeting their 'basic needs', along with the characteristic desire of infants and toddlers to enjoy and return to the familiar. Quotidian inquiry asks us to consider the inventiveness that accompanies the re-meeting of everyday practices; ordinary actions are the space where possibilities are born. When considering the lens of quotidian inquiry with very young children, it is paying attention to those experiences that are characterized by their commonality or familiarity. Richness lies in the seemingly minor, the persistence and resonance of these experiences makes them precious and compelling as they reveal what is valued. Sheringham writes that, 'Attending to the everyday … is not attention to the niceties of individual psychology but to a commonality of experience that is endlessly forming and reforming in human activities and encounters' (2006: 398).

Underpinned by the rich intellectual tradition of thinking and theorizing 'la vie quotidienne' – 'the dimension of lived experience that is involved in everyday life' (Lefebvre 1947, in Sheringham, 2006: 8), the pedagogical documentation shared in this chapter is part of a larger research project aiming to bring visibility to the flow of life in everyday events. Olsson (2009: 112–113) states:

> What takes place in everyday life in time and space is so familiar to us that we take it for granted … When working with pedagogical documentation there is a great risk of just retelling and nailing down the story of the already obvious. But another way of working with pedagogical documentation is established if one is considering that which is not immediately obvious as important.

In keeping with this notion, pedagogical documentation played a fundamental role within this study as a tool with the capacity to make visible the invisible threads that are hidden within the seemingly familiar daily quotidian practices in infants' and toddlers' pedagogical spaces.

To bring visibility to the value of 'everydayness' and its capacity to reveal the development and ways of knowing of young children embedded within quotidian practices, Suallyn (the first author of this chapter) embarked upon an investigation of 'quotidian thinking' in an Australian long day care centre. Working with and alongside children aged 5–38 months and their educators, Suallyn pedagogically documented naturally occurring everyday interactions, through written notes and photographs over a three-month period. Relationships and the richness of a shared dialogue are at the heart of pedagogical documentation; therefore, it is significant to appreciate that the narratives shared within this chapter are underpinned by the value of 'everydayness'. They bring with them, not the observations of an 'outside observer', but the ease and warmth that comes with being a familiar educator.

The pieces of documentation presented in this chapter are part of a collection of over 70 narratives that together build a rich picture of the value of quotidian inquiry. Quite purposefully, each narrative is set squarely in the midst of everyday happenings, routines and habits that weave together 'everydayness'. It is in these 'small events' (Deleuze, 1994: 163) that we see or uncover big ideas revealing the simultaneous play between concepts and concrete experiences that intersect within ordinary actions and interactions (Oken-Wright and Gravett, 2002).

Narrative one: The humble events of everyday life

Emma (1 year 3 months) had followed me into the nappy change room as I ducked in to wash my hands. As I went about my business, I watched Emma go straight to her locker, a space that was respectfully presented to her, with a photograph of Emma to mark this space as her own. Emma was delighted to find her shoes tucked safely in her locker. Emma immediately took out her shoes to show me, 'Shoes,' she said. I responded, 'Yes, Emma's beautiful shoes.' Emma knowingly placed her shoes safely back where they belonged.

Emma then turned to the hats. She looked at the photos very carefully, excitedly identifying the owner of each hat – 'Anne,' she said – pointing to the photo and the hat in the pigeonhole. Emma did not seem to want affirmation; it was more that she was sharing this information with me. When Emma came to Lola's hat, she pulled it out and was very excited to put it on her head. 'Are you going to wear Lola's hat?' I asked. As Emma walked away from me, she was putting Lola's hat on her head and nodding with complete certainty. It was not a day that Lola attended day care, so this was rather exciting for Emma to wear Lola's hat. The gesture seemed to mark a sign of their friendship, that Emma and Lola can still keep company even when Lola is not there.

Figure 4.1   The identity of hats, lockers and shoes

When Anne (1 year 2 months) spotted Emma in Lola's hat, there was complete recognition of the frivolity of this opportunity to swap, or at least share, a part of someone else's identity. Within a flash Anne and Emma returned to the bathroom to peruse the hats. Anne went straight for a hat that was in Clare's pigeonhole, one of the educators at the childcare centre. It was clearly not an adult's hat and more likely a spare, but, nonetheless, it was not Anne's hat. It seems it was this humorous prospect of swapping hats that was the essence of the interaction.

Emma wanted to put Lola's hat on Anne's head, perhaps to share the joy of being Lola for a moment, but Anne had made her choice and was clearly resolute on wearing the jaunty little blue hat. That it was so ill-fitting made it all the more hilarious for the pair. They looked at each other and then at me, and all three of us laughed together at the silliness of the situation.

Figure 4.2　Emma and Anne playfully explore the humour of hats

Within this 'humble event' (Lefebvre, 1958, in Highmore, 2002: 145) of the everydayness of hats, lockers and shoes, we are first of all reminded just how important it is for children to have a place to call their own within a shared community, to have that sense of being an individual within a group. The seemingly small gesture of Emma finding her shoes safely waiting for her brings with it a surety and a knowing that builds a strong connection with herself in this place. It is the foundation upon which to invent a game, to take on the identity of someone else through the opportunity to swap hats. The hilarity, and indeed complete folly, of the game is only possible because Emma knows that she is

recognized as a person with her own ways of being, and significantly recognizing this in others. These two very young children demonstrated their
shared understanding and appreciation of having a sense of their own identity and that of their friends through the humble event of swapping hats.

Every interaction within the everyday is shared with the past and the
future. It is through the touchstone of the familiar quotidian experience
of a young child finding her own hat waiting for her in her own space,
along with the familiarity of putting a hat on before going outside to
play, that Emma and Anne were able to re-invent the possibilities of this
experience. Significantly, what was played out within this interaction was
an expression of the values and beliefs that are shared between educators
and young children alike within this pedagogical space. Everyday
quotidian practices are, indeed, the canvas, the surface upon which the
reality of the lived experience of values, beliefs and culture are expressed.
There are, therefore, two sides to quotidian inquiry, the general and the
particular (Lefebvre, 1987). By 'identifying an infinitely complex social
fact in the minor' (Sheringham, 2006: 140), Emma and Anne's interaction
with the hats reveals the lived experience of the reciprocal culture of
respect and dignity of relationships that underpins the philosophy of this
early childhood setting.

The question arises, how do we know that Emma and Anne have this
knowledge of the shared values of the pedagogical space? What is it within
the pedagogical documentation of the hilarity of simply swapping hats that
reveals their understanding of the value of their own identity within this
community? It is the attitude of the adult, tuning in and giving value to
the voices of Emma and Anne: 'A child's perspective demands an attitude
where adults give value to children's own culture and their own way to
experience and understand the world' (Waller and Bitou, 2011: 16). Simply
more than a game of swapping hats, what can be uncovered by pedagogical
documentation gives us insight into the sensitivities of the service. It is within
this game that the reciprocity of respect and a pedagogy of relationships
valued by the service is made real. Embedded within the inventiveness
of the everyday practice of wearing hats, these qualities are voiced in the
actions of these young children.

Finding voice

Taken literally, voice is usually thought of as a verbal act, but when we
consider the notion of 'voice' within pedagogical documentation, we
understand voice as the conceptual map, rather than the narrative point
of view. Voice can best be thought of as an inclusive concept, not confined

to verbal utterances but rather embracing different ways in which children represent, communicate to others and express their thoughts. Barthes eloquently embraces the expansive concept of voice when he refers to, 'Life as text' (in Sheringham, 2000: 297). Representing the voices of young children, particularly infants and toddlers, requires the capacity to explore unseen dialogue within interactions, the exchange, and the engagement with qualities within pedagogical spaces, the thinking, ideas and values that are embedded within place.

Pedagogical documentation is an attitude, a way of experiencing. The concept of voice is centred in 'listening as a sensitivity' (Rinaldi, 2006: 65), listening to the complexity, joy and constant amazement of young children's ways of being and knowing. Documenting pedagogically requires the documenter to consider listening as an intersubjective act. Unlike the receptive act of hearing, 'to listen is to be straining toward a possible meaning, and consequently one that is not immediately accessible' (Nancy, 2007: 6). To listen, particularly to very young children, is to search for meaning and to believe in young children's right to be heard (Dahlberg and Moss, 2005). It requires the documenter to engage in 'the double act of noticing and understanding' (Bright et al., 2013: 715), bringing into play an intelligent heart that is not looking for 'evidence' that can be quantifiably measured or evaluated by objective means, but, rather, trusts the heart in bringing understanding to the qualities that are being documented.

Significantly, pedagogical documentation embodies the value of subjectivity. It is not the adult who drives pedagogical documentation; it is not an isolated objective act. There is a reciprocity that enables the agency of pedagogical documentation to be a shared construct. Indeed, the attitude of pedagogical documentation can become part of the daily quotidian, as a space for knowledge building within everyday practice. In the following piece of pedagogical documentation we re-meet Anne engaging in another familiar quotidian experience with an educator, Rebecca, and Lola, who through the presence of her hat, also played a central role in the first piece of documentation.

Narrative two: Sharing the viewfinder

There is a much-loved and often-returned-to quotidian experience of shaking the bamboo stems in front of the covered verandah to make the leaves rustle above. Anne (1 year 2 months) crawled over to an educator, Rebecca, who welcomed her with a warm embrace. Anne perched on Rebecca's lap with her body stretching across Rebecca's torso, which put the bamboo shoots right at Anne's fingertips.

Anne began to shake the branches, creating the much-loved rustle above. Without a word, Rebecca joined with Anne in sharing the attention of the rustle of the leaves above that Anne was creating. They smiled and laughed together, captivated by the rustling. Anne swayed across Rebecca, reaching over one shoulder and then the other, playing the bamboo like a large harp, plucking at shoots and creating a symphony.

With Anne stretched and leaning over Rebecca's left shoulder, Rebecca was able to document Anne playing with bamboo with the camera in her right hand. Anne heard the click of the camera and her attention shifted. Rebecca immediately responded to Anne's interest and they sat in close so that they could both look at the images that Rebecca had taken.

Figure 4.3   Anne and Rebecca re-meet the joy of the bamboo

Lola (1 year 2 months) came over and joined the pair. She, too, began shaking the bamboo shoots to make this much-loved sound, motion and light response. When Rebecca began to document Lola shaking up the bamboo, Anne shared in this process. Just as Anne and Rebecca had looked over photos together they were now sharing the viewfinder to document Lola.

Figure 4.4 Sharing the process of pedagogical documentation

Documentation within this context is not something that is placed on top of day-to-day interactions. Rather, pedagogical documentation becomes a way of knowing that is part of the co-creation of knowledge within the social space of the daily quotidian. When young children share in the processes of pedagogical documentation, it supports the development of understandings that bring with them the capacity to recognize each other's place in the world, in particular that we are co-creating subjectivities in company.

Dahlberg states that pedagogical documentation 'embodies the value of subjectivity – that there is no objective point of view that makes observation neutral' (2012: 225). The view that Rebecca and Anne shared through the viewfinder brings with it the recognition that the camera, along with Rebecca, Anne and Lola, has its own subjectivities, its own perspective and its own point of view. Embracing subjectivities is such a phenomenally significant aspect of documenting pedagogically, as we strive to reflect the textures of all players involved in the documentation. The complexity of the pedagogical documentation as a concept is being shared between a very young child and her educator. To have processes of documentation sitting comfortably within the unfolding of the daily quotidian enriches a mutuality between children and educators of the purposes and mental attitude of documentation.

Conclusion: Linking the threads

The two narratives shared in this chapter reflect the capacity of pedagogical documentation to become a value, a shared value that, like other quotidian practices, embraces the culture of the community and what is valued within that community (Rinaldi, 2006; Giamminuti, 2013). Perec (1990, in Sheringham, 2006) believes that the daily quotidian implies community because the everyday is characterized by the interrelationship of all aspects of life. When pedagogical documentation sits sensitively within the daily quotidian, it has a two-fold effect. First, it has the potential to bring visibility to the values and qualities that characterize the pedagogical space. And, second, rather than being suspended above and distant from everyday practices, pedagogical documentation is woven into the mutually constructed culture of the community that is constituted through everyday practices.

Actively played out within quotidian moments, pedagogical documentation becomes part of the culture of the service when embedded within the everyday. This is because pedagogical documentation shares the richness of the lived experience of the values, beliefs and culture of the daily quotidian, the 'collective social text' of the everyday (Lefebvre, 1962, in Sheringham, 2006: 376). Pedagogical documentation becomes a value that is interwoven with the other shared values of the community, such as love, joy, friendship and embracing a sense of welcome.

To delve into quotidian inquiry is not just to bring value to the everyday and to acknowledge the learning and development that happens within the space of the familiar, it is to enter a field of resonance, where we examine the ripple effect of an experience. Rather than overlooking everyday happenings, quotidian inquiry asks us to question and uncover the characteristics or critical potential of these endeavours. What is the development at play within the seemingly ordinary and everyday happenings of young children? What unseen qualities, values and dispositions characterize these interactions? What is the culture that is being revealed within everyday practices? What does this 'everydayness' tell us about our pedagogical spaces? By examining pedagogical documentation through the lens of quotidian inquiry, we not only reveal intersections between big ideas and ordinary actions and interactions, but we also reveal the lived experience of documenting pedagogically.

References

Bright, N.G., Manchester, H. and Allendyke, S. (2013) 'Space, place, and social justice in education: Growing a bigger entanglement', Editors' Introduction, *Qualitative Inquiry*, 19 (10): 747–755.

Dahlberg, G. (2012) 'Pedagogical documentation: A practice for negotiation and democracy', in C. Edwards, L. Gandini and G. Forman (eds), *The Hundred Languages of Children: The Reggio Emilia Experience in Transformation* (3rd edn). Santa Barbara, CA: Praeger, pp. 225–231.

Dahlberg, G. and Moss, P. (2005) *Ethics and Politics in Early Childhood Education*. London: RoutledgeFarmer.

Deleuze, G. (1994) *Difference and Repetition*. New York: Columbia University Press.

Giamminuti, S. (2013) *Dancing with Reggio Emilia: Metaphors for Quality*. Mt Victoria, NSW: Pademelon Press.

Highmore, B. (2002) *Everyday Life and Cultural Theory: An Introduction*. Abingdon: Routledge.

Lefebvre, H. (1987) 'The everyday and everydayness', *Yale French Studies*, 73: 7–11.

Moran, J. (2005) *Reading the Everyday*. London: Routledge.

Nancy, J.-L. (2007) *Listening* (tr. C. Mandell). New York: Fordham University Press.

Oken-Wright, P. and Gravett, M. (2002) 'Big ideas and the essence of intent', in V.R. Fu, A.J. Stremmel and L.T. Hill (eds), *Teaching and Learning: Collaborative Exploration of the Reggio Emilia Approach*. Upper Saddle River, NJ: Merrill Prentice Hall, pp. 197–220

Olsson, L.M. (2009) *Movement and Experimentation in Young Children's Learning: Deleuze and Guattari in Early Childhood Education*. London and New York: Routledge.

Rinaldi, C. (2006) *In Dialogue with Reggio Emilia: Listening, Researching and Learning*. London: Routledge.

Schilling, D. (2003) 'Everyday life and the challenge to history in postwar France: Braudel, Lefebvre, Certeau', *Diacritics*, 33 (1): 23–40.

Sheringham, M. (2000) 'Attending to the everyday: Blanchot, Lefebvre, Certeau, Perec', *French Studies*, 54 (2): 187–199.

Sheringham, M. (2006) *Everyday Life: Theories and Practices from Surrealism to the Present*. Oxford: Oxford University Press.

Waller, T. and Bitou, A. (2011) 'Research with children: Three challenges for participatory research in early childhood', *European Early Childhood Education Research Journal*, 19 (1): 5–20.

5

MAKING LEARNING VISIBLE IN DANCE AND OTHER CREATIVE ARTS

MARC RICHARD

The consideration of documentation in the context of dance and other creative arts in elementary schools may be unexpected. This Canadian example of creative exploration makes visible the ways in which these processes enable the visualizing of dance as language, embodying subjectivities and empowering both learners and teachers.

Introduction

What is the learning that happens in dance and other creative arts in an elementary school setting? Can pedagogical documentation, inspired by the educators of Reggio Emilia, make this learning visible to the various stakeholders in education? This research project investigated the learning for both teachers and students in four elementary schools in the Canadian Province of Ontario. Although the focus of my research was dance, the findings extend beyond dance to other arts such as drama and visual arts. In my pedagogical documentation process, four expert dance educators, who were also generalist classroom teachers, were video-recorded and photographed while teaching creative dance classes. Afterwards, the teachers were interviewed while watching the video documentation. I have included reflections of two of these educators – Emily and Alorani, who were working with the younger children.

Moments of perceived learning were proposed via pedagogical documentation panels using information from interviews, observations, field notes and photographs. The words and pictures of students and teachers were placed on poster-sized, mock-up panels and were used to provoke further dialogue in the form of one-on-one interviews, small group or whole class discussions. In the end I created an exhibit of banner-style documentation panels that summarized the research findings.

Findings suggest that in embodied arts classes (i.e. classes utilizing the body to learn and create), students are learning to develop awareness of the tacit knowledge of their bodies, an intersubjectivity as they engage in collaborative creative processes and discover the interconnectedness of dance as a language of learning. Teachers are learning their unique role as facilitators in creative dance classes and are acquiring an ability to witness thinking that is happening using the body. The methodology of pedagogical documentation is able to make the learning visible in creative arts classes because it provokes students and teachers to revisit and reflect on their learning and to confront issues that arose in the creative process.

Pedagogical documentation, for the Reggio educators (Forman and Fyfe, 1998; Rinaldi, 2001a), is the practice of carefully studying and intentionally recording the process of a student's learning and attempting to animate the process for others. As a methodology, it interacts well with an embodied arts curriculum, which remains a hidden curriculum in most educational settings. Unlike the standard practices of pedagogical *observation* that focus on observing children in order to classify them, pedagogical documentation is about seeing and understanding 'what the child is capable of without any predetermined framework of expectations and norms' (Dahlberg et al., 2007: 146). It seems to fit well with *creative dance* defined by Stinson (1988: 2) as 'an art form that is based on natural movement', and MacDonald (1991: 434) as 'bodily actions that express inner thoughts and feelings and enhance those thoughts and feelings'. Forman and Fyfe (1998: 240) view documentation as a necessary part of negotiated learning, 'a dynamic system of causes, effects, and counter effects'. Making visible the unique moments of embodied learning within a *creative dance* setting may broaden definitions of *education* and *learning*.

Schools in Reggio Emilia refer to a poem, 'No way. The hundred *is* there', written by their founder Loris Malaguzzi, as a basis for their pedagogical practices. The poem inspires teachers to recognize more than one hundred languages of expression, communication and cognition (Edwards et al., 1998: 3). The Reggio educators employ graphic arts (painting, drawing, sculpting and so on) as ways of communicating children's understanding of their world. On a study tour of the Reggio schools in March 2011, I had the opportunity to visit three schools, including the Choreia School, which specifically emphasizes the body as a site of learning. The Choreia educators propose, 'the language of the body enriches knowledge' and 'consider the body of children as the bearer of multiple aspects of knowledge and possibilities for learning' (Cavazzoni et al., 2007: 2–3). The Reggio educators are beginning to document the use of dance as a language in their schools as seen in *Dialogue with Places* (Filippini et al., 2008), their approach suggests that dance could also be used, along with other graphic arts, as a medium for expressing students' expanding knowledge.

If we follow Malaguzzi's (1998: 73) thought that 'teachers must learn to teach nothing to children except what children can learn themselves', then dance and other creative arts should be some of the most apparent languages of learning, ones that children understand from a very young age. Sheets-Johnstone contends that: 'Movement is first of all the mode by which we make sense of our own bodies and by which we first come to understand the world' (2011: xxv). She describes a 'corporeal apprenticeship', in which we are 'apprentices of our own bodies' (ibid.: 195). Rather than viewing bodily language as pre-verbal, Sheets-Johnstone sees verbal language as 'post kinetic' (ibid.: 438).

Tacit knowledge

Pedagogical documentation animated the idea that creative dance experiences in an elementary school setting seem to offer students a chance to re-discover their tacit knowledge of the body. This knowledge refers to the hidden awareness of dance elements (body, space, energy, relationship and time) that students seem to possess innately. The language of the body is perhaps the first language that children understand. As Polanyi (1966: 4) states, 'We know more than we can tell'; and as one teacher, Alorani, explained, 'The elements of dance are fairly human … you have, without any adult showing you, a whole breadth of movement vocabulary that you didn't even know existed.' Students as young as four years old seem to experience a divide between their dancing selves and their role as students in a classroom setting. This can be seen in the following case study.

On the first day Emily, the teacher, provoked the four- and five-year-old students, asking, 'What do we know about shapes?' The students responded using their fingers and arms to demonstrate geometric shapes they had learned in school. Emily prompted them, 'Can you make shapes with another part of your body?' The students almost immediately began to explore whole-body shapes. While watching the video footage of the lesson afterwards, Emily reflected that she was 'giving them permission' to use knowledge their bodies understood but hadn't been invited to use in a school setting. While viewing video-recorded footage of their dance classes, Emily and Alorani demonstrated an *image of the child* that is in alignment with that of the Reggio Emilians; through their creative dance pedagogy, they were recognizing a child who is 'rich in resources, strong and competent – a child who has the right to hope and the right to be valued, not a predefined child seen as fragile, needy, incapable' (Rinaldi, 2001a: 79). As Emily explained, these students 'already know something about the way school and adults work'. Alorani reflected, 'We're conditioned to move through school in a certain way. At each point, there is a "this is what sitting looks like, this is what standing looks like".' These teachers were provoking their students beyond preconceived notions of bodies-in-school and encouraging them to re-discover their tacit knowledge of the body.

Intersubjectivity

For these four- and five-year-old students, one of the most predominant parts of the creative process was that of *exploration and experimentation.* On the first day, Emily offered scarves to the kindergarten children as a provocation. Almost immediately they began to investigate the tactile and transparent nature of the materials. Most placed the scarves over their heads, saying, 'You can see through it!' While watching the video footage afterwards Emily interpreted their actions:

It's like when you first give them any material. When you first give them paint, when you give them clay, there is sort of a play period. There is that free *exploration* period with the scarves where you just want to go crazy. It's fun. They just wanted to see what they could do.

These moments of play were documented in the series of photographs shown in Figure 5.1.

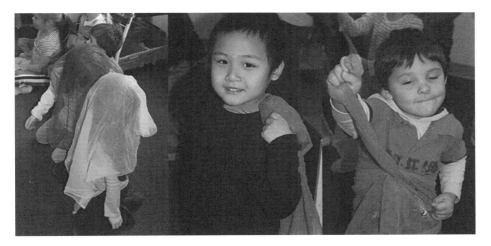

Figure 5.1 Exploring the scarves

For the children, initial exploration using the scarves fluctuated between dramatic-type play and dance-type play. Two girls created a relationship with the scarves over their heads, Ben made a cape out of his scarf, and Tristan intentionally tied his scarf around his waist.

After an initial exploration period, Emily offered suggestions for exploring the scarves, using guided questions:

> Can you dance with curved lines?
> Can you paint the room with curvy lines?

The students immediately began to explore moving their scarves in new ways and exploring the concepts of circles in the air. Upon reflection, Emily recognized that she was honing her skills as a facilitator of learning via these creative dance classes. By actively participating in the creative process with her students, she was a learner herself – not the adult with the right answers but instead someone there to inspire and provoke their development. As Emily reiterated:

> They are doing all these movements ... I am naming it and I'm putting it in a dance context ... I am somehow getting them to see the material of the body as material for dance as opposed to presenting them with material.

In the Reggio Emilia schools where the visual arts are used as alternative languages of learning (but not taught as isolated subjects), Katz (1998: 35) explains that the pedagogista or atelierista offers lessons on how to work in certain media and with certain skills, i.e. artistic technique. However, the emphasis is always on allowing the children to discover how to use the artistic materials to express their own theories about the world. Similarly, in these creative dance classes, Emily and Alorani explained that they arrived at a different type of teacher–learner relationship in which they were co-constructing meaning. There is an affinity between this and what Katz recognizes about the Reggio approach: it alters 'the content of the relationship between adults and children', because it is 'focused on the work itself, rather than mainly on routines or the children's performance on academic tasks. Adults' and children's minds meet on matters of interest to both of them' (ibid.: 36–37).

Another important finding is that embodied learning experiences, such as dance and drama classes, offer a unique learning opportunity: to use touch to communicate with another person, and also to teach how one wants to be touched in return. I witnessed and documented (via photographs) this lesson with Tristan and Isabelle as they played statues, a drama exercise in which you move your partner's body into various positions as if you were a sculptor (Figure 5.2).

At first, Isabelle was handling Tristan fairly roughly and he resisted her touch by moving away and batting with outstretched arms. Their teacher reminded them, 'It's a soft shape.' But Isabelle resisted, 'I don't know how to make a soft shape.' Almost instantly, Tristan started to gently touch the side of his cheek with his hand as though he was petting himself. Their teacher gasped, 'That was nice!' Isabelle stood close and observed Tristan's hand movements. Very gently, she placed her two hands on Tristan's hand as he continued to gently pet his face. It appeared as though Tristan

Figure 5.2 Tristan and Isabelle play statues

were teaching Isabelle how he wanted to be touched. Isabelle seemed genuinely fascinated by this lesson about soft touch as she reached forward almost as if she were blind. It was a powerful moment; learning about touch, trust and empathy. The next day, I interviewed the two children using this set of three pictures. Tristan described it as a moment when they 'were doing gentle things'. Emily described this moment as a physical dialogue – a conversation that gave 'the toucher' some sense of their own physical impact on the other.

This one moment between these four-year-old students animates the theory of social constructivism. Young children are excellent teachers, and a variety of lessons may be taught and learned by students in embodied arts classes. In this moment, Tristan was teaching Isabelle how he wanted her to touch him. When children first come to school, a pervasive message (sometimes overt and sometimes covert) exists that the body is something to be kept still and under control. Students are reminded to place their hands in their laps and not touch their peers. With so much emphasis placed on a *no touch* policy in our schools, how can students learn to touch with a sense of care and respect? Tristan and Isabelle demonstrated that learning to communicate through touch, with an awareness of your impact on your partner, can begin in the early school years – but these lessons can only be learned if there is an opportunity for physical engagement with one another.

The three pictures in Figure 5.2 and the story of Tristan and Isabelle have prompted many important discussions about touch among my community of early childhood educators and embodied arts pedagogues. As Rinaldi (1998: 122) suggests, 'Sharing documentation is in fact making visible the culture of childhood both inside and outside the school to become a participant in a true act of exchange and democracy.' Since documentation is a tangible form (the panels include in-the-moment pictures and transcriptions of real conversations as well as interpretive comments from the pedagogue), it allows for a continual revisiting and reconstruction of the original learning event – *a spiral process*, 'which allows for taking multiple perspectives, for looping between self-reflection and dialogue, for passing between the language of one's professional community (theories and practical wisdom) and one's personal passions, emotions, intuitions and experiences' (Dahlberg et al., 2007: 154). Used in conjunction with embodied arts education experiences, I believe that pedagogical documentation allows teachers to confront biases and assumptions inherent in the professional education community – assumptions about control of children's bodies and minds, assumptions about assessment and evaluation and assumptions about what learning looks like.

Interconnectedness of the arts

Arts experiences for young children often provide opportunities to shift from one mode of representation (language) to another, such as translating from dance into visual arts and visual arts into dance. Something vitally important happens as students translate concepts from one medium into another: they seem to clarify ideas that were amorphous. They also seem to open up to new ideas and possibilities. A translation from visual arts into dance can mean a unique interpretation of a visual pattern, and a translation of dance into visual arts can become a type of notation that can be used to remember a dance.

Emily brought in some shape/symbol cards for her students to interpret. She asked, 'What kind of dancing goes with this card?' Interpreting a card containing a series of dashes – - – – – -, Isabelle explored a pathway in space in which she took a step forwards, then sideways, then backwards, and then sideways in the opposite direction, representing the physical

Figure 5.3 McKayla's step map

pathway she would be making in order to move around these short dashes. She was translating a 'bird's-eye view' of this pathway around the dashes into a sort of physical dentil pattern (small block shapes like the top of a castle). This led Emily to provoke the students into creating their own symbol/shape cards based on something they had done that week. McKayla drew 'a map of her steps' (Figure 5.3).

After drawing her map, McKayla immediately went to the carpet area and interpreted her map through intricate dance steps. She said, 'This is a step map and it helps me remember the steps and where to go.' McKayla offered Emily a full description: 'This is a twirl, this is walking, and this is a turn.' Emily commented: 'It's almost one continuous line,' and she was tracing it with her finger, 'and you go this way and you go that way'. This shift into the domain of mapping (initiated by four-year-old McKayla) provided a form of dance notation by which she could remember the dance she had created. It was her way of documenting her own learning.

The movement map further demonstrated connections being made across modes of representation. The children understood that it was possible to represent their dances through drawing, but also, to translate visual images such as the dashes into dance. As Reedy (2003: 2) explains, these students were *multilingual*, made evident 'when a teacher offers children opportunities to explore, develop, and redefine their understanding of the world through as many media as possible'. Reggio educators recognize that the ability to 'shift from one kind of intelligence, from one language of learning to another' is a possibility for all children, and allows them to recognize *other* theories, given they speak many languages of learning (Rinaldi, 2001a: 81).

Conclusion: How can pedagogical documentation make learning visible in the arts?

As I analysed the data in this research study, I recognized many instances of learning that were uncovered specifically because the research method was pedagogical documentation. Utilizing photographs and text on documentation panels, students were able to revisit and reflect on emerging theories and problems encountered in their work with others. Through video documentation, teachers discovered moments they had missed while in the context of the classes, which allowed them to focus on individual students. As a research methodology, pedagogical documentation seems to expose a

(Continued)

(Continued)

specific kind of learning in these embodied arts classes that might otherwise remain hidden or dormant.

   Video documentation specifically allowed the teachers to discover moments they had missed in the class context. Emily viewed this as looking through another lens:

> You can't see everything that's going on in the room. I always notice things that I didn't see in the moment. That's one of the great things about it [pedagogical documentation], because *it gives you that other eye in the room* …

Alorani saw, through documentation, that learning is happening everywhere:

> I think often *it's where you're not looking that the stuff is happening* – it's symbolic of life … we all miss huge parts of what's going on with people … so definitely there have been some 'aha' moments with those [things] I would have missed otherwise.

Reviewing video documentation provided the teachers with a completely new experience of those classes. As Wien (1991: 60–61) suggests, 'The teacher both reacts to herself as a stranger (seeing herself from the outside) and is intimately connected to every move the stranger makes.'

   We choose pedagogical documentation because, as Lenz Taguchi (2010: 91) suggests, it *intentionally complicates* our understanding of our practices. In the context of this study, pedagogical documentation provided what Reggio educators refer to as a *collective memory* (Krechevsky and Mardell, 2001: 289). It provoked students and teachers to consider things that might otherwise have remained hidden but were made public. Pedagogical documentation not only made visible specific moments of learning but, also, as Rinaldi (2001b: 150) says, made it 'open to the "possibilities", possible interpretations and multiple dialogues among children and adults'. As Dahlberg et al. (2007: 147) suggest, pedagogical documentation as a *narrative of self-reflexivity* offers all stakeholders in education the opportunity to define and re-define themselves through their relationship to the dominant discourses in education. It also allows them the opportunity 'of taking control of one's thinking and practice and creating counter-discourses' (ibid.: 153).

   When we document the integration of bodies into education, through creative dance, and the other embodied arts, a rich source of information about self, other and the world is made available. This offers the opportunity to challenge dominant discourses in education. Common practices such as management, evaluation and obedience transform into discovery, expression, creativity and collaboration.

References

Cavazzoni, P., Pini, B., Porani, F. and Renieri, A. (2007) 'Corpo in movimento … the body in motion', *Innovation in Early Education: The International Reggio Exchange*, 14 (2): 1–12.

Dahlberg, G., Moss, P. and Pence, A. (2007) *Beyond Quality in Early Childhood Education and Care: Languages of Evaluation* (2nd edn). Abingdon: Routledge.

Edwards, C.P., Gandini, L. and Forman, G. (eds) (1998) *The Hundred Languages of Children: The Reggio Emilia Approach – Advanced Reflections* (2nd edn). Greenwich, CT: Ablex.

Filippini, T., Vecchi, V. and Giudici, C. (2008) *Dialogue with Places*. Reggio Emilia, Italy: Reggio Children.

Forman, G. and Fyfe, B. (1998) 'Negotiated learning through design, documentation and discourse', in C. Edwards, L. Gandini and G. Forman (eds), *The Hundred Languages of Children: The Reggio Emilia Approach – Advanced Reflections* (2nd edn). Greenwich, CT: Ablex, pp. 239–260.

Katz, L. (1998) 'What can we learn from Reggio?', in C. Edwards, L. Gandini and G. Forman (eds), *The Hundred Languages of Children: The Reggio Emilia Approach – Advanced Reflections* (2nd edn). Greenwich, CT: Ablex, pp. 27–48.

Krechevsky, M. and Mardell, B. (2001) 'Four features of learning in groups', in C. Giudici, C. Rinaldi and M. Krechevsky (eds), *Making Learning Visible: Children as Individual and Group Learners*. Reggio Emilia, Italy: Reggio Children, pp. 284–295.

Lenz Taguchi, H. (2010) *Going Beyond the Theory/Practice Divide in Early Childhood Education: Introducing an Intra-Active Pedagogy*. London and New York: Routledge.

MacDonald, C.J. (1991) 'Creative dance in elementary schools: A theoretical and practical justification', *Canadian Journal of Education*, 16 (4): 434–441.

Malaguzzi, L. (1998) 'History, ideas and basic philosophy: An interview with Lella Gandini', in C. Edwards, L. Gandini and G. Forman (eds), *The Hundred Languages of Children: The Reggio Emilia Approach – Advanced Reflections* (2nd edn). Greenwich, CT: Ablex, pp. 49–97.

Polanyi, M. (1966) *The Tacit Dimension*. London: Routledge and Kegan Paul.

Reedy, P. (2003) *Body, Mind and Spirit in Action: A Teacher's Guide to Creative Dance*. Berkeley, CA: Luna Kids Dance.

Rinaldi, C. (1998) 'Projected curriculum construction through documentation – progettazione: An interview with Lella Gandini', in C. Edwards, L. Gandini and G. Forman (eds), *The Hundred Languages of Children: The Reggio Emilia Approach – Advanced Reflections* (2nd edn). Greenwich, CT: Ablex, pp. 113–125.

Rinaldi, C. (2001a) 'Documentation and assessment: What is the relationship?', in C. Giudici, C. Rinaldi and M. Krechevsky (eds), *Making Learning Visible: Children as Individual and Group Learners*. Reggio Emilia, Italy: Reggio Children, pp. 78–89.

Rinaldi, C. (2001b) 'The courage of utopia', in C. Giudici, C. Rinaldi and M. Krechevsky (eds), *Making Learning Visible: Children as Individual and Group Learners*. Reggio Emilia, Italy: Reggio Children, pp. 148–153.

Sheets-Johnstone, M. (2011) *The Primacy of Movement* (2nd edn). Philadelphia, PA: John Benjamins North America.

Stinson, S. (1988) *Dance for Young Children: Finding the Magic in Movement*. Reston, VA: American Alliance for Health, Physical Education, Recreation and Dance.

Wien, C.A. (1991) 'Developmentally appropriate practice and the practical knowledge of day care teachers'. PhD dissertation, Dalhousie University, Halifax, Nova Scotia.

6

USING VIDEO IN PEDAGOGICAL DOCUMENTATION: INTERPRETIVE AND POETIC POSSIBILITIES

SYLVIA KIND AND ADRIENNE ARGENT

This chapter offers video as a pedagogical tool in documentation. Building on narratives and video poems from a Canadian children's centre, the authors take a lyrical stance inspired by poets and a Korean-born conceptual artist. Encounters with huckleberries and memory become the focus of joy and discovery, explored through film.

Introduction

This chapter explores the use of video in pedagogical documentation. We are particularly interested in the interpretive and poetic possibilities of video and how the processes of filming, editing, viewing and considering the work together can help us develop deeper attunement and invite more sensitive and diverse ways of knowing, seeing and responding. While video can be used in many ways in pedagogical documentation and in teacher research with children, in this chapter we would like to emphasize the poetic capacities of the medium and that which emerges through the video composition processes. What we are proposing is an enactive approach that tries to animate or evoke the moments under consideration: a practice that 'sings the world' (van Manen, 1997: 13) and engages with the difficult work of noticing (Tsing, 2013). Our ideas in this chapter have emerged from our work together alongside other educators at the Capilano University Children's Centre in North Vancouver, Canada where Sylvia works as an atelierista and Adrienne works as an infant and toddler educator.

A particular kind of noticing

Through the practice of pedagogical documentation we have tried to get close to children's lived meanings; how things matter, how they are experienced, understood and worked through from children's perspectives, so that our work with children might be enriched, expanded and enlivened. This pedagogical practice is process-oriented and interpretive. It requires reciprocity, pedagogical thoughtfulness and tact (van Manen, 1997), an ethics of listening, and an attunement generated through sustained and learned attention. By this we mean that sensitivity to children's processes is not something immediately attained. It is cultivated over time. Additionally, we have tried to situate ourselves as researching *with*, not on or about, children. Thus, our focus isn't about gaining knowledge, rather it is oriented as a collective search for insight and understanding so that we might more closely align ourselves with children's own experimentations, research pathways, and ways of being and knowing. Pedagogical documentation, then, is a particular kind of observing, noticing and documenting. It is not an objective, distanced or evaluative search. This is important in considering how we situate ourselves in the visual processes discussed in this chapter.

This, of course, is difficult work. We are always in the process of figuring things out, never quite arriving, always trying to stay in movement towards greater understanding and awareness. In this, we are engaged in a constant search for other ways of seeing and attending, for perspectives that enlarge our vision and allow for greater attunement. In an effort to see differently, we try to attend to an interplay of materials and the relationality between things. Additionally, we are convinced that pedagogical documentation must be an inventive process so that we are not just reproducing already known methodologies. If our methods make the world in particular ways (Law, 2004), and if the nature of the attention that we give to things shapes that which we are considering, then we need inventive practices to help us get to know things differently and in their complexity. *The ways that we attend to things matter.*

We have engaged with these things through reading articles and book chapters together, visiting art exhibits and considering different artists' processes and approaches. We have also collectively engaged in this search for greater attunement through weekly atelierista meetings. In these meetings, educators and atelieristas, and occasionally pedagogistas, meet over lunch in the Children's Centre foyer to consider selections of video documentation. These 10–20 minute video segments are usually drawn from much longer video recordings and reflect aspects of the week's ongoing processes and projects that are taking place in the studio and the individual rooms. Segments are roughly edited so that they highlight particular ideas, curiosities and questions, and give insight into the videographer's interpretive understandings of what might be happening. The video selections are then discussed, and responses and interpretations generated. After this, there is generally further editing of the video selections so that more refined, shorter or more specific segments can be returned to the children to provoke and engage children's continued explorations and the educators' thinking. The meetings are informal and are attended by any educator whose schedule allows for it. Occasionally, children who are not napping at the time join the circle of discussion as well. In this way, we strive to stay in the movements and practices of pedagogical documentation and create spaces of learning together.

Thinking through video

Over the past three years of gathering together for weekly atelierista meetings and experimenting with ways of using video as part of the pedagogical documentation process, we have tried to interrupt the 'mundane realism that continues to regulate video method' (MacLure et al., 2010: 543). Video can be a detailed form of visual note taking as it is very useful in recording children's conversations, offers insight into how an exploration or event has progressed over time, and helps us record and reflect on what has happened. It allows for a more nuanced record of events and happenings than notes and photos alone. These are valuable ways of using video in pedagogical documentation and we

continue to use video in this way. However, video also has great potential as an expressive, interpretive and artistic medium. The moving
images, moving bodies and materials, gestures, enactments, sounds,
voices and various and shifting perspectives allow for thinking in movement (Manning and Massumi, 2014) and for particular visibilities and
ways of seeing. For instance, through video, we can explore perspectives
other than that of the one doing the recording, disrupting the centrality
of the researcher's 'I' (eye) and offering other perspectives than the single
point and stationary perspective (see Berger, 1977). The camera can be
mounted on a tripod, or passed hand to hand, enabling the videographer
to be both observer and the observed. It can move with the videographer's body and can act as an appendage to the body, expanding the
body's capabilities, seeing what the videographer cannot easily see and
taking perspectives other than what the adult's eye would typically attend
to. It can also move with a child's curious interceptions offering surprises
and unexpected visions. As a 'catalyst of attention' (Grasseni, in Pink,
2007: 251), it uniquely allows for a focus on moving bodies, a world in
motion and intersecting perspectives.

Additionally, this world in movement includes much more than human
movements (Kind, 2010). The potential of video is also in how it can give
glimpses into the materiality of things and how materials and children
move together (Pacini-Ketchabaw et al., 2016). A video camera held low
on the table can follow materials, such as paint, paper, water and brush
as they mix, mutate and move together. Video helps us pay attention
in particular ways and as a result produces particular understandings.
Thus, engaging with video in pedagogical documentation means giving
attention to what the video camera and video processes enable and, as
mentioned earlier, inventing with video's potentialities and possibilities.

Some ethical considerations

As we explore the expressive possibilities of the medium, we are also
compelled by the poetry, sensory, material and embodied nature of
experiences we encounter. If we think of video not as a representation
of the world as it is, but as a creative, composed, particular perspective
on what might be happening, then all we ever have are possibilities for
how things *might* be. For instance, as the videographer selects what to
film and frames a particular view, she or he attends to certain things and
not others (Cooley, 2007). The process of filming, editing and the resulting video segments are also the results of the videographer's 'discursively
positioned actions' (Thompson and Hall, 2016: 119). Right from when the

camera is turned on, decisions are made about what to attend to, what view to take, what will matter and what further understandings the video might generate. We make no claim to truth or objectivity in what is seen and recorded, and acknowledge that we have certain aesthetic, artistic and poetic interests.

As *pedagogical* documentation, video also has pedagogical concerns and orientations. This means that teachers are researching with children with the goal of developing and transforming curriculum, not standing at an objective distance. While the use of video in pedagogical documentation borrows from visual ethnography, it still locates educators in the midst as co-researchers *with* children. This 'with' is important. Certainly in visual ethnography there is a constant concern about the 'othering' potential of visual methods. Yet, as Dahlberg and Bloch (in Olsson, 2009: 42) ask, 'Is the power to see and visualize always the power to control?'

Quite often in visual research with children, this risk of othering is addressed through engaging children as participants by giving them cameras to document and explore their own views, and engaging them in interpretive discussions about what they have imaged and recorded (Clark and Moss, 2011). Along with these researchers, we are interested in 'a redistribution of pedagogical relations and objects in line with a more participatory and emancipatory aesthetic project' (Atkinson, 2011: 89), but find this kind of approach limiting, particularly in our work with infants and toddlers. To produce new pathways and possibilities for learning, we must explore other processes than primarily sharing and discussing video with children with an emphasis on the content of the video or images and interpreting them for meaning. We aim also for a seeing-with (Kind, 2013) that doesn't just look at children and at their engagements, but attempts to join with them in their movements. Thus we strive in ethical and participatory ways to come alongside children, to see with, to follow their lines of movement, and to try, however difficult it might be, to get close to the ways that things unfold and come into being. We try to feel the movements of learning and emerging understandings, and not just reflect on words spoken, drawings made and so on, and in doing this we try to create 'new empathetic routes through which to broker everyday knowledge' (Pink, 2011: 451).

A visit to the gallery

One winter evening, we, a group of educators from the Centre, went to see the exhibition *Unfolding*, a retrospective of the work of Kimsooja, a South Korean-born conceptual artist. Her work engaged with everyday objects, the acts of sewing, and the daily life of textiles, while exploring themes of time, memory, displacement and relationship of the human body and the material world. As we entered the exhibition, we encountered a room filled with long panels of fabric hanging as if from a series of clotheslines. The vibrantly coloured silk swayed and brushed against our bodies as we walked through; pinks, yellows and reds reflected and multiplied along mirror lined walls. It was impossible not to touch and be touched by the fabric. Her video projections created a sensitive form of empathy and embodiment that drew the viewer in as both a spectator and a participant. As we viewed her video installation, *Mumbai: A Laundry Field (2007–2008)*, her images began to work on us. This was not a passive or voyeuristic experience. We became drawn in and caught up in the rhythms and flows of movements, colours, sounds and sensations.

Across four massive screens, the constant presence of brightly coloured fabric served as a form of connective tissue between each film segment. Each screen pulsated with movement, energy, colour and rhythm. These visceral qualities moved the viewer beyond the role of spectator and detached understandings of the harsh realities of poverty and overcrowding, to a more textured understanding that highlighted the beauty and interconnectedness of everyday human existence. Her videos challenged the inorganic divide between art and everyday existence, and brought poetic qualities and dance-like expressions to mundane activities such as washing clothes and hanging laundry.

We were all moved by how this artist had brought to life these everyday rituals and expressed such poetry and rhythm through her video projections. As we gathered in a nearby café after the exhibition, we wondered how we could attend more closely to aesthetics, movements, material moments and everyday rituals through video. We discussed possibilities of using video in pedagogical documentation; using video not as if we were looking back on something that had already happened, rather in ways that brought the moments to life again in the viewing so that the viewer could enter the experience, feeling the movements, sounds and tempo of the repetitions as we had experienced in the exhibit. MacLure et al. (2010) liken this to a process of *animating*, or adding liveliness to, the viewer and the subject under consideration. They insist that, 'video recordings made by the usual hands-off method have limited potential to animate the viewer – to spark new thoughts, sensations, or reflections. They do not interrupt the dead-level tempo of banal repetition – the beat of that which we already know' (ibid.: 246).

We encountered Cooley's (2007) writing on video poems and found an invitation in her work to think differently about how we might use video documentation with children. Van Manen (1997: 13) describes research as a 'poetizing activity', where researchers construct possible interpretations of an experience through a language that 'sings the world'. The resulting text does not become the focus of analysis, rather evokes the experience in such a way that the reader is moved or animated and new understandings emerge.

The American poet Edward Hirsch (1999: 5) writes that 'the lyric poem seeks to mesmerize time. It crosses frontiers and outwits the temporal'. Akin to the work of a poet, who attempts to distil the complexities of the world into words and who, sometimes, brings magnification to some of life's minutiae; we began to consider video documentation and, more specifically, the concept of video poems, in a similar way. Video poems could become artistic tools to encourage a particular way of seeing, bringing not only potency but also sustained and suspended attention to particularities of time–place–movement, and what emerges in the over-lapping spaces. As processes of artistic research, the acts of creating video poems could enable different kinds of understandings. This form of interpretive, experiential, poetic and artistic research could pry openings into the unacknowledged spaces that exist in the lived and multi-layered culture of children's spaces.

The huckleberries

Kimsooja's work left a lasting impression on Adrienne, in particular. Through the vibrancy of Kimsooja's videos, she felt transplanted into the midst of the scenes and felt compelled by the in-between-ness of flow and movement, materials and bodies. She visited Kimsooja's exhibition several times, and each time returned to her role as an educator with a strong desire to re-imagine her classroom and become more attuned to the complex entanglements and intra-acting (Lenz Taguchi, 2009) forces of places, bodies, gestures, language, images and objects. She began to wonder how to acknowledge these dynamic movements as important components of the collective lived experience of a busy toddler class-room and to use video as a way of listening to the rhythms and more nuanced aspects of curriculum. She found herself thinking about how video could animate young children's everyday engagements so that we might be drawn in: in emotional, felt, bodied and haptic ways to the experience and interpretive meanings of the events, and to get closer to the toddlers' relational, intra-active, material, bodied and storied ways of being in and moving with the world. We spent much of the remaining winter and spring discussing these things in atelierista meetings and in a

Teacher as Researcher course that Sylvia was teaching. By summer, Adrienne began to try them out. Compelled by the children's intense fascination with huckleberry bushes in the Children's Centre's outdoor space, she began to consider how huckleberry bushes were meaningful to the infants and toddlers, and how she could become attuned to the daily repetitions of berry picking and the children's particular ways of knowing and being in these spaces.

The Children's Centre, nestled in a coastal forest on Coast Salish territory, is covered by a tree canopy of Red Cedars, Hemlocks and Douglas Fir. This creates the ideal condition for smaller species, such as the huckleberry bush, to thrive. The surroundings have an abundance of huckleberry bushes; in the summer months, these bushes become a vibrant green, their expansive branches dotted with tiny, tart, edible berries. The outdoor space, divided by a chain-link fence, is shared by the preschool age and infant-toddler children, with most of the huckleberry bushes on the infant-toddler side. Each season, children throughout the Centre immerse themselves in rituals of huckleberry-picking, not merely for the delight of berry-foraging, but as a deeply relational event that gathers children and educators together, various children crossing the fence to return to the lush huckleberry grounds. Even in their non-fruit-bearing months, the constant presence of the bushes provokes memories, curiosities and a sense of collective anticipation for the events of searching, reaching, collecting and tasting.

Adrienne spent a summer observing and video recording rituals of berry picking, and through the filming and editing process, many new possibilities and openings became visible. At the base of the huckleberry bushes where the slender stems sprouted out of the earth, she noticed a collection of small objects that lay on the surface of the earth: a small wooden bowl, a silver spoon, a doll, a truck, a scrap of brightly coloured fabric. She could see these mis-placed objects that had come to reside beneath the bushes as traces left behind, echoing the relationship of child and huckleberry bush. Notions of time and memory also began to slowly reveal themselves from the film segments, as older children returned to the place where they once roamed in bare feet as infants and toddlers. This was especially evident as one girl, Kensie, now four years old, opened the adjoining gate and came back to the toddler side to visit. Through the lens of her camera, Adrienne followed her feet. Her feet encircled and carved out a pathway moving swiftly from one huckleberry bush to the next. Other small feet came into the frame, mostly shoeless, and they paused. Toes gripped the earth and the balls of the feet pushed into the ground, heels lifted; a gesture of reaching and pushing into the earth, with arm and hand extended to branch to berry to mouth. Adrienne watched as Kensie quickly became swept up in the familiar flow of walking from bush to bush, searching, reaching, collecting and eating. Returning to this pattern of movements seemed to trigger a memory about, in her words, a 'beautiful red rose strawberry'. As a toddler, she had watched a certain strawberry in the strawberry patch grow and slowly ripen, until, one day, it mysteriously disappeared. Now in the garden again, Adrienne, through the filming and editing, began to see how Kensie's rhythms of walking, the colours of the berries and her bare feet on familiar ground brought the memory of this strawberry to life again along with the potency of its loss. There was poetry in what she was seeing.

Composing a video-poem

In video it is possible to reverse footage, vary the speed, cut and repeat segments, and re-order moments, echoing poetic elements of tempo, pattern, repetition and juxtaposition. Hoyuelos (2013: 165), relying on Levi-Strauss and Malaguzzi, describes bricolage as the effort 'to set, in a structural relation, a series of *pieces* of things that we do not see as united, but rather juxtaposed'. Cooley, in similar ways, relates her video editing processes to Deleuze's concept of assemblage and the related French word *agencement*, which suggests the acts of arranging, laying out, and fitting together. She describes how the process of video editing:

> enacts the process of assemblage as the segments of image and sound are placed in relationship to each other to become not simply the aggregate of these pieces but a dynamic creation that exceeds the quantification of its parts. It is active over time and hence we can know what assemblage is when we know what it does. (Cooley, 2007: 93)

In exploring these possibilities, Adrienne began to notice a purposeful connection between feet–ground–huckleberry bush. Narrow pathways flow from one bush to the next and the engagement of feet to landscape created an embodied sense of knowing where bodies are at work with the landscape as they overlap and intermingle together. She was drawn to the relationship of huckleberry bush to earth and how the very positioning and architecture of the bush seems to guide children in their movements and trajectories. Ingold (2011: 133) writes that 'haptic engagement is close range and hands on. It is the engagement of a mindful body at work with materials and with the land, "sewing itself in" to the textures of the world along the pathways of sensory involvement.' This form of haptic engagement suggests that the presence of the landscape and huckleberry bushes are active forces. They become gathering spaces that put into motion particular affectations and exchanges.

Adrienne tried slowing down the speed of certain segments and repeated the children's gestures of reaching and gazing. Through this, she began to notice an intricate network of forces coming together. Through a process of experimentation with looping, cutting and augmenting sound and motion, she was afforded opportunities to disrupt linear understandings and was compelled to re-think and re-read children's daily rituals as events-in-the-making. Through creative editing, she began to witness and become increasingly more sensitive to the interplay of gesture, sound, light and the liveliness of materials, allowing certain elements to come into view while drawing out qualities that stimulated specific senses and particular ways of knowing and seeing. The editing process became a space of emergence.

Interpretive encounters

Adrienne shared the completed huckleberry video poem during one of our lunchtime atelierista meetings. As she talked about the children's experiences, her processes of composing and editing, and gave insight into her perspectives, several things became apparent. We could see the huckleberry bush as a significant gathering space, feel the poetics of movement and the circular running of the children around the bush, and appreciated the beauty in daily rituals of berry picking, collecting and eating. We noticed the presence and elusiveness of memory, and how for this one child, fragments of memory were combined and recombined, and evoked through movement, colour, touch and taste. We were touched as well by yearning, loss and desire: Kensie's haunting last words in the video as she searched for the lost strawberry, and the final image of her arms outstretched as she lived again its disappearance. We were all very moved by the video. Still, we were left with the difficulty of what to do with it, how to return it in some way to the children, and draw some implications for practice. If, as Pink (2007: 250–251) writes, video invites 'empathetic engagements with the sensorial and experiencing body', how could we create conditions for children's engagement so the video didn't become entertainment or passive watching, and instead invited 'artful attending' (Leggo, 2004: 32). How could we stay in the movement of these video-documentation processes? What do we do with a video poem?

Carl Leggo (2012) asks similar questions about poetry: What is a poem good for? Leggo describes how poetry engages body, heart, mind and imagination, opens possibilities for 'attending to the world and becoming in the world' (2004: 29), and is an 'instrument for embodied experience' (Rich as cited in Leggo, 2004: 32). Bjartveit and Panayotidis (2004: 251), in considering the visual poetics of Shaun Tan's *The Arrival* in their work with early childhood educators, also ask, 'How might we re-envision the work of imagination, the mythopoetic and playfulness in ECE (early childhood education)? And how might one reconstitute and *play* with these stories?' Turning, then, from the desire to draw out from the video children's meanings and understandings, to play *with* the video and huckleberry events, we considered an aesthetic, storied and bodied response.

So, we looked for places of intersection with what was already happening in the Children's Centre, where we could engage with the video bodily, materially, imaginatively and narratively. We connected the emergent 'themes' of gathering spaces, poetics of movement, memory and desire, to other rituals alive in the toddler room of storytelling and collective drawing. We added other interpretive possibilities by bringing in a story of a strawberry snatcher that children had been engaging with as it echoed Kensie's longing for the lost strawberry.

We projected the video poem onto the wall in the toddler room, the moving images larger than life with a collective drawing area to one side and a small half-moon shaped wooden climbing structure to the other side. Long twisted panels of white paper from previous explorations hung from the ceiling and occasionally caught the moving images. Johanna, another educator, sat on the floor with a group of children around a low drawing platform, and while they drew together, used a wordless picture book to retell the story of a woman who tried to steal strawberries. The moving video projections and tempo of the accompanying music wove in together with mark making, strawberry drawing, storytelling, shadow play, running games and fragments of song. Children ran to greet an educator imaged in the video. 'Lily! Lily! Lily!' they cried out in excitement and turned momentarily puzzled as they saw Kensie at once in the video and also entering the room. The gestures of huckleberry picking were echoed in the children's strawberry drawings as they cut out, collected and extended them to others. In these ecologies of movement (Manning and Massumi, 2014), we could see gestures of generosity, children's desire to stay in movement, and what Bennett (2010: 6) describes as 'the curious ability of inanimate things to animate, to act, to produce effects dramatic and subtle'.

We repeated this video-poem event for several weeks, each time with small variances, so we could continue to feel, see and engage with children's responses and re-enactments. In this way, video documentation and the use of video poems in pedagogical documentation practices engage with a propositional and processual methodology (Manning and Massumi, 2014) where research events are enacted, and we are engaged with contending with making sense of what *is* happening, rather than analysing what has happened. We stay in the flow of the movements of curriculum processes and the embodied movements of video. With the children, we are trying to see from within how things move together. What emerges is not a focus on children's theories or ideas or *what* children are exploring and thinking about, although these things are still very important and are attended to, but, rather, an attunement and increasing sensitivity to children's movements, thinking processes and pathways of individual and collective invention, that is, the *how* of children's engagements. We begin to think of video as a poetic-material-pedagogical interplay (Dixon, 2016) and see the possibility of video for creating 'new modes of thought and action' (Manning and Massumi, 2014: 90).

References

Atkinson, D. (2011) *Art, Equality and Learning: Pedagogies Against the State*. Rotterdam: Sense.

Bennett, J. (2010) *Vibrant Matter*. Durham, NC: Duke University Press.

Berger, J. (1977) *Ways of Seeing*. New York: Penguin.

Bjartveit, C.J. and Panayotidis, E.L. (2004) 'Pointing to Shaun Tan's *The Arrival* and reimagining visual poetics in research', *Contemporary Issues in Early Childhood*, 15 (3): 245–261.

Clark, A. and Moss, P. (2011) *Listening to Young Children: The Mosaic Approach* (2nd edn). London: National Children's Bureau.

Cooley, M. (2007) 'Video poems: Seeking insight', *Canadian Review of Art Education Research and Issues*, 34 (1): 88–98.

Dixon, M. (2016) 'Pedascapes: New cartographies of pedagogies', in J. Moss and B. Pini (eds), *Visual Research Methods in Educational Research*. London: Palgrave, pp. 100–115.

Hirsch, E. (1999) *How to Read a Poem and Fall in Love with Poetry*. New York: Harcourt.

Hoyuelos, A. ([2004] 2013) *The Ethics of Loris Malaguzzi's Philosophy and Pedagogical Work* (tr. R. Pisano). Reykjavik: Isalda.

Ingold, T. (2011) *Being Alive: Essays on Movement, Knowledge and Description*. New York: Routledge.

Kind, S. (2010) 'Art encounters: Movements in the visual arts and early childhood education', in V. Pacini-Ketchabaw (ed.), *Flows, Rhythms, and Intensities of Early Childhood Education Curriculum*. New York: Peter Lang, pp. 113–132.

Kind, S. (2013) 'Lively entanglements: The doings, movements, and enactments of photography', *Global Studies of Childhood*, 3 (4): 427–441.

Law, J. (2004) *After Method: Mess is Social Science Research*. New York: Routledge.

Leggo, C. (2004) 'The curriculum of joy: Six poetic ruminations', *Journal of the Canadian Association for Curriculum Studies*, 2 (2): 27–42.

Leggo, C. (2012) 'Living language: What is a poem good for?', *Journal of the Canadian Association for Curriculum Studies*, 10 (1): 141–160.

Lenz Taguchi, H. (2009) *Going Beyond the Theory/Practice Divide in Early Childhood Education: Introducing an Inter-Active Pedagogy*. London and New York: Routledge.

MacLure, M., Holmes, R., MacRae, C. and Jones, L. (2010) 'Animating classroom ethnography: Overcoming video-fear', *International Journal of Qualitative Studies in Education*, 23 (5): 543–556.

Manning, E. and Massumi, B. (2014) *Thought in the Act: Passages in the Ecology of Experience*. Minneapolis, MN: University of Minnesota Press.

Olsson, L.M. (2009) *Movement and Experimentation in Young Children's Learning: Deleuze and Guattari in Early Childhood Education*. London and New York: Routledge.

Pacini-Ketchabaw, V., Kind, S. and Kocher, L. (2016) *Encounters with Materials in Early Childhood Education*. New York: Routledge.

Pink, S. (2007) 'Walking with video', *Visual Studies*, 22 (3): 240–252.

Pink, S. (2011) 'Images, senses, applications: Engaging visual anthropology', *Visual Anthropology*, 24 (5): 437–454.

Thompson, P. and Hall, C. (2016) 'Using film to show and tell: Studying/changing pedagogical practices', in J. Moss and B. Pini (eds), *Visual Research Methods in Educational Research*. London: Palgrave, pp. 116–132.

Tsing, A.L. (2013) 'More than human sociality: A call for critical description', in K. Hastrup (ed.), *Anthropology and Nature*. New York: Routledge, pp 27–42.

van Manen, M. (1997) *Researching Lived Experience: Human Science for an Action Sensitive Pedagogy* (2nd edn). London, Ontario: The Althouse Press.

Commentary 2: Opening Doors and Windows

Stefania Giamminuti

School of Education, Curtin University

Unfolding their narratives with thoughtful grace, Mitchelmore and Fleet, Richard, and Kind and Argent reveal themselves to us as 'specific intellectuals' who work 'not in the modality of the universal, the exemplary, the just-and-true-for-all, but within specific sectors' (Foucault, cited in Cagliari et al., 2016: 24/532). Connected as they are to the 'quotidian' lives of children, they contest the futile and crippling separation that continues to exist between theory, research and practice in early childhood education. Their pedagogical documentation speaks to us with voices imbued with poetry of place, locality and belonging, and shows how the 'freedom to research' (Cagliari et al., 2016: 88/532) can be a catalyst for transformations, extending our understandings of what is possible and valuable in early childhood education and care. These contributions also reveal deeply considered attention to the heartfelt plea that the *Reggiani* extend to those who encounter their experience: to resist the universality of imitation and instead embrace transformation of their own localities. These authors welcome a 'pedagogy of invention' (Moss, 2014), rather than adhering to a pedagogy of imitation, as they reinterpret the possibilities and peculiarities of their own contexts through values which belong to the educational project of Reggio Emilia. Of the many values that are evident in this work, I will focus on three in particular: rich normality, aesthetics and research (Giamminuti, 2013).

Rich normality is revealed in Mitchelmore and Fleet's 'small events', in their celebration of 'frivolity' and their enhancement of 'silliness'. Their encounters with young children remind me of the words of Giuliana Campani, a teacher in Reggio Emilia with over 40 years of experience, who told me in an interview that rich normality occurs within experiences that 'are not necessarily extraordinary', where 'there are events every day' (Giamminuti, 2013: 83). The beautifully explored notion of the quotidian is an invitation to stop and consider whether we recognize everyday 'humble events' as worthy of our attention, so that we are not lost in the search for the elusive extraordinary project. By being attentive to rich normality, we can nurture daily what the Reggio Emilia educators call *pensiero progettuale* – an inventive way of thinking that makes it possible for educators to suggest provocations to children while welcoming uncertainty, as opposed to being driven by the pervasive 'test curriculum, this'll do curriculum, the activity based curriculum, the preparation for school curriculum and lastly, the thematic curriculum' (Robertson, 2006: 44) – the curriculum which, as Richard so aptly surmises, takes control of children's bodies along with their minds and hearts. In threading the value of rich normality through their work, these authors give us permission to dwell in a curriculum of possibilities, liberating us from the humiliating 'prophetic pedagogy', which Malaguzzi so vehemently opposed:

> [a pedagogy which] knows everything beforehand … to the point that it is capable of giving you recipes for little bits of actions, minute by minute, hour by hour, objective by objective … so humiliating of teachers' ingenuity, a complete humiliation for children's ingenuity and potential. (Cagliari et al., 2016: 23/532)

All three of these contributions dwell in 'poetic possibilities', striving towards aesthetics thanks to the inspiration of a town that has made beauty and culture its responsibility and a right for all its citizens. Malaguzzi wrote in 1945 that 'culture needs to enter slowly but surely into the customs of our people. That is why we need to create cultural circles everywhere' (Cagliari et al., 2016: 75/532); the atelier that Malaguzzi invented, and which is so gracefully honoured many years later in Kind and Argent's Canadian setting, is one such 'cultural circle'.

Finally, these three contributions speak of educators as researchers, as 'cultured teachers' who possess 'the culture of research, of curiosity, of working in a group' (Rinaldi, 2001: 88), contesting the dominant image of the educator as 'a self-interested and essentially untrustworthy individual whose performance must be monitored, managed and moulded' (Moss, 2014: 93). They speak of the interconnective value of research (Giamminuti, 2013), of research as an ethic of welcome and relationship (ibid., 2016), as the premise for education:

> Either education is a place of research and the research produces new pedagogy, or it is the implementation of an offering that is delivered to young children, imprisoning them within a message that is somehow constructed or coded in advance. (Malaguzzi, n.d., cited in Strozzi, 2014: 40, my translation)

The pedagogical documentation that is shared by these authors is inextricably linked to that artistic and aesthetic attitude that is *progettazione* and *pensiero progettuale*. This becomes richly evident in Kind and Argent's beautiful documentation of the feet of four-year-old Kensie, captured as they carve a pathway through the huckleberry bushes, made visible through video and becoming a poem.

Thus, we are thankful to pedagogical documentation for the poetic possibilities it offers to create, shape and unfold the experiences of such 'specific intellectuals', who, in far-flung places, are together dedicated to values such as rich normality, aesthetics and research. We are grateful to the educators and children of Reggio Emilia for the possibilities they have suggested through their tools and experiences to uncover voices such as those we have heard in these three chapters, and for their tireless invitation to build 'alliances with children' (Cagliari et al., 2016: 65/532).

References

Cagliari, P., Castagnetti, M., Giudici, C., Rinaldi, C., Vecchi, V. and Moss, P. (eds) (2016) *Loris Malaguzzi and the Schools of Reggio Emilia: A Selection of his Writings and Speeches, 1945–1993* (electronic book). Abingdon: Routledge.

Giamminuti, S. (2013) *Dancing with Reggio Emilia: Metaphors for Quality*. Mt Victoria, NSW: Pademelon Press.

Giamminuti, S. (2016) 'Research as an ethic of welcome and relationship: Pedagogical documentation in Reggio Emilia, Italy', in W. Parnell and J.M. Iorio (eds), *Disrupting Early Childhood Research: Imagining New Possibilities*. New York: Routledge, pp. 9–25.

Moss, P. (2014) *Transformative Change and Real Utopias in Early Childhood Education: A Story of Democracy, Experimentation and Potentiality*. Abingdon: Routledge.

Rinaldi, C. (2001) 'Documentation and assessment: What is the relationship?', in C. Giudici, C. Rinaldi and M. Krechevsky (eds), *Making Learning Visible: Children as Individual and Group Learners*. Reggio Emilia, Italy: Reggio Children, pp. 78–89.

Robertson J. (2006) 'Reconsidering our images of children: What shapes our educational thinking?', in A. Fleet, C. Patterson and J. Robertson (eds), *Insights: Behind Early Childhood Pedagogical Documentation*. Sydney: Pademelon Press, pp. 37–54.

Strozzi, P. (2014) 'I nidi e le scuole dell'infanzia come luogo della ricerca e del pensiero progettuale: Appunti per una ricostruzione storica dell'idea e della pratica della progettazione', [Infant-toddler centres and schools as places of research and 'pensiero progettuale': Notes for a historical reconstruction of the idea and practice of 'progettazione'], *Bambini*, Marzo: 39–42.

PART 3
EMBRACING POSSIBILITIES OF CHANGE

7

COLLABORATIVE DECISION-MAKING WITHIN PEDAGOGICAL DOCUMENTATION

JANET ROBERTSON

Foregrounding the nature of decision-making in pedagogy, the narratives in this chapter illustrate the potentials of ongoing shared documentation for enriching experiences of children and the adults sharing their lives. Making visible the values of an Australian setting, stories of cockatoos resonate with intellectual and environmental respect.

Introduction

In any examination of pedagogical documentation, the role of decisions must naturally arise. Decisions frame everything we do. Decisions made before, during and after a pedagogical experience are platforms on which experiences play out. Everyone involved is a decision-maker: children, adults, materials and the events experienced 'make' decisions.

Those made beforehand support the values and connectivity (Giamminuti, 2013) of curriculum. Those made during an experience are 'process-oriented' (driving the experience), and those made afterwards are perhaps 'reflective decisions', focusing the participants' perceptions of 'what happened'. In this chapter, I examine decisions made before, during and after an experience with four-year-old children at Mia Mia, a 51-place long day care programme on a university campus in Sydney. As with any narrative, it can seem that events, and therefore the decision-making, occurred in a linear fashion. This is far from the case. Time folds, expands and fractures within the life span of pedagogical documentation. The tales I'll tell are *short stories with long beginnings and long endings* (apologies to Eulalia Bosch, 2005).

Long beginnings: Contextual decisions

The long beginning to these cockatoo events are what I'll call *contextual decisions*. As the outdoor teacher, curriculum is derived from that context: the outdoors. Respecting creatures with whom we share our playground is a 23-year endeavour. We don't allow children to chase birds, scare chickens, stamp on ants or pick flowers (unless we are harvesting or pruning). We consider encounters between human and non-human to be rich in possibilities for curriculum engagement. Even in these highly urbanized times, an ancient section of the brain, the amygdala, kicks in, enabling children to be intensely interested in animals and birds, even if their encounters with them are limited. This evolutionary remnant of our past, noticing creatures, is a reflex response to the state of 'eat or be eaten'.

Who makes curriculum decisions? We are co-researchers with children, so their decisions are given weight in our provisions. This too is a given in our philosophy. Children bring ideas, knowledges and passions to us, and of course we consider these in our planning. The choice of what idea to pursue is our responsibility, framed by our understandings of each child, the group and of our collective endeavours. We may decide to go with a big idea gifted to us by a child (or a bird), but the multitudes of decisions thereafter are shaped by our philosophy, values and pedagogical intentions. They may be negotiated in the moment, at curriculum meetings or in quick discussions with colleagues, children and families, depending on the situation. We do have intentions, but with no predetermined path, it is impossible to predict what will happen. Into the 'what happens' is woven the stuff of early childhood education: communication, relationships, foundational learning and so on.

We choose to work with small groups of children, rather than herds, and spaces are staffed accordingly. We consider outdoor spaces to have as much pedagogical and curriculum integrity as the inside, and staff them with a teacher, because any space in which there are young children should have a qualified early childhood teacher.

Over the 16 years that I've been the outdoor teacher at Mia Mia, investigations into what the birds are saying or letters (written on leaves) between the pet rabbit and a wild rabbit, or building a hotel for snails so they won't eat the vegetables, have been typical. Birds are central in our curriculum, as they swoop, soar, sing, quarrel, roost and live above us in the tree canopy, adding another dimension to the lives led here. Acknowledging this natural context, we are creating a *Field guide to the flora and fauna of Mia Mia* as a long-term project. From infancy, Mia Mia children can identify the call of kookaburras, and those rascally cockatoos. Sitting and watching, enjoying the antics of any creature creates treasured moments, 'privileged' within the curriculum, so time and routines are suspended if we are busy contemplating our fellow creatures. This value of sharing the playground, an 'inter-connectedness' as Giamminuti describes it (2013: 255) is one we cherish. We also share Harraway's (2008) valuing of other-than-human animals within our lives.

One such vivid character is the sulphur-crested cockatoo, a large white parrot with a yellow crest, black eyes and an easy relationship with humans. They live to a great age, 60 or more years, are gregarious and nest in holes in trees. Mia Mia has one such flock, living in the surrounding bushland.

Two stories will illustrate some decisions made during a six-month investigation of our life with a flock of cockatoos. The evolution of titles for these stories illustrates the shift in focus inevitable over time. The first story's working title: 'How to Stop the Cockies Eating the Vegies', makes the intent of the initial pedagogy clear, driven both by children and adult decision-making. Its eventual title: 'Ethical Cockatoo Deterrents', gives the reader an indication of the path the investigation took. Pragmatically, the second story was called 'The Cockatoos' Party'. Its eventual title: 'Yearning for the Impossible', describes the arc of ideas, for both children and adults. Title changes are deliberate, indicators to the reader of content, a response to events and pedagogy. Obviously, the content did not exist before the experience, so the original titles were placeholders, something to hang onto, while we worked.

The decision to give something a title is an act of commencement. In naming the idea, we have something to think about together. The practice at Mia Mia of naming pedagogical events began many years ago. This making visible group intention creates a tangible thinking community:

we are the flag designers; *we are* the letter writers to the rabbits; or *we are* rock collectors. This identity acts as glue, announcing '*we are doing this; we did that*'. Working titles help me keep track of who is doing what when, as there are often several large investigations (pedagogical documentation) occurring simultaneously.

I create a digital file with the working title, and a physical one, in which to keep the 'data', the provisions and proposals in one place. This has the added benefit of assisting children organize their 'task-scape' (Ingold, 1993), as well as keeping them in the loop. The data collected – either digital or physical – belongs to that group, and is the engine driving the process forward. We use these materials as memory banks, a catalyst for further thinking, and once an end point is reached, to remember the long endings, a place for reflection. As I write this chapter, I'm musing about what did happen in those heady cockatoo months, wishing I could re-ask a question, or that I had listened more, while contemplating how marvelous children's brains are and what a privilege it is to be in their company when they are puzzling over the meaning of the world and our lives.

The short stories: Collaborative, pragmatic, transgressive and ethical decisions

How to stop cockies wrecking the cabbages: Ethical cockatoo deterrents

In August 2015, a serendipitous moment occurred. I chanced upon three cockatoos ripping up cabbages in the vegetable tubs. Knowing that this desecration would mean the end of the crop, and that children, alerted to the event, were witnessing my response, I decided to stand still and simply take photos, leaving the birds to their fun. If I chased the feathered villains away, I would be behaving counter to our values. This decision, supported by previous decisions about honouring wildlife in our space, was the first of many as together we explored the aftermath of the vegetable ruination. The following few hours set the scene for a collaborative exploration lasting three of the six- month-long investigation.

The next decision was simple, but I think the hardest. It was to listen. As Rinaldi (2006: 65) reminds us, listening is a 'verb'. We, the adults, had to listen, to listen to children's ideas and evolving narratives. And in listening, was also the decision to slow down, not to jump in and remedy the problem, or plan a unit on vegetable protection, agricultural solutions, or scarecrows, all adult ideas no doubt busting to bubble to the surface. Pragmatically finding time and space to 'listen' in the middle of a busy morning required us to juggle usual events, eliminating some and stretching time to accommodate children's enquiries. The further decision to privilege this event over others was made on the run, with few words between the three teaching staff. By mid-morning the photos were printed and early eyewitnesses were excitedly informing latecomers of the disaster, showing them the devastation, using words, drawings and the crime scene photos to illustrate their tales.

We waited, allowing children to absorb what had happened, for ideas to percolate and coalesce. By mid-afternoon, seven hours later, we could see children's theories with some clarity, which helped to establish what to do next. As Rinaldi (2006: 191) wrote: 'We cannot live without theory or practice. We need to be theoretical practitioners, and to be thinkers. And to give to the children the value and the experience of being a thinker.'

Firstly, the children theorized about why the cockatoos had done it. One group was shocked that their favourite birds could accomplish such wilful trashing of their precious cabbages. As Saskia (3.5 years) said, 'They can't do it, we don't like it. They are just here to destroy the plants. They just ate everything. Well, those cockies are really, really naughty and got the good cabbages out and destroyed them!' This image of naughtiness, of transgression, was one that we, at a curriculum meeting later that week, decided to consider and research: the role of anthropomorphic transgressions and children's sense of self.

A second group thought that the cockies made a serious mistake while they were playing. This idea, one of forgiveness and grace, was one we, too, decided to follow as it illuminated anthropomorphic empathy.

The urgent issue of how to stop it happening again occupied another group. I asked, 'What can we do?' This elicited an outpouring of ideas which formed into theories by morning's end. Barrier-construction characterized a few ideas: building over the garden with 'a concrete slab and bricks', or designing a cubby house for cabbages. As I wrote, listened and waited, I found my own ideas mirrored in their thinking. I had thought of barrier techniques, too, netting for one. Others wondered if they were fed birdseed elsewhere, would the cockies not eat our cabbages? A side decision was to go see them being fed upstairs at a feeding station established by office staff. The flaw in this theory was that the cockies are, indeed, so well fed that, consequently, they don't need to spend time and energy hunting for food, and so they get up to mischief instead.

Four children gathered at a table in the afternoon. Deciding group membership criteria was in this instance based on 'who is interested'. These children became the core group. Others were included in later experiences, always to enhance the group's thinking, but also for reasons such as deepening social skills or strengthening communication. I showed them the drawings, and read aloud ideas from the morning. Saskia floated the idea of scarecrows, and an exciting discussion followed. They almost reached agreement, with the slight modification that it would be a 'scare-cockie', when Jojo mentioned that this might frighten the cockatoos. The group pondered this, shocked by the truth. Scarecrows frighten birds. I could see the Mia Mia values of respect and sharing with creatures in the playground disrupting the normative idea of jolly scarecrows in the fields espoused in children's literature.

I remained silent, even at the height of their scare-cockie plans (I, too, had been energized by this possibility and had mentally begun to assemble things we might need), only speaking to make sure everyone was heard, or to clarify a word for the transcript. Returning to the conversation, I asked Jojo to elaborate. 'They live here,' she said. Without another word, they scrapped that plan. To my surprise, another version of 'scaring' was floated: 'We could make a giant cockatoo,' said Saskia standing on a chair to indicate how tall, and again ideas flew back and forth. I wondered if she had this idea from the plastic owls hanging in cafés to scare pesky birds thieving food from customers' plates. In this discussion stage, I expect children to remain together so that all the ideas are heard. I could see several of the children itching to gather papers and materials to 'do' something rather than just talk. Our expectation is that children listen to each other, staying together during discussions, while an adult transcribes and supports the group in respectful listening and engagement. This contextual decision is one already in place, a strategy understood by all, thus supporting decision-making on the run.

Once again, Jojo had been thinking through the repercussions of the plan: 'But maybe they will think it [the giant cockatoo] is their mother, and more will come.' Their pell-mell rush staggered to a halt as they considered the possibility of even more cockatoos. Far from being despondent that yet another idea had been disbanded, they regrouped.

Two further ideas were posed which were immediately adopted. Jojo suggested the first: 'We could make pretend cabbages,' 'With stinky socks inside,' giggled Yosep. They glanced at each other, assessing the plan. It passed muster. Jojo added a word of warning: 'Not too smelly because we might not like it.' Just before they dashed off to make them, Hayley added, 'We could write a sign: "Don't pick the cabbages!"' 'But we don't speak cockatoo', said Jojo. 'I do,' said Casey, sounding out 'ka ka ki ka ceac'.

I agreed with the four. These ideas not only had traction for the children, but for our pedagogy as well. Literacy, text, cross-species communication and the theory of decoy cabbages had validity within Mia Mia values and curriculum. There was also an issue of expediency. It was now 5 o'clock and to avoid another predation, we had to act; these were two quick solutions, do-able by all. So, within ten minutes, the vegetable garden was studded with paper decoy cabbages, and the sign (in both English and cockatoo) was typed up and stuck on a stick.

The decision to listen, wait, support and trust children to come up with a solution was vindicated. Even more so, the next morning, the remaining cabbages sat speckled with dew, proving their theories right: cockatoos could read, and were put off by tasteless decoys.

Over the next few days, children revisited the event, telling and retelling the tale. I worked with small groups, drawing and chatting, and the event became a thing of legend. To formalize the tale, I worked with two groups to 'write the story'. Stories require a beginning, middle and end; so, to craft their tale, I wrote their words, then physically slotted them into the correct sequence, speaking the addition aloud for confirmation from the teller. With each addition, a rhythm emerged, a storytelling cadence in their spoken then transcribed words. This group-narrative was published:

'The Naughty Cockies'

by Kaya, Seb, Lucas, Yosep, Saskia, Cynthia, Jojo and Arvind

Once upon a time there were three naughty cockies and they went to Mia Mia and pulled up all the cabbages and vegetables – and they threw them on the ground.

They chewed, didn't eat the cabbages, just chewed them. Why? Why? Because they were bored. They only wanted to have some fun. But we didn't like it! They flew away to the fence; maybe they wanted to play with our vegetables?

So we had an idea: give them birdseed. Kaya, Lucas, Seb and Yosep went upstairs to look at the cockatoos eating birdseed up there. Jojo said to maybe make pretend cabbages with stinky smelly socks in them that would stop the cockies coming back.

So everyone made paper cabbages and put them in the vegetable garden. And it worked! The cockies did not come back! Just to make sure Casey made a sign in cockatoo language 'ka ka ki Ceac SSSSSha' ('Don't pick the cabbages' in English). The paper cabbages was a great idea, as was the sign – and so was Seb's to feed them seed.

We think that's enough of the story, so we have to say – the end.

But it wasn't the end. At our weekly curriculum meetings, teachers discussed the grand ideas evident in the theory-making: children's respect for other-than-human animals, their collaborative and thoughtful discussions, how hard it had been for adults to avoid giving children solutions and answers, interest in the cockatoos' transgression and 'naughtiness', anthropomorphic understandings of bird life (speaking English, playing, reading), their misunderstood but generalized understanding of bird maturation (giant mother cockatoos = adult human mothers).

Time passed; the cockatoos stayed away from the vegetable tubs. We continued to watch them fly, gather, screech above us, and note evidence of their bored mischief-making with scattered buds, leaves and twigs on the ground after a morning spent in a tree nearby. The teaching staff considered the role of transgressive play and noted it in other games the children were playing.

Yearning for the impossible: Can cockatoos be children?

Another month passed. Jojo, Jacinta and Xiu Ming found two cockatoo feathers on the lawn and, alarmed, ran to the vegetables, finding them intact. They turned to me and asked if they could write a letter to the cockatoos. As part of our 'use what happens on-site' values, I have taught them to use quills from found feathers, so agreed. Settling at the table with newly clipped quills and blue ink (*'Cockatoos like blue, the sky is blue,'* said Jojo), we began. To my surprise, they dictated these words: 'Dear cockatoos, would you like to have a party here?' As they laboriously copied this text onto what was rapidly becoming an invitation, I weighed up the options. I could run with this and include all our curriculum elements into it (we certainly seemed to be ticking off literacy outcomes), and investigate the anthropomorphic tangent, or mention it might not be such a good idea to invite vegetable wreckers to visit again. Seeing more possibilities in the first, I made an on-the-spot decision that we would invest time and thought into what was now not just an invitation, but a fully-fledged party. Following children's interests is not a mindless pursuit of 'letting children decide the curriculum', but a calculated decision regarding *which interest and why*. I was instantly rewarded by the next proposed task:

> Jojo, 'We don't know how to write cockatoo, Casey is away.'
>
> 'You could try,' I say. 'What do they sound like?'
>
> 'Can you say it like they say it?' says Xiu Ming.
>
> I screech.
>
> 'Easy,' says, Xiu Ming. 'Wak waak WAK!'

They elect to type up the translation on the now embellished and digitalized invitation. An hour has passed since the feathers were found; the whirlwind begins to settle and more pragmatic issues arise as they contemplate the completed invitation. Is the invitation to be mailed, emailed or posted somewhere? 'How will the cockies see/get this?' I enquire. Their solution was to take it to the third floor balcony where (as mentioned before) office staff have a feeding station. 'How will we know if they want to come?' I asked. Xiu Ming said, 'They can use this,' indicating the quills and ink. Only at this point was there concern about the cockatoos' ability to read. Jojo is skeptical, while given the success of Casey's signs, Jacinta and Xiu Ming are certain that they can.

The invitation is installed on the window, and ink is provided for the cockies; we return to Mia Mia and wait. I deliberately don't arrange with the upstairs staff to reply, or contrive to guide the outcome. Children's solutions to problems are provisional, an action research cycle of 'try and see'. We return a week later (one of the restrictions on this investigation was that Xiu Ming only attends Thursday/ Friday) to find the inkbottle spilt. They conjecture that the bottleneck was too narrow for the birds to either use their beaks or toes to dip into the ink. Undeterred, they find and leave a pen on the ground. Jojo again voicing her doubt cockies could read, suggested the three children could dress up as cockies, learn to speak cockatoo, and stand on the balcony, personally inviting them to the party. I mentioned I was not sure I/we could make said costumes. Xiu Ming said, 'Well, there is costume hire.'

The next day, there was a reply from the birds, 'No problem. What morning will we have it?' Xiu Ming was the skeptical one, insisting 'a person wrote that', then in the face of the others' certainty, suspended her doubts so the party was not in jeopardy. The reading, writing and translations, in fact the idea the birds would actually like a party, are anthropomorphic beliefs. This vacillation between belief and disbelief was strong for all three, at times a palpable yearning for it to be true.

I was looking at curriculum opportunities, both practical and philosophical problems. At a curriculum meeting, it was decided to have the party, understanding it was a commitment to support the children in organizing and staging the event. From the discovery of two feathers, it had grown to a class-wide experience. We decided that it would be a fitting end to the cockatoo legend, encompassing the months of cockatoo investigations. There was also a finite frame; the year ended in two months.

At the first 'party meeting', I scribed as children verbalized ideas. I suggested that they draw as they talked, making visible these suggestions to others. (This is a standard pedagogical strategy, externalizing thinking.) Clearly, they had been thinking as their experiences of 'party' informed the brainstorming. Ideas tumbled out, quickly forming into four categories:

food, games, attire and decorations. At this stage, it seemed that they expected to host an occasion at which cockatoos and humans would party together, that the worlds of cockatoo and human would not just be parallel, but merge. The scope of ideas was eclectic including water slides, jumping castle, cakes, party hats, games and dress-ups. Woven into this were more realistic understandings of cockies: Would they be scared of the human party-goers? Would they come? Rip up the vegetables, or worse, the rest of the garden? Plans to cover plants, write even larger 'keep off' notices and finally to block off parts of the playground began to derail the more gala aspects. Elaborate plans to manage 'cocky-ness' highlighted differences between the species; their yearning for a together-party was fracturing under their knowledge of avian behaviour. Over the next few days, the party purpose changed: from a party *with* the cockatoos, to a party *for* the cockatoos. Although the party was for cockies, the plans and games were very human, just scaled down and adapted. The venue altered, shifting to the third floor balcony, to accommodate this separateness. Fanciful designs with practical aspects transpired, such as a shallow swimming pool because they were unsure if cockies could swim, or if the birds' claws would puncture the fabric of a jumping castle, 'cause they can't take their shoes off', or to cope with sanitary issues, a cockatoo toilet. No longer would humans and birds share a cake; as the thought of a human cake sprinkled with birdseed was decidedly unpalatable, two cakes were planned.

It was a morning's work to set the party date, as they grappled with the structure of diaries, mornings and afternoons, numerals and previous appointments. This process gave the children an understanding of the scope of the task ahead; it was possible to break down the jobs into catering, games and construction. A revised invitation was posted on the window.

Pragmatics shaped the next meetings with Jacinta, Xiu Ming and Jojo. Assisting them, being their auxiliary memory and showing them the workings of event organization, I used sheets of paper to log in dates, agendas, tasks and who was doing what. This is a common strategy in our teaching: making tasks visible. In this way, the jobs, reminders and timeframes are the agenda's role, not mine. Expecting children to commit, be responsible and stay on-task is a value that I don't have to teach now. It is a way we work from the beginning of their time with us, so it is familiar.

I knew that they would need help, and co-opted two more children, EE and QiQi. The addition of new children to an existing group is a considered decision; personalities, leadership and working styles impact on team structure. We prefer to work with small groups, three to five children, and generally have two or three investigations running concurrently. That EE and QiQi were a good fit was evidenced as the team embarked on making party hats. Xiu Ming made a prototype conical design; quickly adopted, but issues of size, 'Will it fit the birds?' vexed them. EE left the table, returning minutes later with a wooden bird, to act as mannequin.

The issue of inclusion or exclusion of other bird species had to be addressed. On a reconnaissance visit upstairs, a kookaburra was perched on the railing in the party arena. On another occasion, a raven at the birdbath was eavesdropping, so children whispered their plans, because 'maybe ravens will want to come, too'. Social justice is a value Mia Mia holds; we intentionally seek to give children the job of seeing what is fair. Adopting an ethical decision-making stance, I asked, 'Can other birds come, too?' Trusting that they would come up with a just solution, I kept my counsel as a fierce argument oscillated between, 'it's just for cockatoos' and 'every bird can come', and was rewarded by their eventual inclusive invitation, tempered by concern over guest numbers.

Design processes illuminated not only the structures they wished to represent, but also the relationship that children desired. The party table, drawn with food for both humans and birds, had chairs for cockies to stand on, and a toilet with a long queue of cockies waiting.

The last few days flew by in a whirlwind of construction, decoration, cooking and, we witnessed, yearning and dreaming. Once construction of the structures was completed, the edges blurred further, as children played within the play-scape of the jumping castle, cubby, swing and ladder with small cockatoo figurines, speaking cockatoo and English, as they became naughty cockie families. By the party morning, everything was ready, cakes completed, decorations made, balcony bedecked with ladders and miniature jumping castle. Twenty-five human guests arrived. The children vacillated between certainty and uncertainty, experiencing host anxiety, 'would everything go alright?'

I had, as much as I was able to, ensured that the cockies would arrive, by arranging for the office staff to delay their usual morning feeding until the party, and to be present so they could call them. I wanted the cockies to come, as it was the collision between the children's ideas and the reality of what would happen that was to be examined. I couldn't inoculate the trio from any disappointment ahead.

No cockatoos arrived. Disappointment loomed. Ten minutes later, they swooped in, landing on the railing, warily scoping out the novel items in their space. Thirty minutes later, they were brave enough to eat the cake, as on the other side of the window, children tucked into theirs. Replete, the birds flew off, not interested in clambering up ladders, swinging, jumping or reclining on sofas in the cubby. Downcast, Jojo, Jacinta and Xiu Ming summed it up on their return to school, 'I liked the cake, and the jumping castle even if the cockies didn't use it!'

The next week, I retrieved remains of the structures; they looked at them in dismay. 'Did they think the jumping castle was a toilet?' said Jojo, looking at a dropping on top. Regarding the holes ripped in the cubby, Xiu Ming asked, 'Did they think it was food?' Jacinta was aghast at ripped decorations, 'They just pulled them off like this,' flipping the fluttering drawings with her forefinger. We stood surrounded by wreckage. I waited. 'We could make a bigger one, just for us,' said Xiu Ming gleefully.

Conclusion: Long endings, subjective decisions

The long ending is not this 'after the event' narrative, it is the thinking, for all of us, about the event, visible to us individually over years to come. The short story is the pedagogical documentation within the event itself, the data we collected, analysed and together using that data, made decisions about directions to take. As with any short story, the characters – children, cockatoos and adults – create an idiosyncratic plot, one which cannot be replicated.

A strong thread of ethics must tie all decisions into a socially just frame. Some decisions are functional, pragmatic decisions about time, grouping or materials. Others are consensual within the working group, sanctioned by the adult. Often, these decisions have an element of fluidity, placeholders as theories are formed, ideas made visible and evidence obtained. Contextual decisions, informed by a rigorous understanding of the 'why' of early childhood education, shape almost everything that occurs, and is in the hands of participants. As with the Reggio Emilian understanding of the hundred languages of children, there are a hundred languages of decisions, as no one educational experience with young children is the same.

No pedagogy occurs in a blank space; neither does thinking occur in a blank mind. The space or place of pedagogy is a mélange of edited, intentional and unintentional subjective decisions. Every decision-maker brings his or her subjectivity to the event. Although the initial predation of cabbages was a chance event, as Louis Pasteur said, 'chance favours the prepared mind'. We were prepared, prepared to see potential in curriculum, in our values, theory and pedagogy, prepared as a school to expect children to think. We were prepared to engage in small group work, listen, then propose back to children their ideas. Our context was prepared, current in understanding that pedagogical documentation is the engine bringing curriculum to life and creating places for decision-making, theory and practice.

References

Bosch, E. (2005) *Education and Everyday Life: Short Stories with Long Endings*. Victoria, Australia: Hawker Brownlow.

Giamminuti, S. (2013) *Dancing with Reggio Emilia: Metaphors for Quality*. Mt Victoria, NSW: Pademelon Press.

Harraway, D. (2008) *When Species Meet*. Minneapolis, MN: University of Minnesota Press.

Ingold, T. (1993) 'The temporality of the landscape', *World Archaeology*, 25 (2): 152–174.

Rinaldi, C. (2006) *In Dialogue with Reggio Emilia: Listening, Researching and Learning*. London: Routledge.

8

PEDAGOGIC DOCUMENTATION AND STUDENT LEARNING

MICHAEL REED AND NICOLA STOBBS

This chapter offers a case study of the place of pedagogic documentation as part of undergraduate experience for early educators in an English university. It proposes a conceptual model which may assist tertiary tutors and others engaged in professional development.

Introduction

The authors of this chapter are experienced higher education tutors who value the way pedagogic documentation allows a careful examination of learning possibilities for young children. It is an approach which also provides possibilities for the professional development of early educators as it involves close observation of children's learning, an interpretation of that learning and reflection on practice. However, in universities in England, its influence on professional development is less apparent, even though the concept of documenting children's learning is a significant element within early education curriculum frameworks and seen to be important by regulators of early education. Therefore, it would seem important to enhance professional understanding of pedagogic documentation and extend its reach by including its principles and practices within courses for university early education undergraduate students. This targeted strategy positions these students as the persons who will go on to influence policy, practice and quality as well as meeting regulators' expectations. The chapter takes this position and presents a rationale for the design of such a course. Programmes of learning for undergraduate early education students at university require careful construction of learning environments, involving an active induction into both the world of the child, and the systems and societal influences which support the child's learning. This approach usually involves higher-level learning within a college or university as well as in the workplace: a process where learning in one environment is applied in the other.

The intention is to empower students to use pedagogic documentation in order to critically consider children's learning and understand the influence they and others have on shaping learning environments. It is intended to be a way of provoking thinking and attempts to expose a number of issues about undergraduate professional development allied to pedagogic documentation. However, we need to be clear: it is about understanding children's learning *with* pedagogic documentation. It is not about designing a course *on* pedagogic documentation.

Context

There is considerable evidence suggesting that obtaining early education professional qualifications has a pronounced influence on the quality of early education, evidence which is summarized in a report by Hillman and Williams (2015), the All-Party Parliamentary Group (2015) and the House of Lords inquiry into affordable childcare and the quality of provision (2015). It is also supported by research evidence from Mathers and Smees (2014), who examined provision for disadvantaged three- and four-year-olds and found that a well-qualified staff team was associated with higher quality. There are longitudinal research studies which have monitored children's development over many years and explored the contributing factors which influence quality and recognize the influence of training and qualifications (Sylva et al. 2014). The Office for Standards in Education, Children's Services and Skills who inspect early years settings in England also recognize the effect of training (Ofsted, 2015a). They found that early education settings where a high proportion of staff are qualified to further and higher education levels are more likely to be highly rated by inspectors.

Equally important in terms of engaging in a study aligned with practice are the personal qualities which sit alongside such qualifications; for example, those process features and qualities which make up the many day-to-day interactions within a learning community: warmth, kindness, enthusiasm, commitment, trust, compassion and concern (OECD, 2006). To this can be added the qualities necessary to engage with people and form what is called a community of practice, a term often credited to the work of Etienne Wenger (1998). He argues that since human beings started to come together they have been able to work to a common purpose, defined by their knowledge of what goes on and should go on. Each person brings their own set of skills and knowledge, and through general interaction with one another provides a substantial body of knowledge and skills on which they can all draw. They know which day-to-day actions are important and 'what works'. They also know the things which work less well. Consequently, they become embedded and committed to that community and are willing to share ideas and resources.

It might, therefore, be assumed that these two features, pedagogic documentation and undergraduate professional development, are sometimes combined within university courses; there are some published accounts of this occurring. For example, the work of Quinn et al. (2015) provides useful interrogation of a course of professional development orientated towards pedagogic documentation and suggests it is an important facet for student learning. There is also the work of Wong (2010), who researched teacher learning in two childcare centres in Canada and considered the way pedagogic documentation was used to enhance professional development. It appeared to assist educators in raising questions about children's learning and extended their knowledge and practices. Further evidence is somewhat limited, which may be due to pedagogic documentation being assimilated into teaching about the Reggio Emilia approach to children's learning. Leading practice through understanding and shaping pedagogy in an early education context takes some time to permeate its way through to university study.

It is only relatively recently that there has been an introduction of qualifications in England such as Early Years Educator and Early Years Teacher. These are qualifications introduced following a report from the English government entitled *More Great Childcare* (DfE, 2013). The qualifications are allied directly to the early education statutory curriculum in England which clearly articulates the value of observation in practice in order to help plan children's next steps and assist in monitoring progress.

Both qualifications value the social world of children's learning and the concept of collaborating and promoting good practice with others. They are also focused on what effects the learning community, curriculum and the wider community have on learning, in particular taking account of children's interests and dispositions to learn. Ofsted (2015b) sees this approach as involving careful consideration of the many different ways in which adults help young children learn, and interactions which take account of the physical environment and how educators assess what children know, understand and can do.

It would seem appropriate, therefore, to employ a strategy which enables early education university students to engage in study directly incorporating pedagogic documentation. This should extend the reach of the approach to influence policy and practice in the longer term. The key question is, what would such training look like for relatively inexperienced undergraduate students who would apply pedagogic documentation in practice?

Finding an answer involved the help of 85 students at a university and a process based on principles of action research inquiry. The students were introduced to pedagogic documentation and its value in understanding children's learning, and were invited to provide feedback on learning activities which might be integrated into a course of study. This took place within a number of teaching sessions. Their responses were evaluated via a series of questionnaires and open interviews and have been used to inform the basis of course design contained in this chapter. In light of their comments, a variety of ideas for course content as well as teaching materials and teaching approaches were introduced, refined and reshaped. The authors sincerely thank all the participants for their honest reflections.

Students' perspectives

After class sessions where pedagogic documentation had been illustrated using examples from practice, students agreed that it was of value to them and their learning. In particular, students valued the way pedagogic documentation underlined the importance of working with others and leading through the curriculum. They felt that a course of study should provide a gradual progressive learning route focused on teaching at university and placement in an early education setting with a group of other students. This would help to foster inter-student collaboration and allow them to practise the skills of analysing pedagogic documentation in both learning environments. They felt that learning in this way would work best in courses which promoted collaborative learning, and a setting which accepted students and valued their presence. They felt that the attitude of the leader was important in fostering a culture which welcomed close examination of children's learning. In reality they felt it meant an Ofsted-rated 'Good' or 'Outstanding' setting which was known to the university and had a track record of supporting student learning.

They preferred their formal assessment to be based on understanding children's learning and the characteristics of children's learning, and not to rest on producing an example of documentation for assessment. Such examples should only be part of formative learning activities and produced as the course progressed. In terms of materials, slides and teaching techniques, the students particularly welcomed examples of documentation in practice, not as images of ways to illustrate good practice (because practice and interpretations of good practice varies), but to raise questions and engage in analysis and discussion. They also felt that teaching should allow self-directed learning and problem-solving using strategies that were firmly linked to practice.

A rationale

A number of key features were decided at the outset. For example, professional development involving pedagogic documentation should be practice-led. This did not mean that theory should be ignored, because without theory there was danger of only providing tools to manage practice. It was important to ensure that a course invited consideration of how theory informs an understanding of children's learning and implications for practice. Student assessment should be linked to personal and critically reflective accounts of using pedagogic documentation in practice over a period of time, not assessed via a single observation or product. This involved finding ways to propose solutions to problems arising from that reflection. In terms of developing self-directed study and problem-solving, it was decided to use professional inquiry. This is where a theme, event or focus is investigated in practice, usually involving collaboration with others using rigorous, ethically sound approaches to examine practice (McLaughlin et al., 2004; Fleet et al., 2016). It has been evaluated as an effective form of learning within a variety of educational settings, particularly in schools (Lassonde and Israel, 2008). Importantly, it sees inquiry into practice as refining, developing and influencing practice and impacting upon professional learning and personal development, which are often seen as interconnected (Callan et al., 2012; Solvason, 2012; Healey et al., 2013; Reed and Walker, 2014). It is an approach seen as transformative as it promotes critical reflection and can refine and change both attitudes and actions in practice (Newman and Woodrow, 2015). This means that a student is encouraged to describe what they do in terms of pedagogic documentation, raise questions and develop an understanding of children's learning, and the influence of workplace systems and policy. Importantly, it does not have to be a means of directly illuminating or determining if practice needs to be improved or refined. The question may be solely concerned with inquiring into what works and why. This process is valuable not only in terms of scholarship, but also in allowing reflection on practice and a consideration of personal and wider professional values. This means applying self-directed learning and forming a shared responsibility between the student, setting and university. This requires a pedagogy from the university tutors which supports and prepares students to sensitively engage with practice and recognize there are relational, intellectual, ethical and moral practices that exist within a professional learning experience (Dahlberg and Moss, 2005; Moss, 2008; Callan et al., 2012; Cumming et al., 2013). It means engaging in practice in a way that is ethical, has professional integrity, is academically rigorous and contributes to an understanding and possible refinement of personal and professional thinking.

Operational aspects

The proposed course will be enacted over a time period that some universities measure in semesters and others in terms but which will run for the whole of an academic year. Students will alternate between university and placement. This provides time to engage fully with pedagogic documentation, which is itself a useful mechanism for students to practise forging alliances with colleagues as they observe, reflect and converse about children's learning. They will be actively involved in collaborating with parents and with other professionals. These collaborative processes will enable them to develop a shared language with professional colleagues as they observe what goes on; they can move from asking questions *about* practice to those which are *for* practice as they share their observations and consult with others.

Therefore, it is sensible for students to spend their practice placement with others in a small group. This makes the logistics of identifying a number of appropriate settings easier to manage, and promotes conversations between students in both the setting and the classroom. It is important to locate students in settings which contain structures, processes and routines that establish high expectations for children's learning. This requires a close working relationship between the setting and the university to help students understand the importance of not only examining children's learning but also developing ways to engage with others. It involves explaining, classifying, shaping and improving the way people collectively understand and plan learning opportunities within the curriculum. It is about developing an interrelationship between adults, children and the environment within which to explore the barriers which might restrict children's learning and lessen the impact of those barriers. This approach is focused on understanding children's learning and collaborating with others which Ofsted (2013) suggests is an important facet of leading practice.

A teaching framework

The instructional design should allow students the opportunity to discuss what has been observed in practice with their peers and therefore negotiate meaning (Kubiak et al., 2014). This models the way in which professional colleagues come together in practice to reflect upon what has been learnt from documenting children's learning. For this to happen, there is a need to lessen tutor dependency and promote independent engagement. This allows individual and collective views and opinions to be tested in practice. Such an approach draws on the benefits of professional inquiry to allow choice, reflection and self-confidence to emerge. It is a pedagogy requiring a positive interaction between tutors and students to promote decision-making (Lave and Wenger, 1991; Freire, 1973; Wenger, 1998; Stremmel, 2007). While this process may involve tutor transmission of knowledge, it also requires that knowledge has relevance to practice and the tutor has the ability to make visible what is being taught and learnt (Fleet and Patterson, 2001; Jarvis, 2006; Reed, 2011). It enables practitioners not only to *acquire* knowledge but also to *construct* knowledge within their work environment and develop higher-order thinking skills. This is a process which is not seen as solely emanating from engaging in pedagogic documentation but is closely aligned with principles of learning in the company of others and engaging in analysis and reflection on practice. This involves understanding and being responsive to the culture within the setting in order to appreciate the context within which actions take place, an important trait of leading within an early education setting (Siraj-Blatchford and Manni, 2007; Waniganayake et al., 2012). For the student, this means questioning both hidden and explicit practice and forging reciprocal relationships between the people most closely involved. This is because asking reflective, collaborative questions creates spirals of engagement with practice which may have consequences and touch the whole organization (Reed, 2016). This is a questioning approach which can lead to transformational learning, because it alters shapes and refines practice by influencing people, events and actions in organizations. It is reflection on this process over the length of the course which contributes to a written narrative and forms the summative assessment.

A conceptual model

A conceptual model helps to understand and explain the relationship between the component parts of a subject or theme (Creswell, 1994). In this case, the model depicts the design of a course of study aimed at understanding how children learn, which has at its core an approach known as pedagogic documentation. It is a model represented by Table 8.1 based on the work of Reed et al. (2015), which examined the interconnection between course design and student engagement. It is intended as a map for tutors and students and may help in understanding a course design which incorporates a number of interrelated strands and makes a contribution to the ecology of the course and how learning is shaped (Gibbon and Marcangelo, 2012). The horizontal axis represents the estimated student learning experience anticipated as emerging as the course moves forward. The course content is taught via lectures, seminars and online learning and the active use of a virtual learning environment. It starts with a process of induction and a theoretical base underpinned by contemporary discourse on pedagogic documentation sourced from research papers, published conceptual arguments and government reports. The student is then guided to explore what goes on, becoming a self-organized learner. It is supported by a pedagogy focusing on choice, reflection and building self-confidence. The vertical axis indicates a pattern of learning that exposes the principles of pedagogic documentation by making the child a central focus, integrating theory and practice, and exposing the relevance of policy and systems. It foreshadows the emergence of higher learning skills which are a result of working with others in a learning community. Such skills occur when students are engaged in professional inquiry (Potter and Quill, 2006; Reed and Walker, 2014); for example, skills such as evaluating, reflecting, organizing and analysing, as well as drawing issues together and engaging in critical analysis. This means taking account of the views of everyone closely involved with the

Table 8.1 A conceptual model: Patterns of teaching and learning (adapted from Reed et al., 2015)

Key patterns of teaching and learning	Induction	Exploration in practice	Participation in practice	Self-organized learner
Child-focused learning	Child agency, ethics and valuing the child's voice.	Facilitates ways of listening to the voice of the child.	Understanding children's learning and influences on learning.	Able to organize with others and the children when documenting learning.
Theory and practice	Understanding pedagogic documentation. Finding an alignment with practice and regulatory systems.	Understanding and testing out ways to document children's learning in practice.	Understanding professional learning in the company of others.	Understanding the required level of professional capability when using pedagogic documentation.
Policy and systems	Understanding the importance of context and the wider community, including organizational culture and a community of shared practice.	Opportunities and constraints of policy and systems.	Recognizing the interrelationship between the learning environment and children's learning.	Asking questions about what goes on – seeing things differently.
Application of higher learning skills	Evaluating, reflecting, organizing and analysing. Seeing professional inquiry as a way of learning about practice.	Investigation, gathering information, synthesis, reporting. Focusing and re-focusing.	Critical analysis in the company of others. Quality improvement through professional inquiry. Professional accountability.	Able to reflect on issues through the eyes of others including the child. Reflection on, in and for practice as part of professional inquiry.
Pedagogic practice	Understanding what effective pedagogic documentation looks like when colleagues work together. Analysis in the company of others.	Developing as a communicator, listener and shaper of practice with others.	Able to answer questions posed by the regulator, such as: What is it like for a child here? What difference are we making? How do we know?	Professional accountability and understanding the roles, responsibilities and relationships in the learning community.

child and the child themselves. It is equally important to experience ways of improving the quality of children's learning by forging reciprocal relationships between colleagues and playing a part in shaping refinements to practice. However, a note of caution, it may be far too simplistic to suggest these leadership traits, skills and qualities are solely the effects of course design. It is also the professionalism, determination and the inherent qualities of the student teachers which makes a difference. They will be the new graduate professionals and need to be encouraged to develop their own aptitudes and acquired experiences within the learning environment they inhabit (Callan et al., 2012).

Conclusion

This chapter has argued that pedagogic documentation makes a positive contribution to early education pedagogy and practice. Other chapters in this book have developed this argument and shown in detail its relevance to practice. The evidence is quite clear. Pedagogic documentation in itself is a most productive and valuable way to enter the world of the child and understand the way children learn. The chapter also argues that, if this powerful form of learning is combined with a course of professional development, it can empower students to better understand the characteristics of children's learning and become aware of their own qualities as they inquire into and use pedagogic documentation. It does not suggest that this is the only way that a university course can introduce pedagogic documentation to students. It is only intended to provoke thinking, open up debate and raise questions. For example:

- Teaching and learning at university often involves an approach where there is higher-level learning within a college or university and the workplace: a process, where learning in one environment is applied in the other. Should this involve thinking beyond the practical application of an approach to documenting learning, and interrogate why and how this takes place, investing time in listening to children?
- Should pedagogic documentation be introduced by an identified course as described in the chapter, or should the approach permeate the whole of a degree programme? It can be argued its values and principles extend wider than a course or a qualification.
- It is reasonable to assume that personal and professional forms of learning will emerge when investigating practice. They will touch the person and the organization. How it is possible to capture what goes on and has gone on as a learning journey?

- How might it be possible to encourage educators already operating in the sector to take on board the key principles of pedagogic documentation and work with universities to encourage the development of the next generation of pedagogic leaders?

These are questions that will engage course tutors and course designers, but it is hoped that they might also engage students. It is they who are the future; tutors need to work with them to consider what children are learning as well as what children are doing. Therefore, let's return to the start and say once again: this chapter should be seen as a way of understanding children's learning *with* pedagogic documentation. It is not proposing a course *on* pedagogic documentation. Put simply, pedagogic documentation works and is a vibrant and purposeful way to help students learn about children.

References

All-Party Parliamentary Group (2015) *The Early Years: A Report by the All-Party Parliamentary Group on a Fit and Healthy Childhood*. London: APPG. https://gallery.mailchimp.com/b6ac32ebdf72e70921b025526/files/APPG_Report_Early_YearsFINAL.pdf (accessed 15.06.16).

Callan, S., Reed, M. and Smith, S. (2012) 'A pedagogy for educating new professionals: An English perspective', in T. Papatheodorou (ed.), *Debates on Early Childhood Policies and Practices: Global Snapshots of Pedagogic Thinking and Encounters*. Abingdon: Routledge, pp. 95–104.

Creswell, J.W. (1994) *Research Design: Qualitative and Quantitative Approaches*. Thousand Oaks, CA: Sage.

Cumming, T., Sumsion, J. and Wong, S. (2013) 'Reading between the lines: An interpretative meta-analysis of ways early childhood educators negotiate discourses and subjectivities informing practice', *Contemporary Issues in Early Childhood*, 14 (3): 223–240.

Dahlberg, G. and Moss, P. (2005) *Ethics and Politics in Early Childhood Education*. London: RoutledgeFalmer.

DfE (Department for Education) (2013) *More Great Childcare: Raising Quality and Giving Parents More Choice*. Ref: DFE-00002-2013. www.gov.uk/government/publications/more-great-childcare-raising-quality-and-giving-parents-more-choice (accessed 15.06.16).

Fleet, A. and Patterson, C. (2001) 'Professional growth reconceptualized: Early childhood staff searching for meaning', *Early Childhood Research and Practice*, 3 (2). http://ecrp.uiuc.edu/v3n2/fleet.html (accessed 08.10.15).

Fleet, A., De Gioia, K. and Patterson, C. (2016) *Engaging with Educational Change: Voices of Practitioner Enquiry*. London: Bloomsbury.

Freire, P. (1973) *Education for Critical Consciousness*. London: Sheed and Ward.

Gibbon, C. and Marcangelo, C. (2012) 'A PBL evaluation toolkit: Building the evidence-base to understand effective practices', *Procedia – Social and Behavioural Sciences*, 47 (12): 1686–1691. www.sciencedirect.com/science/article/pii/S1877042812026195 (accessed 15.06.16).

Healey, M., Lannin, L., Stibbe, A. and Derounian, J. (2013) *Developing and Enhancing Undergraduate Final Year Projects and Dissertations*. York: Higher Education Academy. www.heacademy.ac.uk/projects/detail/ntfs/ntfsproject_Gloucestershire10 (accessed 08.10.15).

Hillman, J and Williams, T. (2015) *Early Years Education and Childcare: Lessons from Evidence and Future Priorities*. London: Nuffield Foundation. www.nuffieldfoundation.org/sites/default/files/files/Early_years_education_and_childcare_Nuffield_FINAL.pdf (accessed 15.06.16).

House of Lords (2015) *Select Committee on Affordable Childcare Report*. London: The Stationery Office.

Jarvis, P. (ed.) (2006) *The Theory and Practice of Teaching* (2nd edn). Abingdon: Routledge.

Kubiak, C., Fenton-O'Creevy, M., Appleby, K., Kempster, M., Reed, M., Solvason, C. and Thorpe, M. (2014) 'Brokering boundary encounters', in E. Wenger-Trayner, M. Fenton-O'Creevy, S. Hutchinson, C. Kubiak and B. Wenger-Trayner (eds), *Learning in Landscapes of Practice: Boundaries, Identity, and Knowledgeability in Practice-Based Learning*. Abingdon: Routledge, pp. 81–97.

Lassonde, C.A. and Israel, S.E. (eds) (2008) *Teachers Taking Action: A Comprehensive Guide to Teacher Research*. Newark, DE: International Reading Association.

Lave, J. and Wenger, E. (1991) *Situated Learning: Legitimate Peripheral Participation*. Cambridge: Cambridge University Press.

Mathers, S. and Smees, R. (2014) *Quality and Inequality: Do Three- and Four-Year-Olds in Deprived Areas Experience Lower Quality Early Years Provision?* London: Nuffield Foundation. www.nuffieldfoundation.org/sites/default/files/files/Quality_inequality_childcare_mathers_29_05_14(1).pdf (accessed 15.05.16).

McLaughlin, C., Black-Hawkins, K. and McIntyre, D. (2004) *Researching Teachers Researching Schools, Researching Networks: Review of the Literature*. Cambridge: Cambridge University Press.

Moss, P. (2008) 'The democratic and reflective professional: Rethinking and reforming the early years workforce', in L. Miller and C. Cable (eds), *Professionalism in the Early Years*. London: Hodder, pp. 121–130.

Newman, L. and Woodrow, C. (eds) (2015) *Practitioner Research in Early Childhood: International Issues and Perspectives*. London: Sage.

OECD (Organization for Economic Co-operation and Development) (2006) *Starting Strong II: Early Childhood Education and Care*. Paris: OECD.

Ofsted (Office for Standards in Education, Children's Services and Skills) (2013) *Getting it Right First Time: Achieving and Maintaining High-Quality Early Years Provision*. Reference: 130117. www.gov.uk/government/publications/achieving-and-maintaining-high-quality-early-years-provision-getting-it-right-first-time (accessed 25.01.17).

Ofsted (2015a) *Inspection Outcomes for Providers of Childcare on Non-Domestic Premises Where Staff Qualification Information is Recorded*. www.gov.uk/government/publications/inspection-outcomes-of-early-years-providers-by-staff-qualifications—2 (accessed 15.06.16).

Ofsted (2015b) *Early Years Inspection Handbook: Handbook for Inspecting Early Years in England under Sections 49 and 50 of the Childcare Act 2006*. Point: 153 Note 14. Age group: 0–5. Reference: 150068. www.gov.uk/government/uploads/system/uploads/attachment_data/file/458588/Early_years_inspection_handbook.pdf (accessed 15.06.16).

Potter, M.A. and Quill, B.E. (2006) *Demonstrating Excellence in Practice-Based Research for Public Health*. Houston, TX: Association of Schools in Public Health.

Quinn, S.F., Parker, L. and Palser, M. (2015) 'Teaching and learning through pedagogic documentation in initial teacher education', paper presented at the British Early Childhood Education Research Association, Birmingham.

Reed, M. (2011) 'Reflective practice and professional development', in A. Paige-Smith and A. Craft (eds), *Developing Reflective Practice in the Early Years* (2nd edn). Milton Keynes: Open University Press, pp. 278–299.

Reed, M. (2016) *Leading Early Education*. London: PLA Publishing.

Reed, M. and Walker, R. (2014) 'Leading by example: An examination of early education foundation degree students completing research dissertations', *Journal of Early Childhood Educational Research*, 3 (1): 51–64. http://jecer.org/issues/jecer-31-2014/ (accessed 08.10.15).

Reed, M., Musgrave, J. and Prowle, A. (2015) 'How can problem based learning be used as an approach to facilitating student understanding of integrated working with children and families?' (self-organised symposium). 25th ECEERA Conference: Innovation, Experimentation and Adventure in Early Childhood. Universitat Autónoma de Barcelona, Barcelona.

Siraj-Blatchford, I. and Manni, L. (2007) *Effective Leadership in the Early Years Sector: The ELEYS Study*. London: Institute of Education, University of London.

Solvason, C. (2012) 'Expressing personal values and beliefs: The essential position of the researcher', in S. Callan and M. Reed (eds), *Work-Based Research in the Early Years*. London: Sage, pp. 32–45.

Stremmel, A. (2007) 'The value of teacher research: Nurturing professional and personal growth through inquiry', *Voices of Practitioners*, 2 (3). http://journal.naeyc.org/btj/vp/pdf/Voices-Stremmel.pdf (accessed 08.10.15).

Sylva, K., Melhuish, M., Sammons, P., Siraj, I., Taggart, B. with R. Seems, K. Toth and W. Welcomme (2014) *Students' Educational and Developmental Outcomes at Age 16: Effective Pre-School and Primary Education (EPPSE 3–16+) Project*. Research Report No. DFE-RB354. London: DfE Publications. www.gov.uk/government/uploads/system/uploads/attachment_data/file/351496/RR354_-_Students__educational_and_developmental_outcomes_at_age_16.pdf (accessed 25.01.17).

Waniganayake, M., Cheeseman, S., Fenech, M., Hadley, F. and Shepherd, W. (2012) *Leadership: Contexts and Complexities in Early Childhood Education.* Victoria, Australia: Oxford University Press.

Wenger, E. (1998) *Communities of Practice: Learning, Meaning and Identity.* New York: Cambridge University Press.

Wong, A. (2010) 'Teacher learning made visible: Collaboration and the study of pedagogical documentation in two children's centres'. PhD dissertation, University of Toronto, Canada.

9

MAKING THE OUTDOORS VISIBLE IN PEDAGOGICAL DOCUMENTATION

JANE MEREWETHER

Pondering very young children's perceptions of an outdoor environment at a West Australian centre, the author shares thinking about animism and roles of pedagogical documentation in opening conversations about unexplored perspectives. Referencing research~documentation and bricolage from an ethnographic investigation, fresh insights are offered about children's views of the outdoors.

Introduction

This chapter draws from my year-long ethnographic study using pedagogical documentation to investigate two-to-four-year-old children's perspectives about outdoor spaces at their early years learning setting. The chapter includes data fragments from this project as illustrations of how strategies of pedagogical documentation and bricolage (Kincheloe and Berry, 2004) afford educators and researchers opportunities to observe very closely and record what is happening outside, making visible pedagogical potential, or its absence, of outdoor spaces. I use a strategy of 'plugging into' (Jackson and Mazzei, 2013) varied texts to show how pedagogical documentation can disrupt dominant discourses by enabling educators and researchers to uncover and critically explore hidden assumptions and gain exquisite insight into their own thinking, thus offering a way to transgress traditions and find new ways to be outdoors.

Note: Following Sellers (2015), I use the tilde (~) to indicate co-implicated terms~concepts~ideas in a reciprocal relationship, e.g. 'teacher~researcher'.

Moving outdoors

In many parts of the world, opportunities for children to be outdoors are declining due to increased time spent in screen-based activities, and safety concerns (Clements, 2004; Waller et al., 2010; Little, 2015). Widely publicized claims that children are suffering from 'nature-deficit' (Louv, 2008) have focused attention on the role of the outdoors in children's lives; it has been suggested that schools now have an increasingly important part to play in providing outdoor experiences for children (Tranter and Malone, 2004; McBride, 2012). These suggestions are supported by research pointing to the positive effects of nature and biodiversity on school-aged children's attention and cognition (Wells, 2000; Faber Taylor and Kuo, 2011), preschoolers' play (Dowdell et al., 2011), and school-aged children's physical activity (Dyment et al., 2009; Dowdell et al., 2011).

The confluence of concerns has contributed to an emergence of outdoor-focused pedagogical programmes such as 'nature kindergartens' and 'forest schools' in northern Europe (Knight, 2013; Warden, 2010; Bentsen and Jensen, 2012; Williams-Siegfredsen, 2012; Elliott, 2015). In Australia, approaches such as 'bush kinder' (Elliott and Chancellor, 2014) have emerged for outdoor approaches, although 'forest school' is also used (Cumming and Nash, 2015). However, Janet Robertson (2011), who positions herself as a specialist 'outdoor teacher', argues that forests are not necessary for children to have quality experiences outdoors; what is necessary is desire to embrace *everyday* outdoor environments and their pedagogical potentials. Given the sheer number of children in education, remnant patches of forest and bush could not sustain an onslaught of even the most respectful children and educators. Concerns about outdoor experiences are reflected in the growing number of researchers questioning separation of nature and culture (Descola, 2009;

Taylor, 2013). Karen Barad discusses the 'entangled state of agencies' (2007: 23), reminding us that everything in the world is matter, and all matter, human and non-human, is in a constant 'intra-active' relationship. This challenges conventional Western conceptions of agency, subjectivity and the individual, but, in doing so, provides new thinking space for those who work with children outdoors.

Regimes of truth and animism

Foucault has done much to draw attention to the way in which 'discourses' and 'regimes of truth' shape what people believe to be true:

> Each society has its regime of truth, its 'general politics' of truth: that is, the types of discourse which it accepts and makes function as true; the mechanisms and fragments which enable one to distinguish true and false statements, the means by which each is sanctioned; the techniques and procedures accorded value in the acquisition of truth; the status of those who are charged with saying what counts as true. (Foucault, as cited in Rabinow, 1991: 73)

Developmental psychology contributes significantly to regimes of truth about early childhood (MacNaughton, 2005; Dahlberg et al., 2013). In particular, developmental psychologist Jean Piaget's influence remains unparalleled. One Piagetian 'truth' revolves around animism, which Piaget describes as how children 'regard as living and conscious a large number of objects *which are for us inert*' (1929: 169, my emphasis). Piaget uses children's animism to support his well-known developmental stages theory, arguing it is an example of young children's faulty reasoning; a phenomenon 'seen amongst children, savages, animals ...' (ibid.: 234). Anthropologists, however, including Bird-David (1999) and Ingold (2011), have shown that animism is common to many cultures. In light of this, Descola suggests it is 'scientifically risky' (2009: 147) for anthropologists to separate nature and culture and view the non-human world as objects. Bird-David proposes animism as a relational epistemology, where humans 'make their personhood by producing and reproducing sharing relationships with surrounding beings, humans and others' (1999: S73). But Descola points out the challenge of thinking differently for researchers from Western contexts: 'the dualism of nature and culture that Western ethnographers bring unwillingly with them in their intellectual equipment will result in their perceiving the local system of objectification of reality that they study as a more or less impoverished variant of their own' (2009: 148). It is not just ethnographers who face this challenge – it is particularly pertinent in a field heavily imbued with Piagetian epistemologies. These alternate ways of seeing animism offer new possibilities for working with young children's propensity to animate the material world, particularly when outdoors. Pedagogical documentation, to which I now turn, provides a means of exploring children's animism and the dominant discourses that surround it.

Pedagogical documentation

The term 'pedagogical documentation' has been adopted to distinguish between reductionist documentation that is commonplace in education (e.g. checklists; measurement and accountability documents; summative reports) and documentation seeking to understand learning and pedagogy, as undertaken by the educational project of Reggio Emilia (Giudici et al., 2001; Edwards et al., [1993] 2012; Giamminuti, 2013). Pedagogical documentation comprises 'material which records what the children are saying and doing, the work of the children, and how the pedagogue relates to the children and their work' (Dahlberg et al., 2013: 156) and includes but is not limited to: notes made by educators; children's work samples; video and audio recordings; transcriptions of conversations and recordings; photographs. Pedagogical documentation is an effective means of data-generation for researchers in academia and education alike. However, without analysis, these materials are just a collection of artefacts. It is the process of reflecting on and interpreting documentary material that transforms it into *pedagogical* documentation. For example, a collection of photos is not pedagogical documentation. While photos may record what children are doing, they do not show how or what children and adults are thinking and learning.

This analysis makes pedagogical documentation a form of qualitative research, which also involves materials and their interpretation:

> Qualitative research consists of a set … of representations, including fieldnotes, interviews, conversations, photographs, recordings and memos to the self. … [Q]ualitative researchers study things in their natural settings, attempting to make sense of or interpret phenomena in terms of the meanings people bring to them. (Denzin and Lincoln, 2011: 3)

This research~documentation, does not claim objectivity in the way positivist research does. Rather, it involves choices and subjectivity, as Dahlberg et al. (2013: 155) point out: 'documentation can in no way exist apart from our own involvement in the process. Likewise, what we have documented is also selective, partial and contextual' (Baldini et al., 2012). Such research invariably has political intent. In Reggio Emilia, documentation developed in the early days of the educational project as a way to give visibility to the project; it was a deliberate political act, as Loris Malaguzzi's biographer, Alfredo Hoyuelos (2004: 7) explains: 'Behind this practice … is the ideological and ethical concept of a transparent school and transparent education … a political idea also emerges, which is that what schools do must have public visibility.' Dahlberg (2012: 226) also draws attention to the political nature of documentation: 'Pedagogical documentation … opens up a *public space*, a forum in a civic society, where dominant discourses can be visualized and negotiated.' By making pedagogical work in the outdoors visible and open for debate, documentation, with its 'bricolage' of data-generation and interpretative processes, offers a possibility for everyday outdoor spaces in educational settings to gain a new legitimacy. It is to bricolage that I now turn.

Pedagogical documentation as bricolage

Bricolage research, as conceptualized by Denzin and Lincoln (2000) and more fully theorized by Kincheloe and Berry (2004), takes its name from the French artisan, the *bricoleur*, a Jack-of-all-trades who uses whatever is at hand to ply his or her craft (Levi-Strauss, 1966).

According to Derrida ([1978] 2005: 360):

> The bricoleur … is someone who uses 'the means at hand', that is, the instruments he [sic] finds at his disposition around him, those which are already there, … not hesitating to change them whenever it appears necessary, or to try several of them at once, even if their form and their origin are heterogeneous.

Taking a bricolage approach allows documentor~researchers to use a range of tactics, as demanded by the context. Importantly, it allows them to draw on both pedagogical *and* research strategies. Denzin and Lincoln (2011: 4) explain: 'If new tools or techniques have to be invented or pieced together, then the researcher will do this. The choice of which interpretive practices to employ is not necessarily set in advance'. The bricolage provides documentor~researchers working outdoors with young children the necessary on-the-spot flexibility to adapt, mix and match strategies and materials in response to, for example, resources, children's skills and dispositions, and to capitalize on opportunities as they arise.

Interpreting the bricolage

The role of theory in analysis cannot be underestimated: 'To think with theory is not only useful, but essential, for without theory we have no way to think otherwise' (Jackson and Mazzei, 2013: 269). This is the case for all documentor~researchers. In order to think with theory, Jackson and Mazzei (2013) suggest that we 'plug into', or connect with, theory by imagining the theorist is reading our data over our shoulder – What would they say? What would they ask? As well as offering methodological diversity, bricolage also offers the possibility of theoretical diversity: 'The theoretical bricoleur reads widely and is knowledgeable about the many interpretive paradigms ... The researcher-as-bricoleur-theorist works between and within competing and overlapping perspectives and paradigms' (Denzin and Lincoln, 2011: 4). In an earlier study, I asked four-year-old children to show me 'important places' outside; while doing so they launched into elaborate collaborative stories about Gilligan's Island (Merewether, 2015). This presented a challenge to me as researcher; I had a strict research plan that did not include narrative analysis (Engel, 2005) so I missed the opportunity to embrace the children's stories, and interpret their knowledge and experience through the narrative. A bricolage approach to this research would have provided flexibility needed to make the most of this situation.

It is also useful to view analysis as a 'conversation' that does not set out to be the final word on a matter, but instead aims to 'experiment and keep the conversation going' (Badley, 2015: 418). Dewey's 100-year-old advice on analysis is very useful for a bricoleur:

> analysis is conceived to be a sort of picking to pieces, so synthesis is thought to be a sort of physical piecing together ... Every judgment is analytic in so far as it involves discernment, discrimination, marking off the trivial from the important, the irrelevant from what points to a conclusion; ... Analysis leads to synthesis; while synthesis perfects analysis. (1910: 114–115)

This is the documentor~researcher's task in analysis – to deconstruct and reconstruct to create new conversations. The dilemma documentor~ researchers face is the sheer enormity of data; it is simply not possible to take apart and reconstruct all material encountered in a year of research, or even a week of classroom life. It is impossible to read these data alongside all theoretical frameworks, which in any case, would lead to sweeping generalizations. So, as Dewey (1910) advises, we need to make choices; we need to discern the trivial, the important, the relevant, and what leads to a conclusion. Brinkmann (2014: 724) suggests that we choose data that make us 'stumble'; that is, data that cause us surprise, wonder or bewilderment; it is with this in mind that we come to my study.

The study

I begin this section by discussing the study's background, and then share fragments chosen because they caused me to stumble. They are representative of fragments I encountered repeatedly, but at first I didn't notice them; I took what was happening for granted as it matched 'truths' I was not aware I held about children in this age group. It was the act of documenting children's perspectives about the outdoors that led me to notice children's animation of the non-human world, which in turn caused me to wonder and question.

Data for my study were generated during a 12-month period at a suburban early learning setting (hereafter, 'the Centre') with 35 two-to-four-year-old children in Western Australia. The children shared one outdoor space, but because I am interested in very young children's perspectives, I followed the two-to-three-year-olds where possible. University ethics approval and informed written consent were obtained from children's parents, and children provided ongoing oral assent. I reminded children throughout data-generation activities that they could stop or not respond at any time, which they often did when other events such as meals or class meetings were more pressing; most returned without prompting. Over time, some children showed particular interest in the project and became key participants. Adults associated with the Centre – staff and children's families – were also invited to respond to the evolving research.

I used adaptations of well-documented data-generation strategies including observational field notes, photographs, researcher journaling, semi-formal interviews, conversations, and document analysis (including photos and drawings) (Kincheloe and Berry, 2004; Greene and Hogan, 2005; Merriam, 2009). These strategies are analogous to those of pedagogical documentation, which I had used extensively in my previous work as an early childhood teacher~researcher. My interactions with children were designed to be part of everyday pedagogical activities and were grounded in a desire to: 'a) avoid undue intrusion; b) be non-confrontational and participatory; and, c) encourage children [and adults] to be a part of the interpretation process' (Morrow and Richards, 1996: 100). Activities with children included child-led tours, photography and photo-elicitation, conversations and drawing, offering children in early stages of language development a variety of verbal and non-verbal communication possibilities. Conversations, semi-formal interviews and surveys with educators and parents added to the bricolage (Kincheloe and Berry, 2004).

Research began with two-weeks of relationship-building whereby children were introduced to the project, its intent, the voluntary nature of participation, likely audience and so on. This period included informal observations and conversations. Next, children were familiarized with cameras and audio-recorders and were invited to conduct a guided 'tour' inside (Clark and Moss, 2001). After this, pairs of children were invited to take me on tours of the outdoor space at the Centre, photographing what they considered 'good'.

Conversations during the tours were audio-recorded. Children discussed printouts of their photos with me. The photos and conversation excerpts were added to a documentation book that 'mapped' the project for children, teachers, families and me: '[mapping] fosters connections between fields … [it] is open and connectable in all of its dimensions … detachable, reversible, susceptible to constant modification' (Deleuze and Guattari, 1987: 12). I also added children's ideas about outdoor spaces represented using media such as drawing, modelling and clay.

Animations

This part of the chapter presents fragments from the study chosen as they presented a 'transgressive jolt … that force us think again, and more slowly about what is taken for granted' (Maclure, 2006: 229). I offer these fragments not to explore animism in any depth, but as provocation for thinking about how pedagogical documentation may add to conversations about children and outdoor environments.

Fragment 1 (research journal)

Tonight as I pored over the photos taken by Eloise, one photo (Figure 9.1) catches my eye. I am struck by its similarity to one taken by children in Reggio Emilia (Cavallini et al., 2011: 164). I wonder why children on opposite sides of the world take such similar photos?

Figure 9.1   Eloise's photo

Fragment 2 (research journal)

I sit under trees at the Centre with an A4-sized printout of Eloise's photo.

'Do you remember taking this photo?' I ask Eloise. She nods.

'It's the sky and the trees. The trees are talking to the sky. The trees are having a picnic. They have gooey worms and lemonade for their picnic.'

Xavier arrives and looks at the photo.

'I think they [the trees] are saying "Hello" to each other.'

Nearby, Rachel and Amber are playing in the sandpit. They attract my attention and tell me they are preparing a picnic.

'We are making jam and bread. It's a picnic for us,' Amber tells me. Then she looks up to the trees overhead and says, 'The trees are having a picnic at the swings. But they don't have jam and bread for their picnic, they have worms and gooey stuff.'

Fragment 3 (research journal)

Today, I am in Reggio Emilia. I visit the spot where children took the photo of the trees and recreate it (Figure 9.2). I recall the project where children created a bracelet and song for these trees. One of their teachers, Vea Vecchi (2015: 5), says, 'Sometimes I think that when children are born, they have biological wisdom that gives them the perception that they are part of an enormous living network.'

Figure 9.2   My reconstruction of a photograph taken by children in Reggio Emilia

Plugging into theory

These small fragments, and others like them, caused me to stumble and realize that despite my postmodern leanings, I have been reading children's animism with Piaget, seeing it as a stage of development typical of two-to-three-year-old children – a stage they would outgrow. But what if I read with someone else? Plugging into different theories, such as the new animist theories outlined earlier, opens (me) up (to) different stories. Such stories are examples of '"minor politics" ... which seek to engender a small reworking of their own spaces of action' (Dahlberg, 2006: 25). 'Minor politics also have the potential to become more than the sum of their parts through the ability ... to connect up with a whole series of other circuits and cause them to fluctuate, waver and reconfigure in wholly unexpected ways' (ibid.: 25–26).

My comments here will not be extensive because, as Deleuze and Guattari (1987: 114) have said, 'there is no longer any need to interpret, but that is because the best interpretation, the weightiest and most radical one, is an eminently significant silence'. But I want to plug these small data fragments into snippets of theory to show we do not need to have reams of data, or tell 'grand' stories to cause regimes of truth to waver.

I begin with Descola (2009), who describes how various animistic societies view non-humans as 'life', who have kinship rules, ethical codes and ritual activities. In my data fragments, children see trees as 'alive' with their own sets of rules and codes. What might be the implications of this? Reading with Ingold, I learn that 'life', in a new animist sense, does not mean 'an internal animating principle that is installed in some things but not others', but rather, is a *process*, 'and this process is tantamount to the unfolding of a continuous and ever-evolving field of relations within which beings of all kinds are generated and held in place' (2011: 237). What might happen if, rather than insisting that children 'unlearn' their animistic ways of seeing themselves in relationship with their non-human surroundings, we allowed them to flourish? I reflect on Australian Aboriginal researcher Karen Martin's explanation of Quandamooka Ontology, which does not position humans as superior:

> We believe that country is not only the Land and People, but is also the Entities of Waterways, Animals, Plants, Climate, Skies and Spirits. Within this, one Entity should not be raised above another, as these live in close relationship with one another. So People are no more or less important than the other Entities. (Martin, 2003: 201)

Australian Aboriginal culture is the world's longest surviving culture, one that can be traced back for millennia. What then, might be the role of relational ways of knowing in schools and Western culture?

These fragments highlight children's enmeshed relationship with non-human elements. The children in my study do not see themselves as separated from nature or as 'de-natured' as Louv (2008: 31) suggests; rather, the fragments paint a picture of children who see non-human entities as equal fellow travellers in life. And, yet, in a few short years, they will learn from their school and culture, to think about nature and culture separately. Perhaps the time for this dichotomy has ended and we can learn from children rather than dismissing their ideas and ways of knowing as inferior.

Conclusion

The documentor~researcher approach I have taken revealed, in the first instance, children's animistic thinking, but, more importantly, it revealed taken-for-granted ways of thinking about children's animism.

(Continued)

(Continued)

These discourses have their roots in Piagetian theory that proposes animism as evidence of young children's faulty thinking. Plugging into new animist theories disrupts these assumptions and provokes possibilities for working with children's animism in different ways. There are many regimes of truth involving children's experience outdoors; if we are to work differently outside, small stories of minor politics which emerge in outdoor spaces need telling.

Furthermore, these insights emerged not in a forest, but in an outdoor setting on a confined suburban block. While the pedagogical potential of forests is not in dispute, few educational settings have access to forests. This study, on the other hand, points to the pedagogical potential of *everyday* outdoor environments. Through pedagogical documentation, the role of all outdoor environments in supporting children and their teachers' innovative thinking and acting can be revealed. It enables connections to be made between data fragments, research, theory and contexts and provides possibilities for keeping the conversation going. If we are to challenge regimes of truth about the outdoors, we need to use approaches that create spaces in which different perspectives can come together in the spirit of dialogue and exchange. Pedagogical documentation is such a space.

References

Badley, G.F. (2015) 'Conversation piece?', *Qualitative Inquiry*, 21 (5): 418–425. Doi:10.1177/1077800414566689.

Baldini, R., Cavallini, I., Moss, P. and Vecchi, V. (2012) *One City, Many Children: Reggio Emilia, A History of the Present*. Reggio Emilia, Italy: Reggio Children.

Barad, K. (2007) *Meeting the Universe Halfway: Quantum Physics and the Entanglement of Matter and Meaning*. Durham, NC: Duke University Press.

Bentsen, P. and Jensen, F.S. (2012) 'The nature of udeskole: Outdoor learning theory and practice in Danish schools', *Journal of Adventure Education and Outdoor Learning*, 12 (3): 199–219. Doi:10.1080/14729679.2012.699806.

Bird-David, N. (1999) '"Animism" revisited: Personhood, environment, and relational epistemology', *Current Anthropology*, 40: S67–S91.

Brinkmann, S. (2014) 'Doing without data', *Qualitative Inquiry*, 20 (6): 720–725. Doi:10.1177/1077800414530254.

Cavallini, I., Filippini, T., Vecchi, V. and Trancossi, L. (eds) (2011) *The Wonder of Learning: The Hundred Languages of Children*. Reggio Emilia, Italy: Reggio Children.

Clark, A. and Moss, P. (2001) *Listening to Young Children: The Mosaic Approach*. London: National Children's Bureau.

Clements, R. (2004) 'An investigation of the status of outdoor play', *Contemporary Issues in Early Childhood*, 5 (1): 68–80.

Cumming, F. and Nash, M. (2015) 'An Australian perspective of a forest school: Shaping a sense of place to support learning', *Journal of Adventure Education and Outdoor Learning*, 1–14. Doi:10.1080/14729679.2015.1010071.

Dahlberg, G. (2006) 'A pedagogy of welcoming and hospitality built on listening: Ethical and political perspective on early childhood education', *International Journal of Early Childhood Education*, 12 (2): 5–28.

Dahlberg, G. (2012) 'Pedagogical documentation: A practice for negotiation and democracy', in C. Edwards, L. Gandini and G. Forman (eds), *The Hundred Languages of Children: The Reggio Emilia Experience in Transformation* (3rd edn). Santa Barabara, CA: Praeger, pp. 225–231.

Dahlberg, G., Moss, P. and Pence, A. (2013) *Beyond Quality in Early Childhood Education and Care: Languages of Evaluation* (3rd edn). Abingdon: Routledge.

Deleuze, G. and Guattari, F. (1987) *A Thousand Plateaus: Capitalism and Schizophrenia* (tr. B. Massumi). Minneapolis, MN: University of Minnesota Press.

Denzin, N. and Lincoln, Y. (2011) 'Introduction: Disciplining the practice of qualitative research', in N. Denzin and Y. Lincoln (eds), *The SAGE Handbook of Qualitative Research* (4th edn). Thousand Oaks, CA: Sage, pp. 1–20.

Denzin, N. and Lincoln, Y. (eds) (2000) *The SAGE Handbook of Qualitative Research* (2nd edn). Thousand Oaks, CA: Sage.

Derrida, J. ([1978] 2005) *Writing and Difference* (tr. A. Bass). London: Routledge.

Descola, P. (2009) 'Human natures', *Social Anthropology*, 17 (2): 145–157. Doi:10.1111/j.1469-8676.2009.00063.x.

Dewey, J. (1910) *How We Think*. Boston, MA: D.C. Heath & Co.

Dowdell, K., Gray, T. and Malone, K. (2011) 'Nature and its influence on children's outdoor play', *Australian Journal of Outdoor Education*, 15 (2): 24–35.

Dyment, J.E., Bell, A.C. and Lucas, A.J. (2009) 'The relationship between school ground design and intensity of physical activity', *Children's Geographies*, 7 (3): 261–276.

Edwards, C., Gandini, L. and Forman, G. (eds) ([1993] 2012) *The Hundred Languages of Children: The Reggio Emilia Experience in Transformation* (3rd edn). Santa Barbara, CA: Praeger.

Elliott, H. (2015) 'Forest School in an inner city? Making the impossible possible', *Education 3–13*, 43 (6): 720–728. Doi:10.1080/03004279.2013.872159.

Elliott, S. and Chancellor, B. (2014) 'From forest preschool to Bush Kinder: An inspirational approach to preschool provision in Australia', *Australasian Journal of Early Childhood*, 39 (4): 45–53.

Engel, S. (2005) 'Narrative analysis of children's experience', in S. Greene and D. Hogan (eds), *Researching Children's Experience: Approaches and Methods*. London: Sage, pp. 199–216.

Faber Taylor, A. and Kuo, F.E. (2011) 'Could exposure to everyday green spaces help treat ADHD? Evidence from children's play setting', *Applied Psychology: Health and Well-Being*, 3 (3): 281–303. Doi:10.1111/j.1758-0854.2011.01052.x.

Giamminuti, S. (2013) *Dancing with Reggio Emilia: Metaphors for Quality*. Mt Victoria, NSW: Pademelon Press.

Giudici, C., Rinaldi, C. and Krechevsky, M. (eds) (2001) *Making Learning Visible: Children as Individual and Group Learners*. Reggio Emilia, Italy: Reggio Children.

Greene, S. and Hogan, D. (eds) (2005) *Researching Children's Experience: Approaches and Methods*. London: Sage.

Hoyuelos, A. (2004) 'A pedagogy of transgression', *Children in Europe*, 6: 6–7.

Ingold, T. (2011) *Being Alive: Essays on Movement, Knowledge and Description*. London and New York: Routledge.

Jackson, A.Y. and Mazzei, L.A. (2013) 'Plugging one text into another', *Qualitative Inquiry*, 19 (4): 261–271. Doi:10.1177/1077800412471510.

Kincheloe, J.L. and Berry, K.S. (2004) *Rigour and Complexity in Educational Research: Conceptualizing the Bricolage*. Maidenhead: Open University Press.

Knight, S. (2013) *Forest Schools and Outdoor Learning in the Early Years* (2nd edn). London: Sage.

Levi-Strauss, C. (1966) *The Savage Mind*. London: Weidenfeld and Nicolson.

Little, H. (2015) 'Mothers' beliefs about risk and risk-taking in children's outdoor play', *Journal of Adventure Education and Outdoor Learning*, 15 (1): 24–39. Doi:10.1080/14729679.2013.842178.

Louv, R. (2008) *Last Child in the Woods: Saving our Children from Nature-Deficit Disorder*. Chapel Hill, NC: Algonquin.

Maclure, M. (2006) '"A demented form of the familiar": Postmodernism and educational research', *Journal of Philosophy of Education*, 40 (2): 223–239. Doi:10.1111/j.1467-9752.2006.00505.x.

MacNaughton, G. (2005) *Doing Foucault in Early Childhood Studies: Applying Poststructural Ideas*. New York: Routledge.

Martin, K. (2003) 'Ways of knowing, being and doing: A theoretical framework and methods for indigenous and indigenist re-search', *Journal of Australian Studies*, 76: 203–214.

McBride, D.L. (2012) 'Children and outdoor play', *Journal of Pediatric Nursing*, 27 (4): 421. Doi:10.1016/j.pedn.2012.04.001.

Merewether, J. (2015) 'Young children's perspectives of outdoor learning spaces: What matters?', *Australasian Journal of Early Childhood*, 40 (1): 99–108.

Merriam, S. (2009) *Qualitative Research: A Guide to Design and Implementation*. San Francisco, CA: Jossey-Bass.

Morrow, V. and Richards, M. (1996) 'The ethics of social research with children: An overview', *Children & Society*, 10 (2): 90–105. Doi:10.1111/j.1099-0860.1996.tb00461.x.

Piaget, J. (1929) *The Child's Conception of the World*. London: Routledge & Kegan Paul.

Rabinow, P. (ed.) (1991) *The Foucault Reader*. New York: Pantheon.

Robertson, J. (2011) 'Who needs a forest?', *Rattler: The Children's Services Magazine*, 99 (Sept): 10–13.

Sellers, M. (2015) '… working with (a) rhizoanalysis … and working (with) a rhizoanalysis', *Complicity: An International Journal of Complexity and Education*, 12 (1): 6–31.

Taylor, A. (2013) *Reconfiguring the Natures of Childhood*. London: Routledge.

Tranter, P.J. and Malone, K. (2004) 'Geographies of environmental learning: An exploration of children's use of school grounds', *Children's Geographies*, 2 (1): 131–155. Doi:10.1080/1473328032000168813.

Vecchi, V. (2015) 'Children seen as citizens who are active protagonists of their growth and their learning processes: The secret of a raindrop', *Innovations in Early Education: The International Reggio Exchange*, 22 (4): 4–9.

Waller, T., Sandseter, E.B.H., Wyver, S., Ärlemalm-Hagsér, E. and Maynard, T. (2010) 'The dynamics of early childhood spaces: Opportunities for outdoor play?', *European Early Childhood Education Research Journal*, 18 (4): 437–443.

Warden, C. (2010) *Nature Kindergartens*. Auchterarder, Scotland: Mindstretchers Ltd.

Wells, N.M. (2000) 'At home with nature: Effects of "greenness" on children's cognitive functioning', *Environment and Behavior*, 32 (6): 775–795.

Williams-Siegfredsen, J. (2012) *Understanding the Danish Forest School Approach*. Abingdon: Routledge.

10

DIVING INTO THE UNKNOWN: THE EXPERIENCE OF PEDAGOGICAL DOCUMENTATION AT MIA MIA

ANGELA CHNG

Highlighting curiosity without assumptions, this chapter presents an educator thinking aloud about her work with three-to-five-year-olds in an Australian setting. Encounters with paper bags, jigsaws and music provide opportunities for the unexpected, extending children's play genres and thinking repertoires. Pedagogical documentation is illustrated through demonstrations of unfolding philosophical practice.

Introduction

The experience of pedagogical documentation looks different from time to time, depending on context, the participating thinkers and the person reflecting, reviewing and proposing; it can take on many forms and go in various directions. Keeping in mind that it is never a linear process is a good way to begin thinking about it. Recognizing the significance of the moments throughout the day and learning to listen with presence are important aspects of the process. However, being open to the unknown and unexpected is essential throughout the entire pedagogical documentation process, from identifying possible directions and the unfolding of pedagogy to collating a physical write up. When we look and listen closely, the possibilities are endless. Attempting to find or identify a theme (such as astronauts or insects) always appears to be the logical or quick solution in order to consider further research on an investigation. Instead of moving forward, however, categorizing children's questions and wonderings into a 'box' can limit possibilities. There is a wealth of research and knowledge available to us through scholarly research, books, our relationships with knowledgeable others and the internet. We do, however, have to be careful how we use this information as it can narrow our thinking rather than broaden it when it is not used appropriately. Knowing when to pause in the unknown, when to look for more and what to look for is critical and not always easy. The following are three stories from a three-to-five-year-olds' room, to provide provocation and backdrop to the notions of exploring and being in different moments of unknowing. The decisions made during the process of these investigations frame my thinking at a particular moment and an entirely different perspective or focus might occur if I were to revisit this thinking again.

Many theorists and approaches to education influence our thinking and work with children at Mia Mia, one of which is the educational thinking from Reggio Emilia. We continually find other ways of thinking relevant to our teaching that influences our everyday practice. The learning community in the three-to-five-year-olds' room shapes the curriculum and every year, the dynamics of the group changes. The children engage in small group investigations, evolving from both adult and child initiated questions and wonderings. Multiple investigations occur concurrently and their durations vary, ranging from days to an entire year. Our weekly curriculum meetings enable me to begin collecting information about children who are yet to be in my room, building up my understandings of them and what they have encountered prior to being in the three-to-five-year-olds' room. This foundation influences my pedagogical and curriculum decision-making.

Paper: Making space for chaos

Mia Mia has a culture of valuing open-ended, everyday materials as 'treasure'. As part of our learning community, families are invited to contribute to the collection of these materials. 'When we think in terms of the material being just as agentic as humans, we are not locked into an *either-or* thinking, nor into a thinking of *both-and*. Rather, such thinking goes beyond the divide of the discursive and the materials altogether' (Lenz Taguchi, 2010: 29). When presented to children, these open-ended, everyday materials often challenge children to develop new ways of thinking, working and theory-making.

Documentation of children's work with these materials is common, reinforcing their value within our curriculum. Over time, families learn to identify types of materials that might interest us and collect items to add to the school's collections. One day, a parent asked me if I would like some unused large brown paper bags, closed at one end. She explained they were giant-sized (used to hold huge amounts of flour, cement or similar products) and she thought I could probably find a use for them. I embrace such challenges and appreciated the faith this parent had shown in believing I would be able to find a use for the bags. Through experience, I had come to understand that presenting children with an unfamiliar material opens possibilities for learning, as the children do not approach these materials with preconceived notions of what they are or how they can/should be used. These materials also present me the challenge of creating and posing a thoughtful provocation. Did these bags fall into this category? As adults, we may limit children's possibilities unintentionally as we are unable to see beyond our own perceptions of valuable 'learning' processes. An active part of my reflective teaching is being aware of those moments where I might unconsciously communicate my own perceptions and expectations to children. The challenge is to pave the way to enable children to recognize their constructiveness and their natural approaches towards the experience.

A good place to begin is one with no assumptions. I did not want to assume the children's prior knowledge or experiences with paper bags in general or bags in that size so I decided to present the bags in their original form to children and observe what they did with them. I did, however, have in mind some of the possible responses based on my existing knowledge of children. I invited them to engage with the bags. Noting that they were open at one end, the children began to crawl inside, using them like sleeping bags. Some stayed in a bag for half the morning, some lay motionless in it for minutes; others began bringing in dolls and other items, seemingly using it as a house. It was clear that the children owned the enclosed space, which was not a surprising response as children are drawn to small spaces to hide, spaces that give the sense of being 'enveloped'. I began from a place of known facts, trusting their natural attraction to enclosed spaces by presenting them with the bags but intentionally I chose not to be too specific with my expectations. I wanted to gain a deeper understanding of the children's experiences so I went into one of the bags for a firsthand experience. I discovered some unexpected characteristics. It was warm inside the bags as they retained the warmth from the heated floor; the bags also transformed the external lighting and there was a sense of comfort. Perhaps these were the characteristics children were attracted to, or perhaps these were just the tip of the iceberg. I did not have enough data to make any decisions for future directions, so I waited. This 'sleeping-bag' play continued for a few more days and I continued collecting information; taking down transcripts, observations and photographs.

After days of observing this play and reflecting on the information collected, I decided to interrupt this genre of play and attempt to extend the children's repertoire and thinking. Perhaps I could move the children away from enclosed spaces to explore other ways of encountering these bags; or maybe I could challenge whether children's attraction to hiding can only occur in enclosed spaces. I made the decision to slit open a few bags, presenting them as large sheets of brown paper. Immediately the play was transformed. The sheets of paper clearly reminded the children of a different experience and elicited another response. Five took a particular interest in the big sheets of paper. As they moved them around the floor in various arrangements, it did not take long for the children to discover their impact on them. Loud crunching noises were heard as their feet made contact with the sheets. Two of them exchanged knowing looks and it soon became clear that the main objective was to find ways to create loud sounds. The sheets were reorganized, spread across the floor, covering as much surface area as possible. The children ran on the paper and paused to check on my response to their decision and when I simply nodded, they became bolder; taking turns climbing on the bench and making a combination of jumps and tumbles. The crunch brought immense satisfaction, urging the children to continue as they laughed and made loud exclamations. The play appeared chaotic as they spoke in excited, raised voices coordinating the jumps and the positioning of the sheets. This play went on for the entire morning; they named the play 'Circus'. Their play reminded me of their engagements with bubble wrap, with the satisfaction of an immediate response of sound from a material.

I valued the children's 'check-in', their pauses in the midst of their engagement as it revealed not only their awareness of the broad boundaries of the space but also their respect and acknowledgment of me as a part of their explorations. This play was, indeed, very different from the usual indoor engagements and I began receiving doubtful glances from my colleagues. On the one hand, I was deeply intrigued by the children's engagements and saw immense value in the thinking and skills required when they were involved in the experience. On the other hand, however, as other adults became more concerned, it made me question my own pedagogical decision and the value of such chaos within the classroom. How could I articulate to others what I was seeing so they could also see beyond all this chaos? Have I given children enough time and space indoors for children to engage in louder, physical play? Jovanovic and Roder (2012) reflect on the displacement of our existing knowledge as an investigation progresses and pedagogical decisions made. As teachers, comments of the people around us can create both doubtful and thoughtful moments. There are often differences in professional pedagogical valuing and even articulating one's thinking does not always result in complete understanding. It can be a lonely journey, but, most importantly, the main aim of sharing one's pedagogical valuing should be mutual respect and acceptance rather than agreement. These doubts are, in fact, constructive to the process of learning to articulate pedagogical decision-making. The children's play was, indeed, loud and there were other experiences and engagements occurring concurrently within the room. Negotiations were made and boundaries established, such as the children who were engaging in the play were invited into the room first while the others were still engaged in experiences outside so we could 'legitimize' circus play. This play became part of our inside curriculum over the next month.

Another group of children adapted their 'hiding' play to the flat sheets of paper. A new variation of 'sleeping-bag' play was invented and the papers were used as blankets. I created a provocation to extend on their notions of hiding and enclosures by draping a piece over some chairs and invited them to consider constructing their own hiding spaces. This strategy was quickly adapted and soon sheets were positioned over other pieces of furniture to create small child-sized paper cubby houses. Working with paper double their height was not always easy; it required patience, persistence and collaboration with others. They also had to be very mindful when they were inside their cubbies, as they could fall apart easily. The children spent weeks experimenting ways to construct these cubbies and many variations were documented. Their exploration process was pushing them to venture into the unknown as they transformed paper into a building material. Interestingly, the children did not opt for easy solutions such as using string and other binding materials to keep the paper in place; rather, they kept true to improvisation and used only paper.

To further challenge a smaller group of mainly older children, I posed another perspective for them to consider which would complicate their thinking. I took two photographs of each child; one photograph when they were mostly hidden from view under the paper; then I removed the paper and took a second photograph of them 'frozen' in place to show their original position. I wanted the children to gain a deeper understanding of their experience, and in the process attempt to understand how they were thinking about the experience. In addition, I wanted them to consider their perspective when engaging in representations. The photographs were then printed; I invited children to look at the photographs and draw themselves on the first photograph where they were mostly hidden. This was a tricky cognitive task as the children had to illustrate themselves based on what they knew and experienced, yet had to consider how their illustrations could be proportionate and realistic based on the body parts captured in the photograph. Most had to slow down and thoughtfully consider the task. They examined the photographs carefully before making considered marks a little at a time on the photograph to represent themselves. I was interrupting their drawing default such as drawing figures with a circle and lines for limbs, creating time and space for children to think and look (Kolbe, 2007). Often, the children develop individual preferences for drawing and this process made them slow down to consider the complexities and diversity of drawing.

This example of pedagogy is part of a continuum that does not have a definite conclusion. The documentation of the children's experiences and investigations with paper only showcased a little snippet in time and does not signal the end of the story. The process of pedagogical documentation is not always a smooth, straight road, but many times it is one of chaos; it is learning to see through, and in, the chaos where great discoveries are made.

Figure 10.1 Photographs presented to the child and his attempt to draw himself

Puzzles: Complicating through silence

Two children were collaborating on a 49-piece puzzle, but were disappointed to discover that there was one piece missing. They looked everywhere but it could not be found. Presenting me with the 'problem', they sought assistance. I posed the problem back to them and silence fell as they contemplated what they could do to resolve the issue. Asking for assistance from an adult is usually the quickest solution when children encounter a problem, but instead of jumping in with a solution for them, posing the problem back meant I was opening up a conversation for collaboration. This reminded them that they have the capabilities to find a way out and assured them of my support in their endeavour. Looking around the room, one of them came back with a solution. She found a tiny piece of wooden block in the shape of a capital 'H' (the empty space did resemble the alphabet) and placed it in the empty spot. The pair looked at each other and erupted in laughter. The block was clearly not a good fit due to its size and shape. This ignited a new idea; they went over to the drawing table and began work, while I observed, keen to see how they were going to solve the problem (or so I thought).

I soon realized that their focus was not what I anticipated. They were instead creating exaggerated puzzle pieces that were either extremely small or of a totally different shape and size (such as a squirrel or a tiny dot). These paper pieces, despite their obvious misfit, were routinely fitted into the hole, after which roars of laughter were heard. Each time a fit was attempted, they invited me to look. The obvious puzzlement or perhaps even slight disappointment on my face in their first few attempts clearly fuelled their desire to continue. I realized that I had to let go of my agenda and embrace what these two children were showing me, allowing myself to be tickled by their absurd proposals. This went on for the next few minutes and I decided to point out the outline of the missing piece. This did not change their approach, rather, they continued in their endeavour of creating more misfits and I followed their lead. Immersing myself in their agenda, being intentionally silent, surprisingly opened space for reflection (Ollin, 2008). I began to recognize the necessity of this process to eventually arrive at a solution. In fact they knew the solution, but I simply did not recognize the form it came in. This process of intentional mistake-making was a significant process – in order to create pieces that were misfits, they had to have an idea of what would fit and consciously 'switch' their thinking around. In my initial attempts to convince them of heading towards a solution, which was my solution, I missed theirs. It was there from the beginning; their intention was to solve the problem. I began to recognize that this was a necessary process for them to reduce their cognitive load in order to consider solutions to the problem at hand (Kirschner et al., 2011). When encountering an otherwise unusual and uncommon problem, having to focus on multiple aspects of solving the issue requires more effort than we think.

I invited the pair to revisit their experience two weeks later. Time away from the problem appeared to give clarity and the opportunity to consider my proposal. They exchanged a quick giggle and set to work. I was not certain what they would produce and was ready to be surprised. They worked separately and very seriously, examining the hole in the puzzle as they drew on separate pieces of paper. When they handed their prototypes to me, I knew almost immediately they were close matches for the hole. It was a humbling moment; it was as though in their quick exchange, they quietly agreed to 'give in' to my request. Their process of exaggeration had clearly paid off as well; it gave them a concrete estimate of the size and shape of the piece. Even in my bank of possible solutions, I had not considered encouraging them to draw the piece freehand. My focus was on a proper fit and I thought tracing in the hole would have been the quickest way forward. Their detour and my silence made the process a more complex one than the initial route I had in mind. Ollin (2008: 265) proposed a notion of 'silent pedagogy', and explained how making space for silence within the classroom can give both adults and children opportunity to consider and reflect.

Close-to-accurate was enough for the children and, after four prototypes, they went back to their initial exaggerated ones. This was not only a highly mathematical problem as it required an understanding of geometry, it was also a valuable experience for me to understand how these two children assessed the situation at hand and eventually found a satisfactory solution between them. Throughout the entire process, they

Figure 10.2   The children's puzzle prototypes

made 12 prototypes in all; they were all solutions in their own right. The valuable process of this investigation would have been lost if time, silence and laughter were interrupted with my objective.

Singing: Changing the state of the unseen

Singing is a key part of our everyday curriculum; I often play the keyboard to accompany children's singing. This exposure has nurtured joy within the children for singing with others, and has resulted in a group of children who sing tunefully. I often invite children to reflect on their experiences through the use of photographs, transcripts or video recordings and this particular episode was no exception. The children were asked: 'Why do you think people sing?' They were also invited to illustrate themselves engaging in a singing experience. I have to admit that if I were asked to complete these two tasks, I would be really stretched and my mind would be blank. Despite knowing that I would be challenged to respond to such an expectation, I believe deeply in the children's ability to think about these abstract ideas simply and yet profoundly. Providing them with time to think and revisit the questions was an important aspect of this process.

It was not an easy process for the children and many took a few moments to consider the question. Some were hesitant, some needed a conversation to tease out their thoughts, some gave their answer after a few days, while others responded immediately, sure of their answers. Some children who usually had much to say were struggling to find the words, while others who were generally more introspective spoke with ease. Their responses were thoughtful, reflective of their individual connection to the act of singing. The children are familiar with questions like this and their responses are often simple yet reveal the depth of their understanding. Listening is an important aspect of our lives; learning to listen well takes practice (Rinaldi, 2012). Through these exchanges, I came to know some children more intimately, acquiring newfound understanding into their thinking and their perceptions of the world. Their responses revealed the connections they made to their everyday lives and the values they hold towards the experience of singing. These were some of their thoughts:

'People have voices. If they don't sing, their voice will be boring and there'll be nothing to do.' (Cynthia)

'They think it's nice.' (Arvind)

'They want to learn singing … so they know what songs to teach others in their new school … the new school has so many different children … so many different songs.' (Saskia)

'They love to sing … because we love to be at Mia Mia.' (Elena)

'For God … because God tells us to.' (Yosep)

'Maybe we're learning how to sing because we already know how to sing.' (Sebastian)

'They love to sing … because they also love to talk.' (Casey)

'Because it's a little bit beautiful ….' (Jun)

Representing the unseen is always a challenge. Inviting children to draw themselves singing is not merely requiring them to tap into the technicalities of drawing but also to communicate and represent the experience, the emotions involved; and to give form to the invisible. We see the act of singing, the movement of the lips and we hear the sounds but we do not see singing itself, it is invisible – just like talking. I thought that it was going to be a very thought-provoking, tough task. The children, however, were unfazed by it and went straight into their illustrations; even the children who usually find drawing a challenge managed it well. This intrigued me immensely and I spent time reflecting on why this was not perceived as tricky in comparison to drawing something from a reference, a strategy used in still-life drawing. A number of children understood the significance of notation in musical experiences and included those in their drawings to symbolize singing and the presence of music. There were also children who chose to represent singing differently; the use of a wavy line, circles, squares and even the inclusion of a brain as it is required as part of the singing process. The invisible is always a mystery and opens possibilities for us to imagine and reimagine how it might look when given a form. The children's drawings were influenced by their emotional and experiential connection to singing:

> As children communicate their mental images or theories to others, they also represent them to themselves, developing a more conscious vision. This is what 'internal listening' means. By moving from one language to another, and one field of experience to another, and by reflecting on these shifts, children modify and enrich their theories. (Rinaldi, 2012: 237)

This was a reminder for me not to avoid the invisible but look at it as an opening to undiscovered territory.

Figure 10.3   Children's drawings of themselves singing

Conclusion

Diving is not an easy skill; it takes practice, a sense of adventure and a willingness to learn the technicalities involved. In the same way, diving into the unknown of pedagogical documentation requires the same

(Continued)

(Continued)

commitment, a commitment to be open, to be present in the experience, to be brave, to be vulnerable, to desire to understand more, to invest time and intellect. Through pedagogical documentation, we experience multiple unknowns; some we might be comfortable with, while others may cause concern, challenging our thinking and ability to articulate our intentions. The process can present itself in moments of unexpected responses, seemingly ignored proposals, challenging notions, doubtful bystanders or invisible existences. Our responses to these moments can influence the responses of children and other people around us and also creates the opportunity for us to make the choice to see beyond our own box of comfort and understandings.

References

Jovanovic, S. and Roder, J. (2012) 'Disrupting the separation of adult and child worlds: Teachers' identity and the ongoing flow of agency', in A. Fleet, C. Patterson and J. Robertson (eds), *Conversations: Behind Early Childhood Pedagogical Documentation*. Sydney: Pademelon Press, pp. 123–142.

Kirschner, P.A., Ayres, P. and Chandler, P. (2011) 'Contemporary cognitive load theory research: The good, the bad and the ugly', *Computers in Human Behavior*, 27: 99–105. Doi:10.1016/j.chb.2010.06.025.

Kolbe, U. (2007) *Rapunzel's Supermarket: All about Young Children and their Art* (2nd edn). Byron Bay, NSW: Peppinot Press.

Lenz Taguchi, H. (2010) *Going Beyond the Theory/Practice Divide in Early Childhood Education: Introducing an Intra-Active Pedagogy*. London and New York: Routledge.

Ollin, R. (2008) 'Silent pedagogy and rethinking classroom practice: Structuring teaching through silence rather than talk', *Cambridge Journal of Education*, 38 (2): 365–280. Doi:10.1080/03057640802063528.

Rinaldi, C. (2012) 'The pedagogy of listening: The listening perspective from Reggio Emilia', in C. Edwards, L. Gandini and G. Forman (eds), *The Hundred Languages of Children: The Reggio Emilia Experience in Transformation* (3rd edn). Santa Barbara, CA: Praeger, pp. 233–246.

Commentary 3: Posing Big(ger) Ideas and Questions

Maria Cooper and Helen Hedges

University of Auckland, New Zealand

We engaged in lively debate when discussing the contributions of these four chapters. Our debate encouraged us to note their big ideas. Here, we offer our interpretation of these key messages and then pose two bigger questions and conceptual possibilities to draw the chapters together and prompt further critical reflection on embracing possibilities of change.

Chapter 7 reports a chance event that proved to be a catalyst for teachers to engage children in powerful learning. Robertson invites us to remember that our image of children is as competent and confident theorizers, thinkers and puzzlers. This competence was related to teachers' expectations that children would be kind, respectful and live a fair life with humans and animals. She highlights the skills and knowledge teachers require to recognize, respond to and revisit children's ideas and thinking as they bubble up and down over several months. 'We may decide to go with a big idea gifted to us by a child (or a bird), but the multitudes of decisions thereafter are shaped by our philosophy, values and pedagogical intentions' (p. 104).

Reed and Stobbs' chapter in the context of teacher education suggests that assessment of student teachers 'should be linked to personal and critically reflective accounts of using pedagogic documentation in practice *over a period of time*' (p. 121, our emphasis). We link their ideas to those of the other chapters when they make the insightful point that: 'Pedagogic documentation in itself is a most productive and valuable way to enter the world of the child and understand the way children learn' (p. 126).

Merewether suggests that making visible small stories about children's explorations in outdoor spaces promotes potentials for learning. Importantly, she notes that the term 'pedagogical' documentation implies value through recognizing and revisiting connections, dialogue and interpretation. Merewether argues that 'without analysis, these materials are just a collection of artefacts. It is the process of reflecting on and interpreting documentary material that transforms it into *pedagogical* documentation' (p. 134, original emphasis).

Chng presents three examples of children's investigations, reminding us of the importance of being open to and responding to new learning as 'categorizing children's questions and wonderings into a "box" can limit possibilities' (p. 148). She also identifies complexity: 'Knowing when to pause in the unknown, when to look for more and what to look for is critical and not always easy' (ibid.).

We integrate our interpretations of key messages from these chapters as:

- pedagogical documentation is an outcome, a process and an experience of teacher thinking, reflection, reviewing and theorizing
- pedagogical documentation requires acknowledgement that children's future learning pathways are not always known, and an acceptance of the non-linear nature of pedagogical documentation
- decision-making underpinning pedagogical documentation is multi-faceted and intentional, and places children, and teachers' understandings of them, at the centre of the process
- teachers don't 'do' pedagogical documentation; they engage with it as a way to learn about children, teaching and themselves.

We then pondered these bigger ideas in the context of Aotearoa-New Zealand to further embrace and provoke possibilities of change. We pose these questions as follows:

1. How might we conceptualize competent children's interests and inquiries?

The stories in three of the chapters about children's learning are evidence of the depth of children's interests when teachers are prepared to go beyond the surface and realize the potential of children's learning. This links to our own work where we have argued that without conceptual understandings of children's interests and inquiries, the potential of teachers' ability to draw on these rich aspects of children's learning to think more deeply about their own practice may remain untapped.

We have conceptualized children's interests as relating to their curiosity about life and living, and their meaning-making about their identities (Hedges and Cooper, 2016). We have argued that attention to children's 'real questions' (Wells, 1999: 91) and associated inquiries and working theories (Hedges, 2014), assists teachers to make decisions about what might be documented among a myriad of things that inspire children's learning and teachers' teaching.

2. How might the process of pedagogical documentation be made more visible and coherent?

These chapters highlight that teacher decision-making can be identified through pedagogical documentation. What appears less visible is the process of children's learning. We suggest that ideas presented in these four chapters about pedagogical documentation might benefit from being situated within the wider literature on assessment to balance attention to teaching and learning. In Aotearoa-New Zealand, the significant work undertaken on interactive formative assessment (Cowie and Bell, 1999) has foregrounded a holistic and credit-based approach to understanding children's learning (Carr, 2001; Carr and Lee, 2012). We suggest that the interrelated phases of 'noticing, recognising, responding, recording and revisiting' (Carr, 2008: 44) form both a conceptual and practical framing for everyday teaching and learning. Apart from 'noticing', the order of the other phases is not linear, but is dynamic and flexible in response to the organic nature of children's learning and inquiries. These phases involve many of the skills and aspects of teacher knowledge and reflection highlighted in this section but balance attention to children's learning as well as teachers' teaching.

We believe that providing a conceptual basis for children's interests and inquiries and the processes of assessment embedded in pedagogical documentation are important in teacher professional learning. In this way, the serious nature of children's learning can be engaged with and recorded using multiple methods that position pedagogical documentation as a mediational tool for (student) teacher puzzling, reflection and growth.

References

Carr, M. (2001) *Assessment in Early Childhood Settings: Learning Stories*. London: Paul Chapman.

Carr, M. (2008) 'Can assessment unlock and open the doors to resourcefulness and agency?', in S. Swaffield (ed.), *Unlocking Assessment: Understanding for Reflection and Application*. London: Routledge, pp. 36–54.

Carr, M. and Lee, W. (2012) *Learning Stories: Constructing Learner Identities in Early Education*. London: Sage.

Cowie, B. and Bell, B. (1999) 'A model of formative assessment in science education', *Assessment in Education*, 6 (1): 101–116.

Hedges, H. (2014) 'Young children's "working theories": Building and connecting understandings', *Journal of Early Childhood Research*, 12 (1): 35–49. 10.1177/1476718X13515417.

Hedges, H. and Cooper, M. (2016) 'Inquiring minds: Theorizing children's interests', *Journal of Curriculum Studies*, 48 (3): 303–322. 10.1080/00220272.2015.1109711.

Wells, G. (1999) *Dialogic Inquiry: Towards a Sociocultural Practice and Theory of Education*. New York: Cambridge University Press.

PART 4
THE WIDER VIEW

11

KNOWLEDGE AND PRACTICE OF PEDAGOGIC DOCUMENTATION: PROFESSIONAL DEVELOPMENT FOR EDUCATORS

ROSIE WALKER, MICHAEL REED AND NICOLA STOBBS

Building on a literature review and a series of 'training events', these authors propose possibilities for graduate leaders and educators to promote further understanding and implementation of pedagogic documentation through professional development. Using examples of analytic questioning, the centrality of leadership and practical examples in communities of practice are emphasized.

Introduction

This chapter explores the vital relationship between pedagogic documentation and the essential role of a leader in ensuring there is an alignment between theory and practice, developing collaborative reflective questioning and modelling how pedagogic documentation can be applied in practice. It investigates key features which could ideally form part of introducing pedagogic documentation to educators and leaders from a variety of settings. Above all, it firmly places the principles and values of pedagogic documentation within children's learning throughout the construction of professional development activities.

Initially, the authors conducted a review of literature surrounding practitioner/educator implementation of pedagogic documentation and literature on leadership. These sources ranged from day-to-day observations using pedagogic documentation published as blogs, institutional websites, detailed reviews of practice and a sometimes perceptive interrogations of pedagogic documentation in practice. Higher degree theses and research papers were examined as well as books and published commentaries, mostly from Canada, Australia and New Zealand. As a result, a number of key elements were identified; these were introduced to potential undergraduate leaders and experienced educators. They revealed that in England there is a lack of professional development to assist in introducing pedagogic documentation to graduate leaders and educators, particularly as an integrated part of pedagogic leadership. It was in this context that we decided to inquire into potential ways to overcome these resisting factors. The results are some key facets which may be of value to course designers and leaders of early education settings, and may assist in the introduction of pedagogic documentation.

Rationale for introducing pedagogic documentation to professional practice

Making the values and principles of pedagogic documentation visible within professional development is an important part of equipping potential leaders to invest in pedagogic documentation. These include the intention to help understand and promote children's learning through seeing children as capable and competent researchers in their own right. It involves educators within an early education setting observing and documenting children's learning. This information is shared with others and allows a collaborative dialogue and a close consideration concerning how learning is shaped by what *they as educators do* as well as the *environment, context and community* which the children inhabit. Pedagogic documentation may also inform assessment in terms of what children can do, although assessment is not the primary aim of this work, rather it is to become better informed about children's learning. Children are shown that practitioners value their learning and view the process of learning as a collaborative one where multiple voices are heard and acted upon.

This process asks educators to question their practices in order to make connections between theory and practice and to understand and reduce the barriers which might restrict children's learning. Therefore, alignment between theory and practice is a necessary principle and means that one informs the other. This involves the leader playing an integral part in establishing and making these principles visible, highlighting good leadership practice and establishing an environment which goes beyond an application of regulatory frameworks and policy, to critical thinking about why these are in place. The leader must also have a sound understanding of their own values and beliefs as an early years educator (Callan, 2015), within the context of a collaborative team. In terms of course design, it is essential to aid a leader's understanding by presenting clear examples of the principles aligned to the application of pedagogic documentation.

Learning from workshops

In an attempt to find out how pedagogic documentation could become an integral part of course design, a series of training events were held for both educators and student teachers. Through this, it became clear to us that the introduction of pedagogic documentation to this audience required a deeper and more purposeful introduction, particularly to the way it was an integral part of leading practice, framed within the term 'pedagogic leadership'. To this end, our slides and other workshop materials were reviewed, resulting in a deeper, more positive evaluation about documenting children's learning. Materials for use with experienced early educators were re-orientated towards statutory curriculum requirements and regulatory requirements for self-evaluation. This proved to be highly successful. It revealed the value of situating the materials in an organizational and curriculum context, and thus became a valuable way to engage participants in the idea of documenting learning. There was, however, a danger that this skewed the approach towards 'teaching' and seeing pedagogic documentation as a functional form of assessment.

(The work of Stobbs et al. in Chapter 3 gives weight to developing this strategy where they highlight the resistance to pedagogic documentation as a consequence of regulatory requirements.) Time was therefore taken to assure participants that children's learning was the focus and that it was possible to see such learning both within the curriculum requirements and in the inspection procedures. Presenters ensured that pedagogic documentation was seen as a process intended to influence practice and driven by what educators consider to be of value to their local setting as well as responding to the external driving force of the statutory curriculum. This process had both personal and professional consequences for the participants. The prospect of introducing pedagogic documentation required knowledge of not only organizational and curriculum needs, but also was likely to require a detailed knowledge of curriculum requirements and a challenging of assumptions to allow an understanding of regulatory requirements about what children should learn and how they learn. As a result, we identified a number of key issues for the introduction and application of pedagogic documentation in practice.

The first of these related to leadership: it became clear that pedagogic documentation is unlikely to be successfully implemented into practice without pedagogic leadership. This means that the leader empowers others to invest in pedagogic documentation. This is key to developing 'orientational' quality (Wall et al., 2015: 22). This process embeds the principles and values of the approach by a leader who then invests time in motivating and supporting people within a community of practice.

The second was the importance of introducing practical examples of pedagogic documentation. This was considered essential to enable educators and students to begin to envisage the potential of the approach and the part they may play within its implementation. While studying the practical examples, they soon realized that questioning is a higher-order skill which needs to be developed when taking an analytic and critical approach to observation of children's learning. They also appreciated that the views of those most closely involved must always be heard to inform the shaping of practice, whether this be in terms of children's or educators' learning, or course design and construction.

Features of leadership and the inclusion of practical examples are, in themselves, important, but it was also essential for us to underline the principles and values of pedagogic documentation as an examination of children's learning. This reinforced a view which saw children as capable and competent learners. Although each of these issues will now be discussed in turn, it is important to recognize the interrelationship between them as, taken as a whole, they represent the way that the community of practice embraces pedagogic documentation as a way of being.

Leading the community of practice

Participants in the research understood that pedagogic leadership can be seen in terms of a leader who understands what effective learning for young children looks like when people work together. This understanding emphasizes the leader sharing their views with others, developing a collective responsibility towards recognizing problems and celebrating success. Within the research, this allowed the idea of collective discussion and a deep consideration of learning via pedagogic documentation to be more easily understood. It became apparent that significant time was needed to convince educators that the provision of learning opportunities within the curriculum could reveal as well as promote the independent capability of children. In practice, this means educators documenting learning and considering the resources children use. This expectation involves educators asking questions about the physical environment as well as structures and routines which establish the direction and expectations for children's learning. These components required consideration regarding how this would be possible through the curriculum and an inevitable discussion about whether this approach would somehow 'fit' with the regulatory requirements of assessment.

In England, the Office for Standards in Education, Children's Services and Skills (Ofsted) assesses the quality of provision by observation of child–adult interactions. They look to see how far an educator encourages and inspires children to be independent. The leader is doing what Ofsted (2013) recommends as good practice by getting people to think about: *What is it like for a child here? What difference are we making, and how do we know?* In effect, developing a cycle of child-focused observation, reflection and evaluation to improve quality. They are doing what Ofsted (2015) suggests is exploring the *characteristics of effective learning* and using this information to refine opportunities and to work out how best to monitor progress. As Stobbs, Harvell and Reed highlight in Chapter 3, the implication here is for leaders to act as facilitators in developing new ways of working within the curriculum frameworks to encompass these within a pedagogic documentation framework.

The environment facilitated by the leader is key to the child's development and underpins their right to build their own knowledge and relationships. Early childhood educators develop the skills of knowing how and when to intervene in a child's learning as well as recognizing the importance of play in a child's development. It involves an acceptance of a shift in power from adult to child by creating an environment as a means of building knowledge, rather than knowledge as an end in itself, through considering children's individual interests as well as their intellectual, emotional and social needs. There is no right way of observing and documenting children's learning. The intention is not for a leader *to give away authority*, it is about investing time and energy in others so they feel encouraged, capable and inspired to work together. This is a very different leadership stance from 'permitting' people to share their views. For the leader, this means shaping the attitude and energy of those involved so they engage in 'purposeful observational conversations' about children's learning.

The leader within this context asks questions that require more than a yes or no response. This is because the responses are about the real world in which people operate and, therefore, are not clear-cut. It is a world that contains an educational landscape formed and shaped by their effort and experiences. The observations and questions need time to be assimilated. They will touch upon and expose not only organizational and curriculum issues, but also professional roles, responsibilities and relationships. This brings into play issues such as professional trust and professional expectation, as well as the integration of parents and the community into contributing to pedagogic documentation. The leader takes a key role firstly in ensuring that the documentation is visible and accessible to all parents, secondly that community needs are considered, and thirdly that the documentation is situated ethically within the local culture and context of its implementation. This is a view echoed by a leader who researched the implementation of pedagogic documentation in practice as part of her studies. She suggests that: 'It has to be approached honestly and openly by all participants. Most of all, it has to reflect the voice of the child as an individual and as part of their social context' (Corrick, 2015: 47).

Practical examples

The scenario below is a practical example which was used to engage participants in discussion and analysis. It involved documentation of the concerns of two children aged three who were engaged in a freely chosen activity at an early education setting in a rural county in England. This is the conversation between the children as documented by Louisa (the educator):

Philosophy in the sandpit

[*Luke is sitting alone in the sandpit. He uses a funnel to pour sand on a toy ambulance.*]

Luke: 'Somebody died in the back. We need to take him somewhere.' 'Here I am man.' 'Thank you.' [*He uses a funnel and a teapot to make tracks on the raised edge of the sandpit.*]

[*Jacob gets in the sandpit. He brings with him a Rescue Hero figure.*]

Luke: 'Help! I'm broken down. Help! Help! Oh thank you. I've gone to heaven.'
Jacob: 'What? Where have you gone?'
Luke: 'To heaven.'
Jacob: 'How are you gonna get out of heaven? You'll be stuck there forever! Look at his shape.' [*Jacob takes a play person and makes prints in the sand with its feet.*]
Luke: 'Yeah.'
Jacob: 'I'm walking in the mud.'
Luke: 'I can't; I'm sinking!'

Louisa's reflection

By observing the boys' play, I realized how much children's meaning-making is invisible and that so much of what they learn is never taught. The surprise apparent in Jacob's response, and the unconventional way he described getting 'stuck up there forever', makes me deduce that he is not repeating something formally discussed but verbalizing his own thoughts based on overheard conversations.

This is similar for Luke, knowing that people die in the back of ambulances. Most children know that ambulances take sick people to hospital, but there is normally a happy ending. Both boys seem to have been considering 'dying' because they both tune into each other's frame of reference immediately. We never measure children's

(Continued)

(Continued)

awareness of these profound concepts, yet place great importance on the testing of transmitted knowledge such as colours; it makes me wonder how often, as adults, we underestimate children's awareness of bigger issues.

This has made visible to me part of our 'hidden curriculum'. As a staff team, do we have an unwritten rule that subjects such as death are not up for discussion? Yet, children's interest in death has been documented since the Malting House days of Susan Isaacs. What happens in the process of growing up that silences these philosophical conversations?

Commentary

Louisa 'reflects a disposition of not presuming to know … of asking how the learning occurs, rather than assuming – as in transmission models of learning – that learning occurred because teaching occurred' (Wien et al., 2011). Jacob and Luke's cultural and social experiences, framed through a child's lens, are glimpsed through the documentation, as is Louisa's evaluation of her own cultural and social experiences. It has troubled her acceptance of an 'ages and stages' view of development and opened her eyes to the realization that she has underestimated the complexity and depth of children's learning and cultural processing. The intersection of two lenses are made visible: the child's, but also 'in the spaces at the edges of pedagogical documentation is evidence of the teacher's thinking' (ibid.), as it is the teacher who frames the learning and the child's voice through the lens of partiality (Lancaster, 2006; Dahlberg et al., 2007).

What might have resulted if Louisa had taken on the role of assessor, evaluating the observation against normative benchmarks? What evidence is there that learning has taken place? Other than noting that the boys are 'Confident to talk to other children when playing, and will communicate freely about own home and community' (Personal, Social and Emotional Development, Self-confidence and Self-awareness, 30–50 months) (Early Education, 2012: 11); and that they are demonstrating 'engagement – playing with what they know', and 'creating and thinking critically – having their own ideas and making links' (ibid.: 5).

Louisa has questioned the direction of children's learning and exposed an issue of how discussion of death is facilitated with children and how

Table 11.1 Examples of analytic questioning (adapted from Reed, 2016)

It is important to develop ways to involve educators in collaborative analysis and ask questions when engaged in an analysis of pedagogic documentation.	The questions (over time) will create spirals within the setting and community which the leader needs to consider. Answers to such questions may have an impact on professional roles, responsibilities and relationships; as well as potentially refining children's learning opportunities.	Reflective dispositions used by educators may include: inquirer, planner, thinker negotiator, listener, communicator, collaborator reflective investigator, leader, shaper and reflective questioner.
• What was the documented focus? Why was this focus used? What did it reveal? • What do we think and what can we learn about the things that shaped children's learning within the environment they inhabit? • Were the values and identity of the setting visible? • How do we feel? • What difference are we making for children and how do we know? What shall we do? • Is there a way of …?	• How do we explain to our community that pedagogic documentation is about enhancing learning and not just about assessment? • How do we keep our own distinctiveness and values in the midst of possible change to the learning environment? • What personal and professional qualities will be needed to help to shape and refine what goes on? • Is it possible to see a picture of practice and children's learning as it might be – if we changed things? • Will any change mean a change of roles and responsibilities? • How do we keep listening above the noise of change?	They will be classifying, describing, discussing, planning, explaining, identifying, indicating, recognizing, selecting and interpreting, appraising assessing, evaluating, predicting, co-coordinating, developing, modifying, adapting, changing, reflecting, considering, re-arranging and applying.

real world situations are considered and developed. These two outcomes are not mutually exclusive. The regulatory categories can be seen to be 'met' and richly observed, with 'value added'.

Taking pedagogic documentation further: Collective analysis/questioning

One of the key issues to emerge while examining practical examples of pedagogic documentation within the workshops focused on ways to develop analytic questioning techniques as part of documenting learning. These can be used when educators come together to reflect and review the learning that has occurred as an integral part of their provisioning of the learning environment. This analytic questioning involves a collective examination of practice and sharing of values and knowledge. It requires the development of reflective questioning in action which is more than just assessment and maintains the values of pedagogic documentation. The types of questions that may be used by leaders and educators are illustrated in Table 11.1.

As a result of analysis of the workshops in relation to this aspect of the research, it can be concluded that:

- questioning involves responses that include making moral judgements and exposing views which are not solely about practical and organizational features
- questioning can mean looking at existing structures and practices which can expose current roles, responsibilities and relationships
- questioning can mean asking whether the questions only reinforce a particular (and perhaps singular) leadership approach or whether questions are used to transform and refine what goes on by involving others
- questioning may well contribute to a personal and professional transformation for the leader and members of the team as they consider their own actions on, in and for practice.

Therefore, questions have consequences. Asking them imposes a responsibility on the leader: a responsibility to carefully consider and act on what is heard, learning from others, considering what works and why and asking what can be done to extend and improve what goes on. Personal and professional values are examined, as is an ethical understanding of why and how their actions may impact on children

Table 11.2 Responses from participants

Empowerment and investment of the leader	The leader models good practice	I have been encouraged and supported to explore and develop curiosity within children's learning	I have been able to join in discussion and ask questions	I explore issues and concepts through different perspectives	I am less reliant on the leader now – and gaining independence
Educator reflects on pedagogic documentation	I have learnt to ask questions wider than the here and now	I can recognize features of quality practice and potential for shaping change	PD has made me think about the importance of sharing ideas to extend learning	My knowledge and interest in quality improvement has begun a 'wave of change' within the setting	I have just 'got' how complex early childhood really is!
For those involved in vocational study	I am able to promote models and illustrate ways of sourcing and recording information (in and for practice)	I have presented with my peers at the student conference	I can refine content in light of inter-tutor discussion and student feedback	I have fed back to my setting the findings of my data analysis	How I think of myself has changed, I feel more confident as a childminder
Wider aspects and reflection	Ethicality is a major part of all my work now as I understand its importance	I have been helped to understand children's interaction and learnt about how they learn	I now know what actually counts as good quality	I'm also understanding why I'm doing something and not just doing it because I have to	I have come to see the complexity of early childhood and respond positively to change

and families. As this happens, there is likely to be a personal and professional transformation because the leader and others become instruments to investigate practice and must consider their own actions on, in and for practice.

The responses

A snapshot of thoughts of participants involved in the research as they reflected on materials presented to them to introduce pedagogic documentation is presented in Table 11.2. It demonstrates the value of the voices of those most concerned in shaping course design. Their views have been codified to represent the following:

- the role and value of the leader moving pedagogic documentation forward through pedagogic leadership
- the value of questioning
- reflective responses – specific to pedagogic documentation
- value for studies
- reflective responses – about the setting and personal understanding.

Conclusion

This chapter has sought to model values and principles of pedagogic documentation as revealed by research undertaken with educators and students. It has developed these elements in its focus on children's and students' learning rather than on systems. Ethicality, shared communication, community, reflective analysis and valuing of children's learning have featured highly within the findings. Examination of this has the potential to be transformational in the thinking and practice of early educators.

For the leaders of early years settings, this means that their work must be valued not just as keepers of the curriculum, but for the way in which they examine children's learning and give this status and meaning. In terms of university students and potential leaders, the acquisition of higher-order learning skills allows understanding and operation within established practices and procedures as well as challenging assumptions and values as each different issue or contextual situation arises. This means developing the ability to contribute effectively to new approaches, such as pedagogic documentation, at their setting.

It is apparent that regulators and educators have the same vision and goals for children; both have high expectations and a desire to raise aspiration. These may only be realized when documentation is seen as more than a functional aspect of the curriculum. Collectively asking questions helps to define what 'high expectations' really means and ways to provide positive learning experiences for children's learning.

References

Callan, S. (2015) 'The ethical practitioner with children and families', in M. Reed and R. Walker (eds), *A Critical Companion to Early Childhood*. London: Sage, pp. 36–47.

Corrick, G. (2015) 'Pedagogical documentation: A small-scale enquiry into its implementation and viability in a rural preschool'. Undergraduate Independent Study, University of Worcester, Worcester, UK.

Dahlberg, G., Moss, P. and Pence, A. (2007) *Beyond Quality in Early Childhood Education and Care: Languages of Evaluation* (2nd edn). Abingdon: Routledge.

Early Education (2012) *Development Matters in the Early Years Foundation Stage*. London: Early Education.

Lancaster, P.Y. (2006) 'Listening to young children: Respecting the voice of the child', in G. Pugh and B. Duffy (eds), *Contemporary Issues in the Early Years*. London: Sage, pp. 63–75.

Ofsted (Office for Standards in Education, Children's Services and Skills) (2013) *Getting it Right First Time: Achieving and Maintaining High-Quality Early Years Provision*. Reference: 130117. www.gov.uk/government/publications/achieving-and-maintaining-high-quality-early-years-provision-getting-it-right-first-time (accessed 25.01.17).

Ofsted (2015) *Teaching and Play in the Early Years: A Balancing Act?* Reference: 150085. www.gov.uk/government/publications/teaching-and-play-in-the-early-years-a-balancing-act (accessed 25.01.17).

Reed, M. (2016) *Effective Leadership for High Quality Early Years Practice*. London: PLA Publications.

Wall, S., Litjens, I. and Taguma, M. (2015) *Early Childhood and Care Literature Review: England*. Paris: OECD. www.oecd.org/unitedkingdom/early-childhood-education-and-care-pedagogy-review-england.pdf (accessed 01.12.15).

Wien, C.A., Guyevskey, V. and Berdoussis, N. (2011) 'Learning to document in Reggio-inspired education', *Early Childhood Research and Practice*, 13 (2). http://ecrp.uiuc.edu/v13n2/wien.html (accessed 10.11.15).

12

THE POTENTIAL OF PEDAGOGICAL DOCUMENTATION FOR LEADERSHIP ENACTMENT

IRIS BERGER

This chapter furthers the focus on leadership. Using the Canadian frame of pedagogical narration, the author considers the global ECE landscape and offers pedagogical documentation as leadership enactment. Building on storytelling as political action, she questions affirmation of the status quo and offers provocations for rethinking practice. Public participation becomes key.

Introduction

In this chapter, I make a case for thinking about pedagogical documentation as a site for early childhood education leadership. I draw from a research project that explored theoretically and empirically what *new* possibilities for thinking and enacting leadership arise when early childhood educators engage with the practice of pedagogical documentation (or pedagogical narration, as we call it in British Columbia, Canada) (Berger, 2013). Thinking about leadership in relation to the practice of pedagogical documentation entails thinking about leadership differently than it is conventionally conceived and practiced. I unhinge the concept of leadership from its association with administrative power, hierarchical position and control over outcomes, and relate it instead to the act of sharing pedagogical documentation as an *event of interruption* to our habitual and stereotypical understanding of early education, and of its protagonists: children, educators and families.

When educators practice pedagogical documentation as a 'risky business' and when they insert into the public domain *provocative* narratives about significant pedagogical occurrences from their early childhood settings, they illuminate the contingency and complexity of our worldly co-existence with young children (Pacini-Ketchabaw et al., 2015). In doing so, educators enact leadership through subverting conventional thought about what early education is about, while reinvigorating and complicating public conversations about what early education might be.

Time to speak about, and do, leadership in early childhood education

For a plethora of reasons, early childhood educators have traditionally rejected the notion of leadership. A major cause for this phenomenon is that conventional views of leadership, such as forms of leadership that are closely associated with hierarchical structures and a single position that is typically held by a male figure, are deemed by early childhood educators as antithetical to the collaborative and relational experiences which make up a central pedagogical value in the field of early education (Rodd, 1997; Woodrow and Busch, 2008). Challenges to early childhood leadership have been linked to the early childhood educator's professional identity, low social status of the early childhood field, and the gendered nature of the early childhood sector (Scrivens, 2002; Hard, 2004). Rejection of the notion of leadership should not come as a surprise. Early childhood pedagogical creed has leaned heavily on a child-centred practice that situated early childhood educators in semi-passive roles such as unobtrusive observers and facilitators of the developing child (Langford, 2010). To a large degree, these pedagogical traditions relegated the educators' pedagogical work (and its complexity) to the background and often rendered the early childhood educator invisible. Moreover, the professional identity of the early childhood educator has been constructed on notions of 'caring' and 'niceness', rather than on taking a stance or articulating one's position in public (Grieshaber, 2001; Fasoli et al., 2007). Relatedly, when early education is framed as care work, or as service for parents, it has, until recently, been seen as belonging to the familial, domestic private sphere, and therefore not a topic fit for public political debates.

The global ECE policy landscape

Against the backdrop of the historical construction of the identity of the early childhood educator as a maternal, apolitical figure (a construction which works against notions of leadership), there are emerging trends on the global early childhood policy landscape that signify that, rather than rejecting leadership, it has become pertinent to think about and enact early childhood leadership in a radical new way. Over the last two decades, national and provincial governments in a significant number of countries around the world have created centralized early childhood curricula documents (Oberhuemer, 2005; Urban, 2012). An increasing number of ECE scholars link global changes in early childhood policy to the constant seepage of neoliberal agendas into the educational arena (Dahlberg and Moss, 2008; Duhn, 2008; Woodrow, 2008). Neoliberal narratives of early education focus on preparing children for a competitive market, where children's 'educational needs' are often established in relation to economic growth of the knowledge society. Although some policy documents adhere to a progressive approach to early education such as valuing play and a holistic approach to learning, inevitably these global policy meta-narratives reflect particular, and rather narrow, assumptions about the purposes of early education (i.e. increasing competencies and school readiness for young children) (Urban, 2012).

As early education increasingly conforms to established standards and as educators become more accountable for mapping children's experiences into predefined learning outcomes, valuing and attending to the potential of unexpected, complex pedagogical moments to broaden the scope of what early childhood education might be about may become superfluous. The issue with the rise in regulatory ECE frameworks was articulated succinctly by Giugni (2011: 12), who argued: 'I have yet to encounter a curriculum, regulatory or quality assurance document that has captured all the complexities of what early childhood practice can become, perhaps because, to date, this complexity is yet to be successfully expressed in "regulatory language".' In other words, the kind of leadership that is needed for contemporary ECE is leadership that destabilizes standardized thinking about early childhood education, or leadership that makes public and visible, echoing Giugni (ibid.: 12), these 'complexities of what early childhood practice can become'.

It is here that pedagogical documentation enters the scene as a productive site for leadership enactment because it orients practice towards encounters with the contingent, the unexpected and the extraordinary that permeate daily-lived experiences with children. The *raison d'être* of pedagogical documentation is the idea that educational responses cannot be predetermined, but must remain open and be re-thought again and again in relation to unpredictable events that unfold in educational contexts. If we accept Davies' (2011: 121) invitation to enact pedagogical documentation as *a practice of open listening* – 'opening up the ongoing possibility of coming to see life, and one's relation to it, in new and surprising ways' – then pedagogical documentation can create *a zone of emergence* where early childhood education becomes a space for unexpected possibilities, as well as a venue for leadership that draws on 'creative engagement with the not-yet-known'.

Pedagogical documentation: A new vision for ECE practice

Within the contemporary realm of ECE practice, pedagogical documenta-tion has interrupted and forever changed conceptually and methodologically the practice of child observation (Dahlberg et al., 2007). Traditional forms of child observation focused on assessment of individual children along the lines of a predefined set of criteria (devel-opmental stages and/or predefined learning goals), with the underlying assumption that educators are to employ theories and standards external to their context to gain an objective account of what the child can/should do. Alternatively, within the context of the practice of pedagogical docu-mentation, educators' narrative interpretations of children's experiences are no longer seen as direct representation of what happened or as an objective account of who children are. The narratives become an occa-sion for dialogue, through which the diverse perspectives of educators, children and parents enrich, challenge and broaden the possibilities for interpretation and future pedagogical response/action (ibid.). From this premise, pedagogical documentation has implications for leadership that are associated with keeping questions about the purpose of education open by sustaining democratic debates that afford visibility of plurality of thought and continual processes of discussion and disputation about the identities of children, as well as the content and aims of early educa-tion (Rinaldi, 2001; Dahlberg and Moss, 2008).

Most significant for leadership enactment is the idea that pedagogical documentation makes possible a new image of the early childhood educator. Educators of young children can no longer be depicted as merely passive observers of the child; rather, early childhood educators become narrators of unexpected stories that refuse to be contained within frameworks, thereby creating the possibility to transcend universalized categories and challenge assumptions about who children and educators are, what teaching and learning is, and who can participate in public conversations that create and enrich our common world.

Researching pedagogical documentation as leadership enactment

Considering the above – namely, the endemic issues affecting ECE leadership, the global and local movement to frame early childhood education through policy, and emerging pedagogical possibilities for early childhood practice – I have completed a study that aimed to explore the leadership potential that the practice of pedagogical documentation (or pedagogical narration) holds. At the heart of this study was a curiosity about the potential of pedagogical narration to position early childhood educators as storytellers who can instigate (with the narrations) conversations and engage the early childhood community in thinking about children and our common world in new ways.

I studied how pedagogical narration and its leadership potential was enacted across four early childhood settings, and linked acts of leadership with early childhood educators' initiation of dialogic critical reflection about the meanings of narrations pertaining to significant events from children's lived experiences. Some of the data gathered included: observations of occasions when pedagogical narrations were shared with either children, colleagues or parents; interviews with early childhood educators who created pedagogical narrations; and samples of pedagogical narrations collected from each site.

Theoretical framework

To theoretically sustain a concept of leadership that is associated with pedagogical narration, I enlisted the political thought of Hannah Arendt (1906–1975). Arendt's unique conceptualization of political action is highly relevant for theorizing leadership as it is enacted with the practice of pedagogical narration. In her seminal work, *The Human Condition*

([1958] 1998), Arendt explored the political dimension of storytelling in a public space and its significance for sustaining an engaged political community. Arendt's political thought peaks in her writings about political action and its connection to storytelling and leadership. Action, for Arendt (ibid.: 178), entails the capacity to initiate, to begin, through speech and deeds, something 'which cannot be expected from whatever may have happened before'. To act and to lead, for Arendt, means to set something into motion and to bring something new into the world. Importantly, the insertion of something new into the world is intricately linked with what Arendt calls the 'faculty of interrupting'. She states:

> The lifespan of man running toward death would inevitably carry everything human to ruin and destruction if it were not for the *faculty of interrupting* it and beginning something new, a faculty which is inherent in action like an ever-present reminder that men, though they must die, are not born in order to die but in order to begin. (Ibid.: 246, my emphasis)

In other words, Arendt links the possibility for a new beginning with action (or narration, see below) that triggers a discord with the status quo and a move beyond what is already known.

Storytelling as response-ability

Arendt (ibid.: 184) postulated that action – an event that interrupts the status quo and *demands* our responses – 'produces stories with or without intention as naturally as fabrication produces tangible things'. According to Gambetti (2005: 434), Arendt's action 'is the name to be given to that which defies conventional limits and establishes new meanings or inspires new stories'. More poignant is Arendt's claim that action is in danger of disappearance if not noted by spectators and narrated by storytellers. The role of narratives, then, is to transform (unique and unexpected) events into a tangible appearance, to make action public and visible, and endow it with significance and permanence.

Storytelling for Arendt is not about self-expression or transmission of values and knowledge; rather, storytelling is about telling a provocative story that stirs people to think about what they are doing (Disch, 1994). Arendt upheld storytelling as a methodology that affords a response to unprecedented events through an engagement with the 'actuality of the event', without confining the phenomena to established norms and theories. She argued that telling stories about the unexpected was a way to remind ourselves of the worldly experience for which our traditional concepts are no longer adequate. Thus, when stories of unprecedented events are told, they can awaken us and act as an ethical invitation for a collective, vigorous critical mediation on the meanings of our ever changing, precarious plural existence, while at the same time, awaken our responsibility for our common world. Arendt was particularly interested in narratives about unexpected events in which certainties surrounding values and identities are shaken and destabilized, because such narratives illuminate the contingency and complexity of our human condition as they reinstate possibilities for a new beginning.

The public/common world

For Arendt, the public realm connotes a space where people come together to constitute a reality and create a common world by means of robust talk and storytelling about a worldly issue. Stories play a significant role in creating our common world. Disch suggests that Arendt's public space 'emerge[s] not around an action itself but around the various stories that make it a public event' (1994: 85). Inspired by Arendt, Maxine Greene (2001) has written extensively about the importance of creating public spaces in educational contexts. She imagined this space as a realm where multiple perspectives encounter each other with the possibility of making our common existence richer and more complex. As Greene reminds us, a public space, or a common world, is not a given – it needs to be brought into existence and kept alive. To this end, Greene proposes that the teacher becomes a 'challenger' – opening spaces where the taken-for-granted and normalized ways of being are *interrupted* and where new ones are born. With Arendt's conceptualization of storytelling as political action that ushers in political engagement and the creation of a public/common world, we can move to thinking about leadership in association with the faculty of interruption and with a view of the early childhood educator as a challenger whose leadership is enacted by inserting provocative pedagogical narratives into a public domain to preserve 'our ontological potential-for-new-beginnings' (Magrini, 2012: 78).

Pedagogical documentation: From affirmation to interruption

In this section, I share data from the aforementioned study in order to delve more deeply into the complexities of pedagogical documentation, especially in its potentiality either to affirm or to interrupt the status quo.

As pedagogical documentation spread and gained international popularity, a number of authors began to caution that this practice is a powerful technology that needs to be approached thoughtfully, as what is made visible through using this tool is not an innocent or apolitical recording of children's experiences. Davies (2011), in particular, cautioned that pedagogical documentation could become a technology of legitimation, affirming conventional perceptions about early education and fixed identities of children and educators; making visible what is already known and foreclosing the possibility to inquire into what might be.

Analysis of data in the aforementioned study illuminated that a number of participants interpreted pedagogical narrations as a venue for affirming early childhood educators' practice and legitimizing ECE as a valuable field. For example, one educator claimed that pedagogical narrations gave 'the early childhood educators the legitimacy to say: "You are doing great work!" and "Don't underestimate yourself!"' In a similar vein, another educator explained that pedagogical narrations helped 'to justify what we are doing'; while a third contributed that, 'it makes visible [to parents] how our day is spent. So I think that when you document, you are really showing the value of our work and what we are doing with the children on a daily basis.'

While I do not wish to minimize the significance of the use of pedagogical documentation (or pedagogical narration) for gaining appreciation for the work that is being done in early childhood settings, it is important to note that when pedagogical narration is understood and practiced as affirmation of an existing, stable identity for the ECE field, it may limit its potential for leadership enactment. The educators' desire for professional recognition, as seen above, was a reaction to the ECE field's low social status, but not a generative response to the possibilities that the practice of pedagogical narrations holds for *contesting* or *enlarging* public conceptions about what ECE might be about. The issue associated with a desire for affirmation that is linked with legitimation, rather than action, is that pedagogical narrations may become a tool for maintaining the status quo, constraining, rather than opening up, the possibility for pedagogical narration to bring something new into the world.

Next, I share an example from one of the research sites, where Karen's pedagogical narrations distorted conventional thought about the early childhood classroom as a private, isolated, protected, apolitical space, separate from the world and its worldly issues. Karen often took up the challenge to engage deeply with common world issues as they surfaced in her pedagogical work through writing and sharing pedagogical narrations that made visible how children, educators and parents encountered dilemmas surrounding gender, exclusion, freedom, power, ethics and identity. An understanding of

ECE as an integral part of our common world and its existential challenges is important in order to rethink how contemporary early childhood leadership might be enacted, because, as Filippini (2001: 54) asserts, 'the issues of children and childhood cannot be treated separately from the issues of women, men, families, and society'.

What I learned from my observations and conversations with Karen was that construction and sharing of pedagogical narrations that explored volatile, risky topics brought into being a public space because of their hospitable capacity to ignite a multiplicity of viewpoints and opinions. In her pedagogical narrations, Karen purposefully exposed difficult topics in order to de-familiarize and disrupt the normal preschool classroom agenda, while inviting others to ponder and negotiate with her the possible meanings that an engagement with such topics opens up.

A pedagogical narration about love and death as a moment of interruption

On Valentine's Day, Karen asked the children the question: 'What is love?' Karen was intrigued by how a conversation about love was unexpectedly changed by the four-year-old children to a conversation about death, or more accurately, to a conversation about the relation between love and death:

Aaron: Love means you fall in love and you are going to marry.
Beatrice: It means you want to be nice and help your little brother.
Ron: When someone dies, you love them. It means you miss them. You have to find a new family if they die.
Anna: Every single person will die.
Bill: He said you get another family but that's wrong.
Aaron: If someone dies, you turn into a skeleton, then a ghost, then a spirit.
Edna: Love means, if you die, you put something over the hole so you know where they are buried.

Captivated by the children's engagement with these existential questions, Karen documented the children's conversation and sent the content of the conversation with a brief reflection to the parents via email that read:

It would seem that love and death are inextricably linked. I had no idea. Clearly children have opinions on how the death of a loved one would affect them. They have strong ideas about what happens after death. These are not topics we generally discuss with children. Maybe we should start.

To her surprise, the parents' responses were quick to come, and they included stories about how the children and their parents have been exploring the topic of death. In an unexpected turn of events, the documentation of the children's conversation opened up a space for collective thinking and multi-perspectival storytelling among the educators, the children and their families about fundamental forces of human existence: death and love.

For example, one parent shared the following:

> We have conversation about heaven in our house. My husband is from a religious background, so a lot to do with his mom's death had to do with religious stuff, and I come from the opposite side, so we are clear that this is what daddy believes and this is what mommy believes. But it's hard cause Connor says 'so is grandma in heaven like in the stars', and I go 'well, ... that's what some people believe'. So that's how it comes up in our house, more spiritually I guess.

The conversation within the preschool community was sustained by questions about how death inserts itself into our human consciousness and about its relationships with love, loss and loneliness. The educator, along with the children and families, continued to search together for collective responses to these significant philosophical questions. Not unlike the children's insight about the relation between death and love, contemporary philosopher Simon Critchley (2009) has proposed that:

> death comes into our world through the deaths of others, whether as close as a parent, partner or child or as far as the unknown victim of a distant famine or war. The relation to death is not first and foremost my own fear for my own demise, but my sense of being undone by the experience of grief and mourning.

The kinds of discussions that this narration brought to life are evocative of Davies' (2011: 120) mediation, mentioned earlier, that pedagogical documentation may open up 'the ongoing possibility of coming to see life, and one's relation to it, in new and surprising ways'.

What made this narration provocative, risky and therefore a site for renewal, was not only the engagement with the topic of death, which is definitely not a common curricular topic for the early childhood classroom, but also the notion that in the realm of early childhood, a topic such as death is often relegated to the realm of the private. One of the ways in which Karen challenged her community with this narration was to bring into the public domain discussions about a topic that is typically considered suitable for the familial, private domain.

Creating a public/common world

According to Phelan, the Arendtian public space requires provision of opportunities for the articulation of multiple perspectives out of which something common can be brought into being: 'It is a space wherein the opportunity to enlarge one's perspective or change one's mind or change another's is possible' (2010: 326). In the pedagogical narration discussed above, it was initially children who interrupted the conventional 'doing' of Valentine's Day, but it was Karen who recognized 'the moment of grace when unexpected connections become visible' (Davies, 2011: 131) in its potential of becoming a common concern that brings people together to co-create a public space or a common world.

When Karen shared the love and death pedagogical narration with the community, and thus made it public and visible, she invited children, parents, and colleagues to participate in world making. The encounter with multiple perspectives meant that the children, parents and Karen enlarged their understanding about complexities that awareness of death (and especially the death of loved ones) presents in our lives. This *enlarged thought*, as Arendt called it, is significant for two main reasons. It expands the possibilities for co-existence *with* children by generating new insights, realities and relations; while it simultaneously creates a kind of resourcefulness from which new and previously unthought-of responses to the world's challenges are made possible (Arendt, [1954] 1994).

The educator as a challenger

In his discussion about how educational encounters may constitute a public space, in the Arendtian sense of the word, Biesta (2012) argues against a traditional view of the teacher as an instructor or a facilitator. Similar to Greene's proposition of the teacher as a challenger, Biesta (ibid.: 693) argues for a view of the pedagogue as 'someone who *interrupts*'. Not unlike the actions that Karen initiated with the love and death pedagogical narration, the pedagogue interrupts by introducing an element or an event that opens for the community dimensions of our common world that were previously invisible or silenced. By doing so, the pedagogue creates an educational space that is permeated with stories that propel movement towards new relations with life and with the world.

Pedagogical narration as interruption requires early childhood educators to position themselves politically in relation to the world by thinking of pedagogical documentation as a venue to inquire into life's difficulties, tensions and ambiguities and by making these difficulties, tensions and ambiguities public and open for disputation. The power of the narratives lies in the conversations that they initiate and in their potential to cultivate care for a common/public concern, as well as for creating occasions for experiencing the commonality of our existential struggle.

Conclusion

In this chapter, I imbued the practice of pedagogical documentation with ECE leadership that is concerned with expanding possibilities for imagining new identities for early childhood education and its protagonists. I argued that the potential of pedagogical documentation for leadership enactment is inextricably linked with what Arendt ([1958] 1998) termed *'the faculty of interrupting'*. I also demonstrated the power of narratives about unexpected events to ignite dialogue and thinking that breaks away from the status quo, thus bringing new dimensions of the realm of early childhood education into the world.

This view of leadership calls into being a new image for the early childhood educator: one who challenges her or his community with pedagogic narratives that inquire into life's difficulties, tensions and ambiguities and who asks her or himself: How can I share stories from practice that open up the world for others as a place for new beginnings?

References

Arendt, H. ([1954] 1994) 'Understanding and politics (The difficulties of understanding)', in J. Kohn (ed.), *Hannah Arendt Essays in Understanding, 1930–1954: Formations, Exile, and Totalitarianism*. New York: Schocken Books, pp. 307–327.

Arendt, H. ([1958] 1998) *The Human Condition* (2nd edn). Chicago, IL: University of Chicago Press.

Berger, I. (2013) 'Narration-as-action: The potential of pedagogical narration for leadership enactment in early childhood education contexts'. PhD dissertation, University of British Columbia, Vancouver.

Biesta, G.J.J. (2012) 'Becoming public: Public pedagogy, citizenship and the public sphere', *Social and Cultural Geography*, 13 (7): 683–697.

Critchley, S. (2009) 'Being and time part 6: Death', 13 July. www.theguardian.com/commentisfree/belief/2009/jul/13/heidegger-being-time (accessed 15.06.16).

Dahlberg, G. and Moss, P. (2008) 'Beyond quality in early childhood education and care: Languages of evaluation', *New Zealand Journal of Teachers' Work*, 5 (1): 3–12.

Dahlberg, G., Moss, P. and Pence, A. (2007) *Beyond Quality in Early Childhood Education and Care: Languages of Evaluation* (2nd edn). Abingdon: Routledge.

Davies, B. (2011) 'Open listening: Creative evolution in early childhood settings', *International Journal of Early Childhood*, 43 (2): 119–132.

Disch, L.J. (1994) *Hannah Arendt and the Limits of Philosophy*. Ithaca, NY: Cornell University Press.

Duhn, I. (2008) 'Globalising childhood: Assembling the bicultural child in the New Zealand early childhood curriculum, Te Whāriki', *International Critical Childhood Policy Studies Journal*, 1 (1): 82–105.

Fasoli, L., Scrivens, C. and Woodrow, C. (2007) 'Challenges for leadership in Aotearoa/New Zealand and Australia: Early childhood contexts', in L. Keesing-Styles and H. Hedges (eds), *Theorising Early Childhood Practice: Emerging Dialogues*. Sydney: Pademelon Press, pp. 231–249.

Filippini, T. (2001) 'On the nature of organization', in C. Giudici, C. Rinaldi and M. Krechevsky (eds), *Making Learning Visible: Children as Individual and Group Learners*. Reggio Emilia, Italy: Reggio Children, pp. 52–57.

Gambetti, Z. (2005) 'The agent is the void! From the subjected subject to the subject of action', *Rethinking Marxism*, 17 (3): 425–436.

Giugni, M. (2011) '"Becoming worldly with": An encounter with the Early Years Learning Framework', *Contemporary Issues in Early Childhood*, 12 (1): 11–27.

Greene, M. (2001) 'Foreword', in M. Gordon (ed.), *Hannah Arendt and Education*. Boulder, CO: Westview Press, pp. ix–x.

Grieshaber, S. (2001) 'Advocacy and early childhood educators: Identity and cultural conflicts', in S. Grieshaber and G.S. Cannella (eds), *Embracing Identities in Early Childhood Education*. New York: Teachers College Press, pp. 60–72.

Hard, L. (2004) 'How is leadership understood in early childhood education and care?' *Journal of Australian Research in Early Childhood Education*, 10: 123–131.

Langford, R. (2010) 'Critiquing child-centred pedagogy to bring children and early childhood educators into the centre of a democratic pedagogy', *Contemporary Issues in Early Childhood*, 11 (1): 113–127.

Magrini, J. (2012) 'An ontological notion of learning inspired by the philosophy of Hannah Arendt', *Philosophy Scholarship*, Paper 34. http://dc.cod.edu/philosophypub/34 (accessed 15.06.16).

Oberhuemer, P. (2005) 'International perspectives on early childhood curricula', *International Journal of Early Childhood*, 37 (1): 27–37.

Pacini-Ketchabaw, V., Nxumalo, F., Kocher, L., Elliot, E. and Sanchez, A. (2015) *Journeys: Reconceptualizing Early Childhood Practices through Pedagogical Narration*. Toronto: University of Toronto Press.

Phelan, A. (2010) '"Bound by recognition": Some thoughts on professional designation for teachers', *Asia-Pacific Journal of Teacher Education*, 38 (4): 317–329.

Rinaldi, C. (2001) 'Documentation and assessment: What is the relationship?', in C. Guidici, C. Rinaldi and M. Krechevsky (eds), *Making Learning Visible: Children as Individual and Group Learners*. Reggio Emilia, Italy: Reggio Children, pp. 78–89.

Rodd, J. (1997) 'Learning to be leaders: Perceptions of early childhood professionals about leadership roles and responsibilities', *Early Years*, 18 (1): 40–44.

Scrivens, C. (2002) 'Constructions of leadership: Does gender make a difference? – perspectives from an English speaking country', in V. Nivala and E. Hujala (eds), *Leadership in Early Childhood Education, Cross-Cultural Perspectives*. Oulu, Finland: Department of Educational Sciences and Teacher Education, University of Oulu, pp. 25–32.

Urban, M. (2012) 'Researching early childhood policy and practice: A critical ecology', *European Journal of Education*, 47 (4): 494–507.

Woodrow, C. (2008) 'Discourses of professional identity in early childhood: Movements in Australia', *European Early Childhood Education Research Journal*, 16 (2): 269–280.

Woodrow, C. and Busch, G. (2008) 'Repositioning early childhood leadership as action and activism', *European Early Childhood Education Research Journal*, 16 (1): 83–93.

13

WEAVINGS, WALKS AND WONDERINGS: STORIES OF THE LIVELINESS OF PEDAGOGICAL NARRATIONS

B. DENISE HODGINS, DEBORAH THOMPSON AND KATHLEEN KUMMEN

Moving beyond retelling stories and informed by postfoundational perspectives, these Canadian authors challenge normative practice. Valuing dialogic and multi-vocal approaches, three different contexts across sites and age groups invite consideration. Traces, entanglements and video all contribute to the 'liveliness' of the unfolding narrations, telling more than is 'known'.

Introduction

This chapter explores the *liveliness* of pedagogical narrations, a documentation practice. We begin by contextualizing our work, including how we understand and engage with the process and how postfoundationalism shapes our engagement. We follow this with three stories focusing on the dialogical. Denise shares moments from a textile inquiry with young children and educators. Deborah's story follows a workplace professional development process involving early childhood educators. Kathleen provides an exploration of pedagogical narrations in the post-secondary classroom. We conclude with considerations about how we work to *create the conditions* for this kind of practice.

Placing our stories

We work in different capacities in early childhood care and education (ECCE) within British Columbia, Canada: Denise as a research associate in an action research project, Deborah as a programme manager in a large child-care service, and Kathleen as a university instructor in an ECCE department. While the focus of our work varies, we each engage with pedagogical narrations, a research methodology inspired by pedagogical documentation.

In 2008, the provincial government of British Columbia released the *Early Learning Framework* (Government of British Columbia, 2008a) and its companion guide (ibid., 2008b), to support adults in facilitating children's early learning and development. *From Theory to Practice* presents pedagogical narration as a specific tool 'to engage in critical reflection through observation' (ibid., 2008b: 13). It is described as a cyclical process that involves observing and documenting moments of practice; interpreting documentation individually and collectively to make learning visible; deepening the interpretation through sharing and making public the description; linking the narration to pedagogical practice; and evaluating, planning and starting the process again (ibid.: 14). The word *narration* highlights the dialogical aspect of this tool.

We conceptualize pedagogical narrations as a methodology for research (e.g. with children, with educators and caregivers, with student teachers). We use the plural, *pedagogical narrations*, with intent to underscore the ongoing and multiple nature of the process. As a methodology, pedagogical narrations present a distinct rationale for the methods put to work (e.g. capturing images through video or photography, constructing problems through creative arts and play, observing and note taking, dialoguing in groups and with individuals). In other words, we understand pedagogical narrations as a method *philosophy* rather than a step-by-step action plan (see Hodgins, 2012, 2014).

The postfoundational perspective that we take within our work shapes our conceptualization. We wish to challenge a dogmatic, rote application of pedagogical narrations aimed at retelling ECCE practices 'as they are'. We are concerned that the practice of pedagogical narrations is often interpreted as producing a single presentation of one person's or one team's interpretation of ECCE moments. One presentation misses the dialogical and multi-vocality underpinnings of pedagogical narrations and buoys the modernist recognizing and representative aspects of documentation, where 'what really took place' is discoverable (Olsson, 2009).

Presentations as single stories work to fix a record of a past event, closing it down to the truths of that event, rather than opening multiplicities. We argue that ECCE is itself lively, steeped in multiplicity and relationality, and that pedagogical narration is a lively methodology for co-constructing ECCE curriculum and pedagogy in a relational, learning collective. We present our argument through sharing three stories, one from each of our practices. We contend that sharing (making public) stories of complexities in practices generates new knowledges for actualizing new material realities.

Denise: Warps, wefts and weavings

My story is about the process of pedagogical narrations within a textiles inquiry with preschool-aged children and their educators that took place over the course of one academic year. I participated in the project as a pedagogical facilitator and researcher with two other colleagues, wherein we followed the children and educators' interests in fabrics, costuming and performance. We started with curiosity about textiles but an unknowing of how exactly the project would unfold and whether it would generate sustained interest, collaboration and knowledge. To our collective delight, the inquiry ended up being a lively, engaging and complex eight-month project that continues to linger with/in the centre's practices.

There are numerous stories from/in/about this project, some of which have already been shared in varying ways. By re-visiting my memories of the project and some documentation generated during the inquiry, I have produced new stories which I share here. They are entangled stories of dialogue – with people, ideas and materials – that attend to the mattering of practice. While they are overly simplified (condensed) for the scope of this chapter, they are intended to illuminate the practice and production of pedagogical narrations as a *lively knowing-doing*.

Tangible traces of our collaborative inquiry took many forms, and were visible during our project in several different ways. The educators mounted photographs of inquiry-moments on walls and tables where the project was taking place, an atrium space joining the entryways of three childcare classrooms. These were adapted throughout the project. We also displayed in the atrium creations from the morning's work and materials to be re-used next time. At one point, an educator placed single printed-out words (e.g. entanglements, knots, connection) beside photographs and textiles/creations. A few weeks later, I added quotes that spoke (to me) to the carefully chosen and evocative words. Video clips of project moments were also displayed during inquiry mornings, at our educator professional development evening seminars, and in team meetings with participating educators and researchers. The materials that we chose to bring in (e.g. fabrics, natural dyes, twig-deer, a textile book, printed words, articles to read) and the artefacts generated through the inquiry (i.e. photographs, video, children's and educators' creations) were displayed for purposes of *engaging with*; they acted as provocations for dialogue. The process and products of pedagogical narrations, importantly our numerous and varied dialogues, *mattered* our collective inquiry.

Traces of inquiry work

When we began, the educators and pedagogical facilitators sensed that two lines of inquiry were happening with the children, one that we described as big and moving (loud), where children collectively made long lines that they stretched, pulled, ran beside, climbed over/under and tied around things. The other we recognized as small, close, concentrated and more individual (quiet), where needles were threaded, and fabric carefully sewn, cut and knotted. We discussed and worked towards facilitating both 'kinds' of experimentation. Returning to video documentation illuminated that what we (the adults) seemed to experience as separate lines actually crossed over numerous times during our inquiry mornings. With this, we began paying attention to exchanges between these 'two lines', the relationship between big and small, loud and quiet, fast and slow, collective and individual.

Noticing that the materials called to the children and educators differently, some experiencing what could be labelled a process-oriented exploration, while others experienced an exploration for purposes of producing *something*, added a knot to the fabric of our inquiry. Through our discussions with the educators and children, in dialogue with the many material provocations, it became increasingly evident that it really mattered how much *what* was being produced, as well as the process of its production. We (the adults) then worked (harder) to attend to children's requests to create particular things, to dye fabrics with particular colours, to drape textiles in particular ways, not simply for the process of the experience but because the actual material product was important. This noticing led to our reading and discussing Ingold's work (2011) to help us to think more (differently) about the product/process binary and re-consider our understandings of skill, making (process) and objects (products).

Thinking with the project provocations generated questions about our pedagogical and curricular actions in terms of everyday choices that we make, but also in terms of the ethics and politics of what we do. We began to wonder where the materials that we were using actually came from. How were they produced? What waste was generated in their production and eventual disposal? How 'natural' were these used fabrics that we were re-purposing? How is it that we had so much stuff that we could re-purpose in the first place? These wonderings led to researching and reading about cotton growth and production, as well as textile manufacturing waste generation, which led to further discussions about the tensions we were experiencing *using* materials in this project for/with children. We also explored traditional understandings and practices related to textiles, including processes for natural dying and felting. Researching and celebrating histories of traditionally feminine, undervalued 'crafts' (i.e. weaving, sewing, dying), existed alongside tensions that I felt about possibly promoting consumerism, beauty and fashion.

These ethico-political questions were generated through our collective dialogue with the materials, histories, experiences and affects that we (both educators and children) brought to the project and the artefacts generated through our inquiry. Our challenging questions, as well as our deep interest and excitement in the project, were interwoven with the children's desires, curiosities and conflicts. The textile project was not singularly or only about children's interests, knowledge or development. Pedagogical narrations illuminated the *inseparability of the materials, children and educators' engagement*, and the always-present ethico-political questions about how we respond and live in/with this world.

Deborah: Walking new paths

Here, I tell a story about some early childhood caregivers' engagement in/with a professional development process. The process involved researching, through pedagogical narrations, an organizational question: 'How do we [the organization] conceptualize care?' The process found us struggling with the how, the what and the why, of pedagogical narrations

(PN) methodology, while we grappled with our question. Like my other PN experiences, lines of flight (Deleuze and Guattari, 1987) erupted as we proceeded, producing a jumble of conceptual paths to follow. The tidy, organized, even linear process I imagined and planned became a messy, fragmented, tangled multiplicity.

The story takes place at the large childcare service where I work as a manager. The organization includes 25 centres, employs more than 120 early childhood educators/caregivers. Like many other childcare centres, to cover child–adult ratios, the centres' early childhood caregivers work shifts. This staffing structure means that caregivers rarely have opportunities to meet and reflect with each other on their work, including their pedagogical understandings and the complexities of theory–practice intra-activity (Lenz Taguchi, 2010). My role includes supporting the centres' programme development and offering professional development with our caregivers. Our question emerged from my interest but also from various group discussions about purpose, vision and pedagogy. To engage with this question, which linked to our named identity – Child *Care* Services – I decided to introduce pedagogical narrations as our inquiry methodology.

We began with reading about 'care' and collecting artefacts of ordinary moments to revisit. Groups of educators from different centres met for an hour at a time. While we tried to have the same people together each time, our large staff combined with our limited availability (five hours per month for several months) created a complicated structure. As we progressed, we revisited and reviewed the same artefact in each different group.

In one session, we considered an artefact that included photographs of, and a caregiver's reflections about, a walk she and a group of toddlers took. A child who had been given a choice between a few destinations opted for a distant coffee shop (and hot chocolate) as the most desirable plan. The caregiver, Sharon, agreed and they invited three more children to walk with them. Between the centre and the coffee shop lay a meadow, a playground and a housing complex with a community centre. Along the way, the group encountered and engaged with mud puddles, some construction and the playground. Sharon also changed a dirty diaper and another child's soiled underwear in the community centre's bathroom. Flexibility and spontaneity characterized the walk. Sharon's reflections revealed her uncertainty as well as the intuitions guiding her decisions as the group's leader. In her emerging artefact/becoming/PN, she described her unfolding inferences about the capacities, feelings and desires of each child and how those inferences influenced her actions. Eventually, she decided that emerging demands of hunger and fatigue meant that some children wouldn't be able to make the journey as planned. She carefully renegotiated with the original child a closer coffee shop as the end destination. A child, as they encountered resistance at the coffee shop, remarked, 'Sharon, you're a little bit cranky' (with the cafe worker). Finally, the children had hot chocolate and one small, quiet, previously seeming-timid child concluded, 'This is awesome!'

In our meetings, we reviewed this ordinary moment (Forman et al., 2001), sometimes with Sharon present, sometimes without her. As a group, we tended to respond to the described moment with a positive evaluation of Sharon's practice. Everyone had been on similar walks with children in the same role as Sharon and perceived potential challenges in her description. Most evaluated her as being very calm and able to allow children both 'space' to explore and 'control' of the experience. Her understated bathroom-event description led to positive assessments of her practice and to wonderings about how we would have responded in the same situation. Through the pedagogical narrations process, we explored concepts of freedom, respect and child competence. We read about and considered the idea of emotional labour (Osgood, 2010). However, we did not dig deeper into our understandings of this concept about what guided our practice. We did not critique our underlying assumptions about care and caring practices.

Our experience demonstrates the difficulty of moving beyond describing and evaluating a past event towards an openness to the liveliness of the event. Our process produced professional development through our reflections. We expanded our capacity to describe and evaluate. Many saw a different way to do a familiar practice (going for a walk). However, we only slightly dipped into ethico-political critical analysis of care, caring, our purpose, or how care/caring connect to early childhood pedagogical practices. We (positively) evaluated one caregiver's practice and began to interrogate our own practices. We did not trouble or interrogate care/caring truths. We created ground to do so, but our overall structure constrained our ability to grapple with the philosophical, political and ethical values and beliefs contained within our question.

The experience, however, produced a crack. As I became aware of what might be described as a failure (we did not answer our question), I also became aware of a different path. Rather than fretting about an inconclusive (and maybe dead) end, I repositioned our experience as a new lively beginning, as a multiplicity. We continue to work together with pedagogical narrations, but I revised our process. We are focusing more on the processes of pedagogical narrations, letting the questions (cracks) that erupt become the paths we follow. Echoing the walk story, we have slowed down and are attending to the new. Our challenges with/in *doing* pedagogical narrations cracked open a new path for us to explore. Together, we are reading *Journeys* (Pacini-Ketchabaw et al., 2015), meeting for discussions while bringing artefacts to our meetings to revisit. We have no end in mind, but will instead follow this path.

Kathleen: What are little children made of? White bodies, sunshine and all things fine ...

My incomplete and partial story shares processes that emerged as a group of first-year undergraduate students in early childhood care and education and I engaged *with*, and *in*, the pedagogical practices of pedagogical narrations as we attempted to make visible and disrupt the hegemonic images of childhood that we held. I began by inviting students to bring in artefacts in the form of visual images capturing their understandings of childhood. Each student showed her image to others in small groups without any explanation or background information. The other students wrote down their thoughts, questions and assumptions, focusing on what understanding of childhood was portrayed by the image, what the image's origins were, and how the concepts of natural or normal childhood were understood (MacNaughton, 2005a). We repeated this process until all students had shared their images with the small group. The forum then opened up to allow the group to engage in dialogues that contested existing understandings and knowledges.

Public sharing of images, ideas and questions is critical to this story about a process of embodied experiences of disruption filled with moments of collective tensions and surprises. My field notes hold images of students sorting images on the basis of similarities and then discovering that one image was left standing, isolated from the other images by a difference. Observing students as they sorted images into various categories provoked me to create a collage of images to bring to the next class. My intention was to begin the class by revisiting the images; therefore, for reasons of efficiency, I decided to put all images of human children (both photos and drawings) into one collage and all nonhuman images into another. I was somewhat disturbed by the collage, and yet could not articulate the source of the disturbance. As I looked at the collage, in my mind I could see the view from the front of our classroom. From that position, I looked out at a classroom filled with 20 students who self-identified as students of colour and 12 who self-identified as white. As I juxtaposed the image of our class in my mind with images in the collage, the overwhelming 'whiteness' in the collage of children became evident. As I closely examined each photo, there were children who appeared to be non-white, yet an overwhelming 'whiteness' was visible. There were 23 images of children, and I could only discern three children who, from my perspective, were children of colour.

As an apparatus of meaning-making (Barad, 2007), pedagogical narrations became entangled with/in me, the students and producing a collage – an artefact. This artefact itself then had an effect: its presence unexpectedly invited a conversation about race where, without its presence, race had been silenced. In response to this disruption, I reassigned the readings for the next few weeks and asked students to read a chapter by Glenda MacNaughton and look at her notion of seeking 'the otherwise'. I was curious as to how students would respond when they revisited the images after they had thought about MacNaughton's question, 'What is your relation with whiteness' (2005b: 187). Would we/ they invite race and colour into the discussion? Would the whiteness of the images call out to them?

My field notes reflect my wandering around between groups as they shared their responses to the collage. The text and images were pushing us to attempt to rework race in our classroom; we resisted by pushing back with our use of/being with race. Our words re-enacted the text that we had read in MacNaughton, about a child (non-white) and a doll (white). Students wondered if there were reasons other than race for the non-white child to choose that particular white doll. I moved through groups, listening and joining in their conversations. In each group, I asked them to look at the collage and consider whether this was the only image of children in our classroom. What message would the poster relay to people entering our classroom? What would the collage tell people about our relationship with whiteness?

As I later revisited the students' narratives as artefacts that were part of the practice of pedagogical narrations, I could feel the disturbance of the collage as it reverberated in our thinking, feelings and being. Sitting on colonized land (the university sits on the traditional unceded lands of the Tsleil-Waututh and Squamish Nations), with students whose ancestors were the colonized and the colonizer, with students whose families had been subjected to head taxes and internment camps within our province, the artefacts created turmoil in our thinking. Group F confessed to a past omission of race as they wrote: 'As we look back at the majority of our images we now understand that there are specific equity issues. With the majority of images being Caucasian, white, middle-class children, is this what we believe is our "perfect childhood"?' Following the collage and the reading, the recorder for Group B shared the following childhood memory:

> When I was younger I did not understand why people like to group different racial groups by colours. Until that one time in elementary school, I was practicing my writing on the chalkboard during break, a girl classmate came up to me and said, 'You don't know how to write in English, you don't belong here, go back to China!' I was really upset about her comment but I didn't know why. At that very moment I wanted to be like her, a white Canadian. Now looking back at that situation my story is very similar to Kim's story. I wanted to change myself to fit in, and no child should want to change itself to fit in. (Yi-Min, Group B, 2011)

These texts and the other narratives then joined the collage as artefacts to revisit, coming out at other times in the term in ways that haunted us and challenged us to re-image our notions of race. Race continued to be present in our classroom through the new images and new narratives that entered, and through students' re-remembering of childhood experiences that spoke of new understandings and meanings. Understandings of childhood moved beyond issues of play, laughter and innocence to include issues of race, colonization and white privilege.

Postfoundational possibilities

We have situated our understanding of pedagogical narrations within a postfoundational lens and shared three stories evoking complexities – multiplicity, relationality, liveliness – of early childhood education practices. Postfoundationalism is an umbrella term for theoretical positions that: (a) trouble modernist assumptions such as truth, generalizability and essentialisms; and (b) interrogate their effects (see Lather, 2013; St. Pierre, 2013). Postfoundational theories challenge modernist understandings of subjectivity and action as fixed, knowable and 'unfettered by values, beliefs, politics, and power' (Pacini-Ketchabaw et al., 2015: 206). Recognizing our *knowing* and *being* in/of the world as always already heterogeneous, fluid, unfinished and ethico-political, significantly shapes our pedagogical and research practices, including our understanding of and approach to engaging with pedagogical narrations (see Hodgins, 2014; Kummen, 2014; Thompson, 2015). We conceptualize material documents (e.g. photographs, video, narratives, artwork) as traces of ECCE practice that dialogically aim for multiplicity and multivocality, rather than consensus and single truths. We wonder: Who gets to observe? Who and what is documented? Which documents are shared and with whom? Whose interpretations are documented and shared? Which actions are taken, for whom and what?

Our postfoundational conceptualization builds upon theorizing and practices of pedagogical documentation in the preschools of Reggio Emilia (see Dahlberg and Moss, 2005; Rinaldi, 2006; Dahlberg et al., 2007), and its take-up by educators and researchers outside of Reggio Emilia (see Olsson, 2009; Lenz Taguchi, 2010), including pedagogical narrations in British Columbia (see Pacini-Ketchabaw et al., 2015). Dahlberg and colleagues (2007: 60) suggested that the pedagogical work in Reggio Emilia has 'anticipate[d] various themes of postmodernity'. Lenz Taguchi's (2010: 67) description of pedagogical documentation as '*alive* and from which we can produce a multiplicity of differentiated knowledge from a specific event' and 'as a movement or force in itself – a verb – and which can only be identified by what it produces' deeply informs our work with pedagogical narrations. Stengers' (2005: 186) conceptualization of an 'ecology of practice' suggests that practices ought not be described 'as they are' but rather 'as they may become'. We propose that pedagogical narrations as a methodology is a relevant tool for such a task in ECCE, challenging the power of unopposed habits and decisions. 'The relevant tools, tools for thinking, are then the ones that address and actualize this power of the situation, that make it a matter of particular concern, in other words, make us think and not recognize' (ibid.: 185).

As a pedagogical practice that British Columbia's government promotes to early childhood educators through the *Early Learning Framework* (Government of British Columbia, 2008a, 2008b), challenging the take-up of pedagogical narrations as a dogmatic, static, truth-telling device (see also Elliot, 2010; Hodgins, 2014; Kummen, 2014; Thompson, 2015) becomes critical for ECCE research and pedagogical practices. We offer stories from our practices not as a road map for 'doing' pedagogical narrations but as provocation for (re)thinking pedagogical narrations as a lively, relational, *knowing-doing* methodology. In our stories, the processes and products of pedagogical narrations materialize particular realities, possibly making visible habitual practices and beliefs, and disrupting held (dominant) understandings. While the stories that we share highlight varying ways that liveliness manifests in our work, commonalities may be productive for considering how we *create the conditions* for this kind of pedagogical practice.

Each story describes reading beyond our discipline. Thinking with philosophies, theories, research and practices from outside ECCE brings new questions, possibilities, understandings and actions to our pedagogical and curricular choices. All three stories contain dialogue and storytelling among a group, highlighting Rinaldi's (2006: 184) conceptualization 'of dialogue not as an exchange but as a process of transformation where you lose absolutely the possibility of controlling the final result'. Each also points to the critical importance of time: to build relationships, to dialogue together, to read, to process, to (collectively) critically reflect and to act. The materialized realities in the shared stories that emerged through/ with pedagogical narrations are not free of tensions, questions and the ongoing challenges in our ECCE pedagogical and curricular beliefs, assumptions and actions. Each story shows pedagogical narrations as a methodology enmeshed in complexities of emerging relationalities; none points us towards a straightforward pedagogical practice.

There are dangers within the methodology of pedagogical narrations and the sharing of stories of practices (for more, see Hodgins, 2014; Kummen, 2014; Thompson, 2015). There is a danger that certain described practices (e.g. which materials to bring to an ECCE place, which ways of engaging with children on a walk, or which images to include in a collage about *the image of the child*) will get adopted as dogmatic practice recipes. The danger lies in the take-up: that a project with textiles engaging with materials becomes good ECCE practice, that child-choice and caregiver flexibility become the markers of a good ECCE worker, that representing racial diversity on a poster becomes a good ECCE student production. We believe that enacting ECCE as emerging and relational makes actualizing recipes for practice impossible. We position pedagogical narrations as a lively methodology enacted with/for/in practices of complexities.

Conclusion

The stories we tell in pedagogical narrations always contain more than we intend/know on our first telling. Readers and listeners always bring something different to the story. Revisiting through storytelling produces a new story, like the new story we have produced here. Multiplicity and multivocality in dialogical processes hold potential for different ethics and different politics (Dahlberg and Moss, 2005). King (2003: 164) puts forward both a caution about stories and a claim about their great potential. He writes, 'After all, we've created them. We've created the stories that allow them to exist and flourish. They didn't come out of nowhere. They didn't arrive from another planet. Want a different ethic? Tell a different story.' He also reminds us that, 'it doesn't take a disaster to destroy a literature. If we stopped telling the stories and reading the books, we would discover that neglect is as powerful an agent as war and fire' (2003: 98). We suggest that pedagogical narrations as dogmatic and prescriptive neglect the potential living within the methodology, the potential to tell another story, to tell a story differently, or to hear a familiar story in a new way, and risks losing the literature. We contend that the methodology of pedagogical narrations creates openings to other (more) ethics-politics in early childhood care and education.

References

Barad, K. (2007) *Meeting the Universe Halfway: Quantum Physics and the Entanglement of Matter and Meaning*. Durham, NC: Duke University Press.

Dahlberg, G. and Moss, P. (2005) *Ethics and Politics in Early Childhood Education*. London: RoutledgeFalmer.

Dahlberg, G., Moss, P. and Pence, A. (2007) *Beyond Quality in Early Childhood Education and Care: Languages of Evaluation* (2nd edn). Abingdon: Routledge.

Deleuze, G. and Guattari, F. (1987) *A Thousand Plateaus: Capitalism and Schizophrenia* (tr. B. Massumi). Minneapolis, MN: University of Minnesota Press.

Elliot, E. (2010) 'Thinking beyond a framework: Entering into dialogues', in V. Pacini-Ketchabaw (ed.), *Flows, Rhythms and Intensities of Early Childhood Education Curriculum*. New York: Peter Lang Publishing, pp. 3–20.

Forman, G., Hall, E. and Berglund, K. (2001) 'The power of ordinary moments', *Child Care Information Exchange*, September: 52–55

Government of British Columbia (2008a) *Early Learning Framework*. Victoria, Canada: Crown Publications, Queen's Printer for British Columbia.

Government of British Columbia (2008b) *Understanding the British Columbia Early Learning Framework: From Theory to Practice*. Victoria, Canada: Crown Publications, Queen's Printer for British Columbia.

Hodgins, B.D. (2012) 'Pedagogical narrations' potentiality as a methodology for child studies research', *Canadian Children*, 37 (1): 4–11.

Hodgins, B.D. (2014) '(Re)Storying dolls and cars: Gender and care with young children'. PhD dissertation, University of Victoria: British Columbia. Retrieved from UVicSpace: http://hdl.handle.net/1828/5740 (accessed 25.01.17).

Ingold, T. (2011) *The Perception of the Environment: Essays on Livelihood, Dwelling and Skill*. London: Routledge.

King, T. (2003) *The Truth and Stories: A Native Narrative*. Toronto: House of Anansi Press.

Kummen, K. (2014) 'Making space for disruption in the education of early childhood educators'. PhD dissertation, University of Victoria: British Columbia. Retrieved from UVicSpace: http://hdl.handle.net/1828/5632 (accessed 25.01.17).

Lather, P. (2013) 'Methodology-21: What do we do in the afterward?', *International Journal of Qualitative Studies in Education*, 26 (6): 634–645.

Lenz Taguchi, H. (2010) *Going Beyond the Theory/Practice Divide in Early Childhood Education: Introducing an Intra-Active Pedagogy*. London and New York: Routledge.

MacNaughton, G. (2005a) *Doing Foucault in Early Childhood Studies: Applying Poststructural Ideas*. London: Routledge.

MacNaughton, G. (2005b) 'Seeking the "Otherwise": Remeeting relations of "race" in early childhood classroom histories', in G. MacNaughton, *Doing Foucault in Early Childhood Studies: Applying Poststructural Ideas*. London: Routledge, pp. 110–140.

Olsson, L.M. (2009) *Movement and Experimentation in Young Children's Learning: Deleuze and Guattari in Early Childhood Education*. London and New York: Routledge.

Osgood, J. (2010) 'Reconstructing professionalism in ECEC: The case for the "critically reflective emotional professional"', *Early Years: An International Research Journal*, 30 (2): 119–133.

Pacini-Ketchabaw, V., Nxumalo, F., Kocher, L., Elliott, E. and Sanchez, A. (2015) *Journeys: Reconceptualizing Early Childhood Practices through Pedagogical Narration*. Toronto: University of Toronto Press.

Rinaldi, C. (2006) *In Dialogue with Reggio Emilia: Listening, Researching and Learning*. London: Routledge.

St. Pierre, E.A. (2013) 'The posts continue: Becoming', *International Journal of Qualitative Studies in Education*, 26 (6): 646–657.

Stengers, I. (2005) 'Introductory notes on an ecology of practices', *Cultural Studies Review*, 11 (1): 183–196.

Thompson, D. (2015) 'Caring, dwelling and becoming: Stories of multiage child care'. PhD dissertation, University of Victoria, British Columbia. Retrieved from UVicSpace: http://hdl.handle.net/1828/5939 (accessed 25.01.17).

Commentary 4: Situating Pedagogical Documentation in a Democratic Context

Andrew Stremmel

South Dakota State University

In his classic book, *Leadership without Easy Answers*, Ron Heifetz (1994) claims that leaders must be risk-takers who can move an organization beyond the conventional and the status quo. He suggests that leaders must have courage to foster the difficult conversations that members of organizations avoid or lack the skills to begin. When reading the three chapters in this section, I was struck by how Heifetz's ideas on leadership resonate with the ideas presented. In Chapters 11 and 12, educational leadership is portrayed differently than it is conventionally understood and practiced. Educational leaders are encouraged to reposition themselves and teachers, and to develop in teachers adaptive capacity, or the ability to address problems of practice according to values and purposes that move beyond conventional thinking about what early childhood education is towards public conversations about what early childhood education might be. This theme is present throughout each chapter. The authors, Walker, Reed and Stobbs (Chapter 11) and Berger (Chapter 12) embrace this idea of leadership, utilizing the methodology of pedagogical documentation (or pedagogical narration, as it is known in British Columbia, Canada), to question practice, think critically about regulatory frameworks and policies, and to make visible ways children think, learn and make meaning of their experiences. The authors of Chapter 13, Hodgins, Thompson and Kumman, challenge typical 'dogmatic' conceptualizations of pedagogical narration to focus on the dialogical and 'multi-vocality' of pedagogical narrations to move educators from forming a single perspective on what is, to creating multiple perspectives on what may be possible.

The key methodology in all three chapters is pedagogical documentation, founded on the pedagogy of listening, the careful paying attention to children's ideas and experiences in order to make visible their learning (Rinaldi, 2006). As both product and process that seeks to represent in words and images the activity and learning of children in groups and as individuals, documentation always yields partial findings, mere traces of experience. More importantly, as these authors illustrate, documentation makes visible not only what teachers and other adults interpret about children, but how they make sense of what is seen and heard as they observe. It allows educators to reflect on how learning is proceeding so that they can base their teaching on what children want to learn, not on what teachers want to teach.

The authors of Chapter 11 rightly point out that the role of early childhood leaders is to move pedagogical documentation forward through questioning, valuing and respecting what children bring to learning, and understanding this as a collective process of the sharing and examination of multiple perspectives, values and understandings. I believe that this last point is absolutely critical to understanding processes of pedagogical documentation. Dewey (1902: 191) cautioned that the child's present experience is in no way fixed or final, but transitional, merely a sign of certain growth tendencies. As long as educators confine their observations to what the child does in the here and now, they will be confused and misled. Pedagogical narration, as described in Chapters 12 and 13, enables educators to understand children and development from many viewpoints to 'produce a multiplicity of differentiated knowledge from a specific event' (Lenz Taguchi, 2010: 67). Thus, as Dewey suggests, what educators observe is children as they are, as they were and as they will be – their simultaneously, waning tendencies, new thinking and interests, and the dawning of capacities that will shine brightly in the future.

Pedagogical documentation does not only make children's experiences and learning processes visible, it makes teachers' perspectives and interpretations explicit and contestable through debate, dialogue and negotiation (Rinaldi, 2006). It is not a search for consensus. As the authors in this section suggest, documentation is a social process in which individual meanings give way to socially constructed ones. Its aim is not to objectively describe or explain what is, but to get close to the child's way of thinking and seeing reality (i.e. what may be). Therefore, the ideas and perspectives of others, including parents, may help educators to see what might not have been seen otherwise.

I find these chapters to be refreshing and affirming of what education can and should be. As practiced largely in the United States, education is an individual commodity, a business competing in a market to sell products of instruction and care. School is a site of technical practice, to be evaluated against its ability to reproduce knowledge and identity and to achieve uniform and consistent criteria. In this frame, teaching is about testing and producing certain outcomes that will allow students to progress to the next rank or position in an assembly line. Alternatively, the educators whose thoughtful work is represented here seem to understand clearly that education is about helping students reach their full human potential and preparing them for democratic participation. Schools and classrooms are first and foremost public spaces for ethical and political practice – places for encounter and relationships, interaction and dialogue among those living together in community. Teaching is about fostering learning and learning capacity, engaging in authentic community-building activities with liveliness, audacity and vision, and exercising human minds and hearts. As a tool for democratic meaning-making, pedagogical documentation is an ethical and subjective means of assessing what children know and understand, in contrast to a process for measuring and judgementally scrutinizing children's work in relation to some standard of acceptability. In essence, pedagogical documentation is important because it repositions teaching as scholarly enterprise and the teacher as someone who questions, challenges, theorizes, researches and generates the knowledge on which classroom practice is based. It moves us from a position of certainty to a position of questioning, wondering and seeking possibilities.

References

Dewey, J. (1902) *The Child and the Curriculum*. Chicago, IL: University of Chicago Press.

Heifetz, R. (1994) *Leadership without Easy Answers*. Cambridge, MA: Harvard University Press.

Lenz Taguchi, H. (2010) *Going Beyond the Theory/Practice Divide in Early Childhood Education: Introducing an Intra-Active Pedagogy.* London and New York: Routledge.

Rinaldi, C. (2006) *In Dialogue with Reggio Emilia: Listening, Researching, and Learning*. London: Routledge.

14

PEDAGOGICAL DOCUMENTATION: WHERE TO FROM HERE?

JANET ROBERTSON, ALMA FLEET AND CATHERINE PATTERSON

Sifting through the narratives that were told and the issues that were raised, this chapter highlights complexities while leaving readers to make their own sense of the provocations being offered.

Introduction

In this book, we have offered perspectives across a range of people invested in pedagogical documentation, from the youngest children being part of their own documenting, to four-year-olds dancing their interpretations, to processes associated with supporting educators in this work. Pedagogical documentation has been positioned as a 'wicked problem' and portrayed as a site of curious, respectful and constantly unfolding decision-making. These decisions have been shown to respect materials as diverse as bamboo reeds, large paper bags and video clips. It is noteworthy that there are as many events shared from outdoors experiences as there are from indoor events, presenting a challenge to educators to assess the extent to which learning potentials outside are as valued as those indoors. Canadian huckleberry bushes acquire poetic significance; approaches to teaching are problematized alongside critiques of assessment. Pedagogical documentation takes on a role of mediator in interactions, of facilitator in professional learning, as provocateur for investigations and as memory-keeper. These components, we suggest, sit naturally within the ambit of pedagogical documentation.

Looking back to move forward

Although visible to the informed other, pedagogical documentation is not solely a product because that is not the purpose of pedagogical documentation (see Fleet in Chapter 1, p. 21). In their discussion of pedagogical documentation, Dahlberg and Moss note:

> the idea is simple – making practice visible or material, thence subject to research, dialogue, reflection and interpretation (meaning-making). But its application, doing documentation, is anything but simple, as are its consequences. For it acknowledges and welcomes subjectivity, diversity of position and multiple perspectives: in short, it values plurality. (Dahlberg and Moss, 2010: xiii)

The characterization of pedagogical documentation as a living process which appears in concrete forms may perhaps best be re-visualized by highlighting aspects of the cockatoo conversations that evolved alongside the work shared by Robertson in Chapter 7.

Transgression: Tales of danger

This story began with the working title: 'Cockatoo Puppets'. This changed as the children's puppetry scripts evolved and it became: 'Transgression: Tales of Danger':

> To gain more data, the decision was made to construct cockatoo puppets, to allow children to 'be cockatoos' in a dramatic sense. At Mia Mia, we use puppetry as its elements of drama: focus, tension, space, time, movement, language, dramatic meaning, character, climax and plot, afford children opportunities to create loose scripts and engage in big ideas. However, the puppet theatre is not the traditional one; it is

a simple frame on which a backdrop is placed. This is intentional, as the theatre's 'space' is open ended, at times one side only is used as in traditional shows, while at others, children stand on opposite sides as the puppets 'talk' to each other. The puppets are a combination of laminated photographs on a stick, supplemented by drawings children added when a new character/plot is required.

As we observed the cockatoo puppet dramas, the transgression theme began to dominate children's plots. The puppets, at first only wrecking the gardens, soon engaged in naughty behaviour, breaking other Mia Mia rules or social norms. New characters were added, including a hapless 'Janet puppet' to whom the cockie puppets behaved badly with guilt-free abandon. We saw children try out and rehearse the rules of our community, showing they know them well in their depiction of transgression. The transgressors were forgiven their mistakes in the dénouement of each plot, with a 'happily-ever-after' ending. As with any dramatic play episode, freed from the constraints of reality, puppeteers were animated, vocal, stepping in and out of character, collaborating and building on each other's scripts.

This example of thoughtful, ongoing 'seeing' of children's problem-solving illustrates pedagogical documentation through collaborative pedagogical conversations around evolving daily encounters. As with the investigation of 'war and peace' in Chapter 1, some readers may not be comfortable with such overt explorations of social justice in early childhood settings. Nevertheless, as has been made clear previously (Fleet et al., 2006, 2012), children have a right to socially just practice. In considering the political contexts in which early childhood education unfolds, Moss noted that:

> legitimate subjects for inclusive political dialogue and contestation, can readily be extended: the *politics of childhood*, about the image of the child, the good life and what we want for our children; the *politics of education*, about what education can and should be; and the *politics of gender*, in the nursery, the home and elsewhere. Pedagogical documentation can provide one means of contesting dominant discourses, through making this one of the tasks of interpreting practice made visible. (2014: 128)

Engaging in transgression requires knowledge of the rules, the norms. In education, these rules and norms are slippery. For teachers to leave behind what is known and comfortable, can at times be transgressive. Lenz Taguchi noted her 'theorising on pedagogical documentation as an "ethics of resistance"' (2010: 96), firmly grounding the discussion at the intersection of ethics and transgression. In this context, subtle shifts in the discourses of power regarding ownership of curriculum and pedagogical decision-making are becoming apparent.

These conceptualizations require pragmatic application, grounded in philosophical strength. Knowing what a site, setting or school values is foundational. And then? There is often the need for 'the pause' – stepping back from over-hasty record-keeping in order to ask: 'What am I seeing here? Why does it matter? If it doesn't matter, why am I /are we taking the time and energy to record it?' There are multitudes of moments in each child's day. Deciding what to 'save' and/or think more about requires some criteria of selectivity – perhaps noting the importance of the encounter for a particular child or groups of children, the richness of delight emerging from an unexpected source, or, indeed, an aspect of socially just practice which is hovering on the edge of an event of exclusion, bias or other form of power-play evidenced in children's spaces. Having noted an interaction/relationship/puzzlement, perhaps on a small notepad or Post-it note, then there is the commitment to find the (perhaps) ten minutes to stop, look and listen to the messages underlying the observations. Are there patterns of behaviour? Dispositions being demonstrated? Curiosities to be nurtured? Possibilities as diverse as tracking developing friendships or explosions from a 'Big Idea' can invite stepping back, discussing with others, recording an analytical reflection, and then action. Each of these pieces is a component of the professional decision-making foregrounded throughout the previous chapters.

While the explorations in this book have been threaded across more than half a dozen countries, that geopolitical spread is a microcosm of Planet Earth. There is therefore no claim of coverage or universal applicability. The **LiLi** schema has been offered to support the *local interpretation of larger ideas*, an acknowledgment that there are key elements to these processes, but that they are heavily contextualized. In addition, writing from multiple geographies and broad perspectives, the commentators have offered both analysis and thoughtful provocation to scaffold unfolding dialogues. Rather than seeing early childhood education as 'a search for the one right answer … the application of a universal best practice or a definition of good quality', Dahlberg and Moss explain that early childhood education should be seen 'as a continuous process involving border crossings, the introduction of new perspectives and the creation of new understandings' (2010: xiii).

To move our thinking forward, we suggest the continuation of a questioning orientation to accountability requirements, of approaches that seek authenticity in climates of constraint. The chapter authors have illuminated the power of diverse points of entry to the processes of working pedagogically, but always recognize the centrality of children's voices, perspectives and everyday experiences. Rather than being strangled by routines, the processes of pedagogical documentation enable educators to be strengthened by their relationships with the quotidian.

It is perhaps here that we can frame pedagogical documentation as a transgression, an engagement with the 'wicked problem', pedagogy stepping away from *teacher as technician*. As Malaguzzi noted, the antithesis of pedagogical documentation is the role of teachers as melancholy implementers of a syllabus removed from relevance, children's learning styles and ideas (Giamminuti, personal communication, 2015). This desire to shift teaching and learning from 'outcomes' and narrow realms of facts is not new.

In 1899, a young woman named Alberta Hammer was graduating from the teachers' college of her day, a 'Normal Training Institute' in Butte, Montana. As this achievement was recognized with pride, the local paper, the *Anaconda Standard*, published on 17 May presentations by graduates. In her address, Miss Hammer spoke passionately, including the following:

> Many old theories of education are being mercilessly discussed and many new theories claim the places of the old. The classical scholar still claims for the ancient languages the greatest educational power. The advocate of modern languages says life is too short to study dead things; that modern languages furnish enough discipline, and are, besides, useful. To the scientist, science is God of all, even of education. To him, no man is properly educated unless his mind is stored with scientific ideas and trained by the scientific methods of the 19th century. Languages, ancient and modern, mathematics, science and philosophy all advance their claims to be the best educators of the coming man.

On hearing this strong young voice, we recognize that the politics of gender have moved on. This educator was only able to take up her new appointment for a few months because, with her imminent marriage, she was required to withdraw from the teaching career for which she had prepared. The argument she raises, however, was echoed almost a century later in the words of Loris Malaguzzi (1993: vi), advocating from Reggio Emilia, Italy, for the voices and rights of children:

> The child has a hundred languages
> (and a hundred hundred hundred more)
> But they steal ninety-nine.
> The school and the culture
> Separate the head from the body.

> They tell the child:
> To think without hands
> To do without head
> To listen and not to speak …

Many of the topics being raised, explored, challenged here, will provoke discussion and perhaps controversy. Perhaps, while looking forward, it is also helpful to listen to these voices from the past, which resonate as strongly now as they did then.

The challenges inherent in these ideas are reflected by Pascal and Bertram, who call for a 'praxeological' world view to progress the aim of 'social and practice transformation' (a meld of reflection, action, ethics and power). They note that:

> Progress in listening better to children's voices and achieving more democratic practice continues … However, the deeper changes in values and attitudes required to realize this commitment for all children in all early childhood settings are much harder to make a reality … Many children are not listened to … (2014: 271)

To hear children's ideas, to build and consider them as the heart of the curriculum in early childhood, requires courage. Children have complicated ideas; they deserve teachers who can cope with complexity.

Conclusion

It would seem that the tension between what is education, learning and knowledge within education sectors and the community, is alive and kicking. Nevertheless, this book brings a wealth of positions from which children, as agents of their own learning, are placed at the centre. Agentic children are shown to be supported by thoughtful, ethical and researching teachers who remain accountable for provision, evaluation and creation of programmes using the device of pedagogical documentation. That is our invitation in this book – an opportunity to look at approaches to documenting learning in educational settings through fresh eyes, to consider ways of thinking and being with children as integral to learning, teaching and assessment – to meet the demands of accountability while expanding visions of what is possible in early education. Hammer questioned in 1899, 'Who is the best educator of the coming man?' To give this a more current and ethical flavour, we can ask: Who is the contemporary child? The contemporary teacher? What is contemporary education? Imagining these questions is an act, but not only of transgression – it is a collaborative, democratic endeavour to find the voice of the child, the voice of the future and to address the 'wicked problem'. The same passion that Miss Hammer expressed is mirrored in the writings and pedagogy of teachers, researchers and students within the chapters of this book.

Perhaps there has always been a need for transgression in the form of sensible, timely advocacy. Pedagogical documentation can have a role in opening eyes, giving voice, challenging mediocrity and offering futures; that potential is here, now.

References

Dahlberg, G. and Moss, P. (2010) 'Introduction by the series editors', in H. Lenz Taguchi, *Going Beyond the Theory/Practice Divide in Early Childhood Education: Introducing an Intra-Active Pedagogy.* London and New York: Routledge, pp. ix–xx.

Fleet, A., Patterson, C. and Robertson, J. (eds) (2006) *Insights: Behind Early Childhood Pedagogical Documentation.* Sydney: Pademelon Press.

Fleet, A., Patterson, C. and Robertson, J. (eds) (2012) *Conversations: Behind Early Childhood Pedagogical Documentation.* Sydney: Pademelon Press.

Lenz Taguchi, H. (2010) *Going Beyond the Theory/Practice Divide in Early Childhood Education: Introducing an Intra-Active Pedagogy.* London and New York: Routledge.

Malaguzzi, L. (1993) 'No way: The hundred is there', in C. Edwards, L. Gandini and G. Forman (eds), *The Hundred Languages of Children: The Reggio Emilia Approach to Early Childhood Education.* Norwood, NJ: Ablex, p. vi.

Moss, P. (2014) *Transformative Change and Real Utopias in Early Childhood Education: A Story of Democracy, Experimentation and Potentiality.* London: Routledge.

Pascal, C. and Bertram, T. (2014) 'Transformative dialogues: The impact of participatory research on practice', in A. Clark, R. Flewitt, M. Hammersley and M. Robb (eds), *Understanding Research with Children and Young People.* Los Angeles, CA: Open University and Sage, pp. 269–284.

INDEX

Åberg, A., 38
Aboriginal peoples, 2, 6, 141
action research, 120
adaptive capacity, 12–13, 23
agentic children, 216
amygdala function, 104
analysis, nature of, 136
analytic questioning, 173–4
animism, 133–4, 138–42
anthropology, 133
anthropomorphism, 107, 110–11
Arendt, Hannah, 183–5, 189–90
Argent, Adrienne, xi, 86, 91–4, 98–9; *co-author of Chapter 6*
Atkinson, D., 89
assessment, 47, 50, 51, 79, 120, 159, 160–1, 167–9, 172–4, 182, 209, 212, 216
attunement, 86–7, 91, 96
Australian context, 2–4

Badley, G.F., 136
Barad, Karen, 133
Barthes, Roland, 68
Basford, J., 50
Bath, C., 50
Bauman, Z., 37
Bellamy, J., 12
Bennett, J., 95
Berger, Iris, xi, 207
Berry, K.S., 135
Bertram, T., 216
Biesta, G.J.J., 189
Bird-David, N., 133
Bitou, A., 67
Bjartveit, C.J., 95
Bjervås, Lise-Lotte, xi, 55; *co-author of Chapter 2*
Botero Lopez, Viviana, 14–17
bricolage, 93, 131, 135–6
Bright, N.G., 68
Brinkmann, S., 137
Britain *see* United Kingdom
British Columbia, 179, 194, 203

Cagliari, P., 99–100
Campani, Giuliana, 98
Canadian context, 5–7

Carr, M., 14, 161
Cavazzoni, P. 75
child-centred practice, 180
children's interests, 160–1
children's perspectives, 86, 89
Chng, Angela, xi, 159–60; *author of Chapter 10*
Choreia School, 75
circle time, 31
cockatoos, 105–14, 212–13
co-construction 3, 50, 78, 195
co-creation of knowledge and understanding, 70
collaborative learning, 121–2, 166
collective memory, 82
communities of practice, 119, 168–70
community-based provision, 4
conceptual models, 124–6
construction of knowledge, 123; *see also* co-construction; co-creation
contextual decisions, 104, 114
Cooley, M., 90–1, 93
Cooper, Maria, xi–xii, 159–61
cooperative learning, 37–8
co-researchers, children as, 1, 104
course design, 167
creative arts, 74–5
cultural circles, 99

Dahlberg, G., 37–8, 48, 50, 70, 74, 82, 134–5, 140, 212, 214
dance, 73–5, 78–83
Davies, B., 182, 186, 188
de Certeau, Michel, 62
death, engagement with the topic of, 172, 188–9
decision-making in pedagogy, 55, 103, 151, 160, 211
Deleuze, Jacques, 61, 64, 66, 93, 138, 140
democratic meaning-making and participation, 208–9
Denzin, N., 135
Derrida, Jacques, 135
Descola, P., 133–4, 141
Development Matters document (2012), 45
developmental psychology, 133
Dewey, J., 37, 136–7, 208

dialogue, Rinaldi's concept of, 204
Disch, L.J., 185
diversity, 2, 7, 37
documentation
   of children's learning, 3, 32, 37, 42, 46–8,
      123, 135, 149, 167–70, 207–8; *see also*
       pedagogical documentation
documents
   nature of, 55–6

Early Learning Framework
   (British Columbia), 194, 203
Early Years Foundation Phase (Wales), 48–9
Early Years Foundation Stage (England),
   44–5, 50–1
Early Years Learning Framework
   (Australia), 2, 18
education, definition of (Dewey), 37
embodied arts, 74, 79–83
empathy, 107
enclosed spaces, 149–50
England, 4–5, 44–5, 49–51, 166, 169
Eskelinen, M., 5
ethical considerations, 88–9, 114
ethnography, 89, 133–4
evaluation 68, 80, 83, 86, 169, 172, 208
see also assessment
'everydayness', 62–4, 67, 71

Ferraris, M., 56
Filippini, T., 187
Fleet, Alma, ix, xvii,, 13–14, 20, 55, 98; *author
   of Chapter 1, co-author of Chapters 4
   and 14 and co-editor*
forest schools, 132
Forman, G., 74
Foucault, Michel, 98, 133
Foundation Stage (Northern Ireland), 49
Fyfe, B., 74

Gambetti, Z., 184
Giamminuti, Stefania, xii, 98–100, 105
Giudici, C., 25
Giugni, M., 181–2
Greene, Maxine, 185, 189
Guattari, F., 138, 140

Hall, C., 88
Hammer, Alberta, 215–16
haptic engagement, 93–4
Harraway, D., 105
Harvell, Janet, xii, 55, 169; *co-author of
   Chapter 3*
Hedges, Helen, xii, 159–61

Heifetz, Ron, 207
'hidden curriculum', 172
higher-order learning skills, 124–5, 176
Hillman, J., 118
Hirsh, Edward, 91
Hodgins, B. Denise, xii, 194–7,
   207; *co-author of Chapter 13*
Hoyuelos, Alfredo, 93, 135
huckleberry bushes, 85, 92–5, 212
Hujala, E., 5

Ingold, T., 93, 133, 141
'inscriptions', 56
'internal listening', 156
interpretive encounters, 94–6
interrupting, faculty of, 184–5, 189–90
intersubjectivity, 76–9

Jackson, A.Y., 136
Jovanovic, S., 151

Kalliala, M., 50
Katz, L., 78
Kimsooja, 89–91
Kincheloe, J.L., 135
Kind, Sylvia, xiii, 86, 98–9;
   co-author of Chapter 6
King, T., 204–5
Kocher, Laurie, xiii, 5–7
Kummen, Kathleen, xiii, 194, 200–2, 207;
   co-author of Chapter 13

leadership
   concept of, 179–80
   pedagogic, 5, 42–51, 121, 166–70, 174,
      179–87, 190, 198, 207–8
'learning journeys', 46
learning possibilities for young children,
   117–18, 126, 129
learning stories (New Zealand), 46
Learning to Learn document (2012), 49
Lee, W., 14
Lefebvre, H., 62–4, 71
Leggo, Carl, 94–5
Lenz Taguchi, H., 37–8, 82, 149, 203, 208, 213
Levi-Strauss, Claude, 93
LiLi (local interpretation of larger ideas) 11–13,
   20–5, 214
Lincoln, Y., 135
Lipponen, Lasse, xiii, 55–6
listening to children, 106–7, 155, 182,
   207, 216
local interpretation of larger ideas (see **LiLi**),
Louv, R., 141

MacDonald, C.J., 74
Mackellar, Dorothea, 2
MacLure, M., 87, 90, 138
MacNaughton, Glenda, 201
Magrini, J., 185
Malaguzzi, Loris, 42, 74–5, 93, 99, 215
Manning, E., 96
Martin, Karen, 141
Massumi, B., 96
Mathers, S., 118
Mazzei, L.A., 136
meaning-making, 38, 171, 208–9
Mei Lee, Suet, 14–19
Merewether, Jane, xiii, 159; *author of Chapter 9*
Mia Mia Child and Family Study Centre, 104–5, 212–13
    values of, 108, 110, 113, 148–9
'minor politics', 140, 142
Mitchelmore, Suallyn, xiii, 64, 98; *co-author of Chapter 4*
More Great Childcare report (2013), 119
Moss, P., 37, 45, 51, 98–9, 212–14

Nancy, J.-L., 68
neoliberalism, 181
New Zealand, 14, 46, 160
Northern Ireland, 49
noticing, 68, 86, 161, 197
Nutbrown Review (2012), 45

observation of children, 5, 21, 43, 46, 47, 49, 64, 70, 74, 117, 119, 150, 169, 170, 172, 182, 194, 208, 214.
Office for Standards in Education (Ofsted), 46, 48, 118–21, 123, 169
Ollin, R., 154
Osgood, J., 45
'othering', 89
outdoor environments, 131–8, 142, 159, 211–12

Pacini-Ketchabaw, V., 14, 201
Panayotidis, E.L., 95
parental involvement in pedagogical choices, 36, 38
Pascal, C., 216
Pasteur, Louis, 114
Patterson, Catherine, ix, xvii; *co-author of Chapter 14 and co-editor*
pedagogical choices, 28–9, 36, 38
pedagogical documentation
    and aesthetic attitudes, 99
    and collaborative decision-making, 103–6, 114

and dance, 73–4, 79–82
definitions of, 12, 13–14, 134
and the educational environment, 33–5
and educational leadership, 179–85, 190
and the everyday, 62–4, 67–71
as a form of research, 55, 64, 74, 81, 86, 89, 91, 92, 96, 98–100, 104, 107, 111, 131–8, 141–2, 194, 197, 202, 216–7
at Mia Mia, 103–115, 147–58
in outdoor spaces, 92, 104–5, 131–42
and professional development, 165–77, 197–200
and relationship-building, 21–22, 28, 35, 37–8, 64, 67, 71, 78, 82, 99, 104, 123, 126, 170, 204, 208
and the *status quo*, 185–6, 190
and student learning, 117–27
in the UK generally, 42–6, 50–1
and use of video, 85–90
pedagogical moments, 181
'pedagogical narrations', 179, 183, 189–90, 194–5, 197–204, 207
    and educational leadership, 186–7
    potential and dangers of, 204–5
pedagogy of invention and *pedagogy of imitation*, 98
pensiero progettuale, 98–9
Phelan, A., 189
Piaget, Jean (and Piagetian theory), 133–4, 140, 142
Pink, S., 89, 94
placements for students, 122
'plugging into' theories, 132, 140, 142
Plum, M., 45
poetic possibilities, 85–6, 90–6, 99
Polanyi, M., 75
politics of childhood, politics of education and *politics of gender*, 213
postfoundationalism, 194–5, 202–3
postmodernity, 203
praxeological world view, 216
problem-solving by children, 153–4
professional development of teachers and student teachers, 118–21, 126, 165–77
professional inquiry, 121, 123–4
Prowle, A., 49
public spaces, 185, 189
puppetry, 212–13

qualifications and personal qualities of teachers, 118–19
Quandamooka ontology, 141
questioning approach to teaching, 124

Quinn, S.F., 119
'quotidian inquiry', 62–4, 67, 71, 98

record-keeping, 23–4
Reed, Michael, xiv, 4–5, 55, 124–5, 159,
      169, 173, 207; *co-author of Chapters 3,
      8 and 11*
Reedy, P., 81
reflection walls, 33, 35
Reggio Emilia, 1, 7–8, 13–14, 21, 23, 73–5,
      78, 81–2, 98, 100, 114, 119, 134–5, 148,
      203, 215
regimes of truth, 133, 142
relationship-building, 37–8
rich normality 98–9
Richard, Marc, xiv, 98; *author of Chapter 5*
rights of the child, 19, 42
Rinaldi, C., 42, 68, 79, 82, 99, 106–7, 156, 204
Robertson, Janet, ix, xvii, 2–4, 132, 159, 212;
      *author of Chapter 7, co-author of
      Chapter 14 and co-editor*
Roder, J., 151
Rosendahl, Gunilla, xiv, 55;
      co-author of Chapter 2

Samuelsson, L.P., 50
Scotland, 5, 48–50
self-directed learning and self-
      organized learners, 122, 124
Sheets-Johnstone, M., 75
Shepherd, Wendy, xiv, 2–4
Sheringham, M., 62–4, 67
'silent pedagogy'(Ollin), 154
singing at school, 155–7
Siraj, I., 49
Smees, R., 118
social constructivism, 79, 208
social justice, 213–14
staying on task, children's capability for, 112
Stengers, I., 203
Stinson, S., 74
Stobbs, Nicola, xiv, 55, 159, 168–9,
      207; *co-author of Chapters 3, 8 and 11*
storytelling as methodology, 183–5
Stremmel, Andrew, xiv, 207–9
Sweden, 27
Sylva, K., 44
Syrian conflict, 15–19, 22, 24

tacit knowledge, 75–6
Tan, Shaun, 95
Te Whāriki curriculum, 46
teachers
      education and training of, 7, 159
      role of, 208–9
theory
      alignment with practice, 167
      need for and role of, 121, 136
Thompson, Deborah, xiv, 194, 197–200, 207;
      co-author of Chapter 13
Thompson, M., 56
Thompson, P., 88
touching, learning about, 78–9
transformative learning, 124
'transgression', 212–17
transmission model of learning, 50, 172

undergraduate students on early
      education courses, 117–18
Unfolding (exhibit), 89–91
United Kingdom, 4–5, 41–6, 49–51
United Nations Children's Fund (UNICEF), 19–20
university courses, 126

van Manen, M., 86, 91
video, use of, 85–96
      as an expressive, interpretive
            and artistic medium, 88
      for showing the materiality of things, 88
video documentation, 82
video poems, 91, 94–6
visual research, 89
'voice', concept of, 67–8
Vygotsky, L.S., 42, 55

Wales, 48–9
Walker, Rosie, xiv, 4–5, 159, 207;
      co-author of Chapter 11
Wall Report (2015), 5
Waller, T., 67
war, children's exploration of, 15–19, 24, 213
Wenger, Etienne, 119
'wicked problems', 12, 14, 211
Wien, C.A., 82, 172
Williams, T., 118
Wong, A., 119
Woodcheck, E., 51